Introduction to
Turbo Pascal

Introduction to
Turbo Pascal™_____

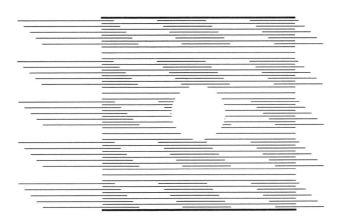

Douglas S. Stivison

SYBEX® Berkeley • Paris • Düsseldorf • London

Cover art by Nicolae Razumieff
Book design by Sharon Leong

Library of Congress Card Number: 85-71778
ISBN 0-89588-269-8
Printed by Haddon Craftsmen
Manufactured in the United States of America
10 9 8 7 6 5 4 3 2

For Di Eigen

Acknowledgments

This book could never have been written without the total commitment and unwavering encouragement of my family.

I owe a great debt to the late James R. Fisk, W1HR, founder and editor of *Ham Radio Magazine*. In writing this book, I have tried to measure up to his standards and to remember the lessons he taught.

I wish to thank Jerry Levitz of the Harris Corporation. As a teacher and as a friend, Jerry has no equal. There were many obstacles in the path to completing this book. Jerry's training in the art of "making things happen" served me well in overcoming every obstacle.

I thank all the talented people with whom I work at Seybold Publications. In particular, I want to thank John Seybold for his initial—and continuing—faith in me. I want to thank Steve Edwards and George Alexander for carrying much of my editorial work load while I worked on this manuscript and for their good comradeship always.

I wish to acknowledge my debt to Rodnay Zaks, whose *Introduction to Pascal* is still the most lucid treatment of traditional implementations of Pascal ever written. It has served as both a model and ideal for this work.

By working in the electronic cottage, I have been able to see the results of other people's creativity and dedication, but without getting to know the people who made the contributions. Nonetheless, I am genuinely indebted to many people at SYBEX for all their contributions. Nick Wolfinger did the technical review, Bonnie Gruen provided editorial assistance, and Valerie Robbins and David Clark did the word processing. Karl Ray oversaw the editorial process. Sharon Leong designed the book and Janis Lund typeset and proofread it. Bret Rohmer and Elizabeth Thomas oversaw the production process. A special word of thanks goes to Carole Alden and R.S. Langer, who supported the concept of this book from its original proposal.

I also thank Jim Compton, the editor of this book. In editing this book, he never deviated—nor let me deviate—from a commitment to clarity. Jim is a true professional, and his contribution to this book is huge.

We all owe a debt to Philippe Kahn, founder of Borland International. It is his concept of Turbo Pascal that has made obsolete the concept of selling small numbers of expensive but lackluster language compilers. He believed that if he treated customers fairly by offering them an excellent product at a fair price, he would be treated fairly in return. Turbo Pascal is not copy-protected, yet he has been vindicated by the hundreds of thousands of users who have chosen to purchase Turbo legitimately. Without Philippe Kahn there would be no Turbo Pascal.

Contents

Chapter *3*

Common Tools and Techniques   *53*

Chapter *4*

Advanced Data Structures   *117*

Introduction

This book was written to help readers develop, as quickly as possible, the ability to write problem-solving programs in Turbo Pascal. It should also help readers develop an understanding of structured programming along the way.

Existing books on Pascal do not address the unique facets of Turbo. Turbo's extensions and nonstandard features are not mere minor syntactical variations. In Turbo Pascal, Borland has grafted a huge set of extensions and simplifications onto the elegant framework of Niklaus Wirth's theoretical Pascal. Standard Pascal, and the books describing it, mirror the technology that spawned Pascal. The language was originally developed in an academic world using large, batch-oriented, time-sharing computers. The unheard-of power and availability of personal computers shattered many of the restraints of earlier Pascals, and permitted the unprecedented innovations of Turbo. This purely Turbo-oriented, hands-on guide was written to help more people take advantage of these unique innovations.

The capabilities of Turbo are too powerful to be ignored, too elegant to be buried in obscure documentation, and too capable to be left entirely to frustrating trial and error. Moreover, Turbo's blending of standard features, universal extensions, and further machine-dependent features is a triumph of consistency and user-friendliness. Some other PC-based Pascals have earned the unfortunate reputation of being merely "grouchy BASIC." No description could be more inaccurate for Turbo, and we hope this book shows just how easy to learn and user-friendly Turbo is.

This book does not have syntax diagrams nor an appendix of Backus-Naur Form expressions. Turbo is a uniquely approachable language and the author refuses to put academic hurdles in the way of new users. This book is an unashamedly try-it-yourself guide. Readers who get hooked on Turbo will find a raft of works available to explore the computational theory behind in Pascal. But these books (some of them are listed in Appendix A) serve best as references once you are comfortable making everyday programs work.

For Whom This Book Was Written

This book provides a balanced and comprehensive treatment for programming students, business persons looking for a tool to solve everyday problems, and for hackers looking for the next creative challenge.

In particular, we hope our readers include college and high-school (AP) students for whom Turbo's low cost makes it the most accessible form of Pascal. The text describes the fundamentals of Turbo for all the different machine implementations, although the details of system-specific operating calls will only be illustrated for the most popular implementation, MS-DOS.

This book is also written for those people who have only recently been attracted to the world of personal computers, yet feel that they have already reached the limitations of interpreted BASIC. For these readers Turbo provides the tools to push their machines to handle larger files, generate faster graphics, and solve far more ambitious problems.

For the programmer who has used other Pascals, this book should provide a painless transition to a world of programming ease and power unavailable in any other PC-based implementation.

Organization of the Book

Chapter 1 presents a brief overview of the philosophy behind Turbo Pascal, to disclose the unifying pattern to its structure. Pascal is an exceptionally precise, logical, and consistent language. The syntax and structure, far from being an intimidating body of rules, punctuation, and arbitrary constructions, form a consistent *pattern*. In learning a natural language, we quickly make informed guesses on how to express complex new ideas based on simpler, past patterns. Similarly, in writing complex Turbo programs, there are many complex control and data structures that function exactly as the programmer would expect based on the operation of simpler structures.

Chapter 2 uses simple working programs to familiarize the reader with the basic structure of a Pascal program. To readers coming from unstructured languages like BASIC and FORTRAN, the appearance of a Pascal program can be initially perplexing. We hope that a few guaranteed-to-work programs will make the transition to Pascal format intuitive rather than mechanical and vaguely perplexing. This chapter also covers the additional terminology and fundamentals to help readers begin writing, compiling and running many small programs on their own.

Chapter 3 expands upon many of the workaday procedures, functions, control structures, and simple data structures that make up the major part of almost every Turbo Pascal program. This chapter also addresses some of Turbo's greatest strengths: the areas of string manipulation and user-created functions.

Chapter 4 deals exclusively with advanced data structures, including records and files. It is universally agreed that the greatest of Turbo's many strengths is its set of flexible data structures, which mirror the "natural" realatonships between data. In addition to describing techniques for using external data files, this chapter covers the range of data structures from arrays to linked lists using pointers. This is an area to which most Pascal students return again and again as they gain more programming experience.

Chapter 5 is a brief look at Turbo's commands for creating sound and graphics. Here are the screen and sound tools for making programs more inviting. Beginning programmers in Turbo will continue to discover applications for the techniques and procedures in this section.

Chapter 6 covers topics of interest to advanced Turbo programmers. These include the operation of the Turbo compiler and ways to access powerful routines offered by the computer's operating system. This chapter also explains and compares the different techniques for managing and linking large programs.

Finally, there are two appendices. The first describes some of the resources available to the Turbo user—the user's group, "bulletin boards," and suggested further reading. The second is a listing of the complete mailing-list program, portions of which appear in slightly different form throughout the book.

What This Book Assumes

The reader is expected to have some experience with another programming language such as FORTRAN or BASIC. No prior knowledge of Pascal or any structured language is assumed. We assume the reader can refer to the Borland manual and instructions for the mechanics of installing and booting the Turbo software on his own system.

We further assume that there is only one way to begin to use Turbo Pascal:

"Ladies and gentlemen, start your engines!"

The
Fundamentals of
Turbo Pascal

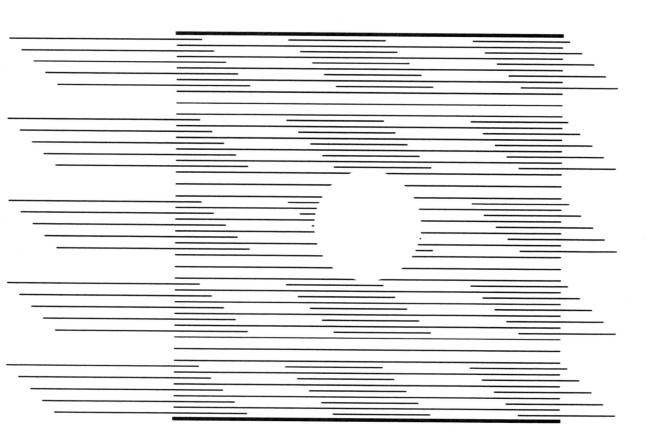

Chapter *1*

A Background to Turbo Pascal

Turbo Pascal is not merely a different set of commands for expressing the same ideas as expressed in BASIC. Instead, Turbo (like all other Pascals) represents a fundamentally different approach to programming; indeed, a fundamentally different way of thinking. If you spend a few moments exploring the theory behind Pascal, learning the details of the language will be much easier, as everything fits into a logical framework.

Using Turbo requires a disciplined thought process. The most obvious sign of this discipline is its orderly block structure. By contrast, a language like BASIC has an amorphous line orientation. Turbo programs are written block-by-block, with each block addressing a specific, clearly defined purpose. The commands, the syntax, the tests, the loops, the very appearance of a Turbo program all reflect this fundamental orientation toward breaking complex operations into manageable pieces.

Niklaus Wirth, the creator of both Pascal and Modula2, has written a book entitled *Algorithms + Data Structures = Programs* (Englewood Cliffs, N.J.: Prentice-Hall, 1976). The title reflects

Wirth's fundamental conviction that efficient programming involves solving two distinct but related problems. The first is to define the *data structures:* what kinds and how much information will be processed? What is the most convenient, natural, and efficient way to arrange it? The second problem is creating the *algorithm:* What is the best step-by-step procedure to transform this data into the desired result?

The need to address these problems informs Turbo Pascal and serves to explain the logic behind most of its commands and syntax. It also explains the logic behind Turbo's tools for structuring data, which go beyond the capabilities of earlier languages. First-time Pascal programmers often regard these new data types and structures merely as complications of the familiar concept of BASIC arrays. In reality, they are genuinely innovative tools for describing real-world situations in terms that can be understood and acted upon by a computer.

Turbo programmers quickly develop the ability to create algorithms by thinking of *processes,* functioning on clearly defined data structures. By comparison, most good BASIC programmers have to work hard at overcoming the line-by-line thought pattern of that language if they want to see the larger logical picture. Clear thinking is necessary for good programming in any language and Turbo's philosophy, structure, and syntax combine to foster this clear thinking process.

When this philosophy has been understood and assimilated, the syntax and punctuation become not arbitrary rules to be learned like a catechism but the most natural ways to express clearly defined, manageable processes.

Throughout this book, these two Turbo Pascal principles will be emphasized: that programs are organized into blocks, and that blocks are algorithms working on data structures. This emphasis will help demonstrate the elegance and consistency of the language.

A Demonstration Program

Before we get into the details of creating a Turbo program on your own computer, let us look at a sample first program:

PROGRAM PrintAGreeting;

```
BEGIN
    WRITELN ('Good Morning')
END.
```

This trivial program merely prints the message

Good Morning

on the screen. Even so, it illustrates several fundamental principles of Turbo. First, all Turbo programs—even those not "documented" with comments—should provide a sense of what they are all about. To this end, Turbo allows the programmer considerable freedom in naming program elements and in physically arranging the lines of code on the screen or printer listing. It is up to the programmer to take advantage of this freedom, by using meaningful names to describe what a procedure does or a variable represents, and by indenting lines and adding blank lines to make the logical structure of the program apparent to anyone reading the listing.

Program Parts

Even this trivial program is made up of two modules or blocks. The first part:

PROGRAM PrintAGreeting;

is called the *program heading*. It names the program and, optionally, can say where input and output will be found. Unlike standard Pascal, Turbo makes this part of the program entirely optional. It is still recommended, however, because giving a program an informative name can save a lot of commenting and contribute significantly to overall clarity. Is there any question that the purpose of this program is to print a greeting?

The second part of the program is the *program block*, containing the code that will accomplish the task at hand. Obviously, it is not optional. In our example, the program block consists of this:

```
BEGIN
    WRITELN ('Good Morning')
END.
```

This block is typical of Turbo in that some data (the message) is processed (written to the screen). Notice that certain words appear in **boldface** type. This is another tool for indicating program structure. Even without any study of Turbo commands, you can see from the indentation and boldface words like **PROGRAM, BEGIN,** and **END** what the program is about (printing a greeting), and where to look for the actual work to take place—surely between the beginning and the end! BASIC programmers should also notice that there are no line numbers; they are unnecessary when a program is organized in informatively named blocks with unambiguous beginning and ending points.

The Turbo package includes a program called CALC.PAS. It is an ambitious spreadsheet program, consisting of many modules and capable of doing a tremendous amount of calculation as well as screen manipulation. If you were to look at a listing of the program, you would probably be pleasantly surprised to see how much of it makes sense to you right now, without any real study of Turbo. While the details of the program may still be obscure, the lists of variables and the names of the procedures immediately give you an idea of the task at hand.

Although this book will not examine the CALC.PAS program in detail, you should refer to it as different topics are introduced in this book. You'll quickly understand individual modules, and you will be stealing ideas from it for your own programs.

Installing Turbo

The Borland documentation explains how to install Turbo on your own computer and how to use and customize the program editor. (The section on installation is one of relatively few good tutorial explanations in the manual; for the most part, it is a reference work, and it is often difficult to extract useful information from it.) Be sure to make several backup copies of the distribution diskette so you need not worry about accidentally destroying vital files as you experiment.

Also, as a devoted user of the XyWrite word-processing package, I have reconfigured the program editor to operate much more like XyWrite than WordStar. While this reconfiguration has made the Turbo editor easier to use, the process is not described in this book. Explicit instructions can be found in sections 1.8 and 1.9 of the

Borland documentation. Users of Version 1.0 should be aware, however, that there are several bugs in the editor-customizing program that, while not affecting its usefulness in its WordStar-like form, do prevent significant modification. The bugs were fixed in all later releases.

Similarly, Borland provides very straightforward documentation on its program lister, TLIST. Because all source-code files are stored in simple ASCII format, you can list programs using any word-processing program. This capability is handy when you occasionally need a printout with running headers, footers, and special print features, or when you include listings within other documents. For routine listings, however, TLIST does the job.

Appreciating the Turbo Program-Development Environment

Turbo is not just a language compiler, but a completely integrated program-development environment—a departure from all other implementations of Pascal and the most fundamental reason Turbo is so easy to use. Other Pascals, like all higher-level languages, require the programmer to jump between the computer operating system, a text processor, a one- or two-stage compiler, and a task-builder. Making a trivial program change not only takes time, but offers a raft of opportunities to do something wrong.

Running the single task called TURBO accesses a menu from which you can create and edit programs, do all compilations and linkages, test and debug programs, and finally create finished tasks which can run outside of the Turbo environment. Only those who have debugged programs in other languages or versions of Pascal can appreciate the savings in time and frustration this integration offers.

Incidentally, the term *task* sometimes leads to confusion. Traditionally, the task-builder program took several input programs—perhaps individual modules and libraries—and produced a single program, which could actually be executed on the target computer. The task builder took into account all references to external libraries, and resolved all questions of where the executable program was to reside and begin in memory. The Turbo compiler takes care of all these operations for you when you ask it to produce a .COM or .CMD file. Programmers who learned the business in the days before personal computers still sometimes use the term *task* as a synonym for any program that can be run by itself. By this informal definition, any Turbo file ending in .PAS or any interpreted BASIC file would not be a task, because they must use either TURBO.COM or the BASIC interpreter to actually run and do anything useful.

Here is a typical program-development scenario in Turbo. At the DOS prompt, the programmer types

TURBO

The Turbo editor is then chosen with a keystroke (E) and a source file displayed quickly for editing. Changes are made and with two more keystrokes the program is immediately recompiled and run. When errors are found by the compiler, you can jump into the source code at the approximate location of the error for an immediate fix. Again the program can be recompiled, run, and tested. The cycle can be repeated until the program runs as desired. At that point, still within Turbo rather than DOS, you can create a .COM file (.CMD in CP/M-86), which can be run outside of Turbo.

In normal programming, the typical editing, compiling, task-building, and running cycle needs to be repeated at least several times. On a thirty-line program, comparable Pascal compilers normally take three to ten minutes per cycle, where Turbo takes a few seconds. On more ambitious programs, the difference becomes even more pronounced. Just imagine how frustrating it is to go through a twenty-minute process simply to find that you forgot a semicolon! That is common in many Pascals but absolutely unheard-of in Turbo. Not only is Turbo's method easier on your nerves, but it also lets you devote yourself to creative program development rather than concentration-robbing mechanics.

The major reason Turbo is so fast is that all but the longest programs are edited, compiled, run, and debugged entirely within the computer's high-speed, RAM memory. This method is many times faster than conventional approaches, which incur delays moving the text editor, program files, libraries, compiler, and linker back and forth between disk and RAM memory.

A few minor limitations are imposed by Turbo's "fit-it-all-into-memory" approach. For example, there is no automatic generation of listing files or object-code listings. But these items are generally of interest only to the professional programmer. The TLIST program prints the listings most users need; professionals can always use Turbo to write an object-code lister if they ever actually need one.

Elementary
Programming
in Turbo Pascal

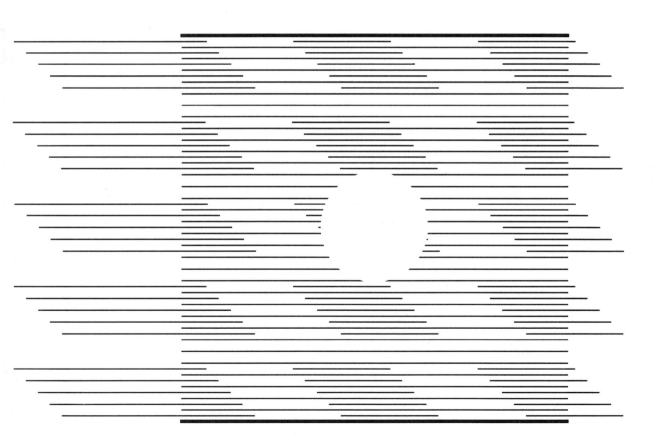

Creating and
Running a Simple Program

It's time to roll up the sleeves, fire up your computer and create a Turbo program. From here on, it is assumed that Turbo is installed on your computer according to the Borland documentation. Type

TURBO

at your system prompt. Almost instantly you are asked if you want error messages. Most other Pascal compilers don't offer the option of asking for informative, plain-English error messages; instead, they force the programmer to search through the manual for the explanation of cryptic error codes. Answering this prompt with a Y tells the system you want descriptive error messages. In installations with very limited memory, the error-message file (TURBO.MSG) can be deleted to save space. Keep the file on disk if at all possible, though. The messages are like programmers' training wheels in that they make life easier while building up your programming confidence.

The screen changes instantaneously to the main Turbo menu. Any command is chosen by typing the single highlighted mnemonic character for that function. To create our first file we choose W (to name a Working file). We'll type the file name

FIRST

The reassuring message

New file

appears, telling us that we have typed everything correctly and that no file called FIRST.PAS already exists and is to be edited. Typing E jumps us into the WordStar-like program editor. For all of Turbo's innovation, here is one place in which Turbo is just like every other programming language: the blank screen does not fill itself. At this point, we become Turbo programmers.

Type the sample program from Chapter 1:

```
PROGRAM PrintAGreeting;
BEGIN
    WRITELN ('Good Morning')
END.
```

The Turbo editor accepts any combination of upper- and lowercase characters interchangeably. Case matters only where you care about it; in text that is written to a file or output device (screen or printer, for example).

Also, the spacing and indentation conventions discussed in Chapter 1 and illustrated above are solely for your convenience. Even if you see no need to follow these conventions, follow them anyway in consideration of the person who may someday try to make sense out of your code. The Turbo editor has a simple feature that indents code automatically; with a bit of experimentation you will master it. From the computer's point of view, the program would run just as well if it were formatted as follows:

```
BEGIN WRITELN('Good Morning')END.
```

For people used to interpreted BASIC, this flexibility is a major distinction. In BASIC, there is only one program file, so the program that accomplishes a task is the same file that contains all of your comments and blank lines. If you add lots of comments, or if you break complex operations into separate lines, each doing one task, it makes the BASIC program much easier to read. Unfortunately, it also makes the program larger and somewhat slower. In small programs, speed doesn't matter. In ambitious BASIC programs like those for sorting and communications, however, the extra size can significantly slow down the program execution. And it is precisely these larger programs that need the most comments and clearest structure to be at all understandable.

Turbo Pascal is a *compiled* language, which means that a separate file is created, based on your source file but consisting of just the machine-language commands necessary to execute your program. It is the size and structure of this machine-language file (sometimes called a *task file,* and ending with the .COM extension in MS-DOS and CP/M-80, or .CMD in CP/M-86) that determine how well your program runs and how much memory it takes up. In making this task file, however, the Turbo compiler strips out all your comments, blank lines, and indentations. Even the nice, long variable names are efficiently converted to simple memory addresses. As a result, your source program can be laid out cleanly and thoroughly commented without paying any penalty in program performance. Here you have clarity for the human programmer and efficiency for the computer. This is as close as you are ever likely to come to the mythical free lunch.

Getting back to our first program, once you have typed the program, end the editing session with WordStar's familiar Control-KD sequence. You have now created your first Turbo source file. To compile and test-run it, type R (for Run). If you have typed everything correctly, and if you have version 1 or 2 of Turbo, the screen should go blank and then the words

Good Morning

should appear on the screen. (If you have version 3, the screen will not clear first.) The message will be followed by the Turbo prompt (>).

Saving Your Programs

You have now created, compiled, and run your first Turbo program. However, the program exists only in memory. It has not been written onto disk. If you turned off the computer at this point, no trace of your program would be left. When using Turbo, therefore, you must remember periodically to write the current file onto a disk. If you try to exit normally from Turbo with an unsaved file, Turbo will courteously ask you if you wish to save the current file first.

Working in the fast-paced Turbo environment, the risk generally isn't of forgetting to save a file on exit. More often, the problem arises as you ricochet between editing and test-running a program. It is such a quick and automatic sequence from altering the source code (editing) through compilation and task building into testing, that you can lose track of when a file was last recorded on disk. Occasionally, an editing change may have some strange effect and put the computer into a loop that cannot be exited by a normal Control-Break sequence. At that point, all you can do is reboot and return to the last version of the program written to disk. In a hot-and-heavy debugging session, the last recorded version might be missing many subsequent changes.

In short, developing the habit of typing S (for Save) before each compilation is a habit worth cultivating.

Running Compiled Programs Under Your Computer's Operating System

Having run our program successfully, we can display it on the screen for additional editing simply by typing E (for Edit). Alternatively, now that we know the program works, we could type S to save it to disk. Once it is saved, we still have only a file called FIRST.PAS. This file can only be run in the Turbo environment. To create a version that can be run at any time outside of Turbo, type O (for the compiler Options). Type C (to Compile a .COM file) and then Q (to Quit the options section). Typing C at this point creates a file called FIRST.COM. Exit from Turbo entirely by typing an X (for eXit). You should now have your operating system prompt (A> for MS-DOS or CP/M). Type

FIRST

and hit Return. The message

Good Morning

should appear.

At this point you have created a source file, compiled it, tested it in a debugging environment, and recompiled it into a form in which it can be run on any computer that uses your operating system—even if that computer does not have a copy of Turbo Pascal. Here is another fundamental difference between Turbo and interpreted BASIC. If someone else wants to run a BASIC program you created using, say, your copy of Microsoft BASIC, that person also must have a compatible copy of the same Microsoft BASIC interpreter. To someone without any BASIC interpreter, your file called FIRST.BAS is useless. And to somebody using a different interpreter, say for Apple BASIC, a certain amount of translation would be necessary to make the program run on that interpreter.

Turbo, on the other hand, allows you to create standard .COM files, which can run on any other computer using the same operating system. I have successfully used Turbo on my IBM PC/XT to create files that were telecommunicated and run on several other computers, none of which had a Turbo compiler.

With the exception of programs that use extraordinary amounts of memory or exploit Turbo's features to interact closely with a specific computer's hardware and operating system, compiled Turbo files are highly portable. This portability makes Turbo an exceptionally attractive language for programmers who wish to write commercial software. If the programmer simply avoids some of the more esoteric Turbo commands, programs can be written that run without modification on a wide range of computers. Also, the range of Turbo compilers available (currently almost every popular 16-bit, MS-DOS and CP/M-86 machine, and most of the popular Z80-based CP/M machines) means that a source file created on one machine can be transferred to a computer with a different operating system and simply recompiled on the Turbo compiler designed for the target machine.

Turbo's portability, however, does not carry smoothly into other Pascal compilers. As mentioned earlier, it is normally not too difficult to translate between, say, Microsoft BASICA on the IBM PC and Radio Shack BASIC running on the Model 4. It is generally much more tedious to convert a Turbo source file to be compiled by other Pascal compilers, such as Microsoft's MS Pascal, Digital Research's Pascal/MT + 86, or any of the versions of UCSD p-System Pascal.

The incompatibility problem is not just a fault of Turbo. Historically, Pascal was devised as a theoretical language designed to teach structured programming. When it was implemented on some real computers, Pascal appealed to users with its ease of learning and flexibility. But it also frustrated them with its weaknesses in such important areas as input/output and string processing. Many different Pascals arose to bridge the gap between a theoretical, pedagogical language and a machine-dependent language intended to accomplish practical programming tasks. This proliferation went on for several years without the formulation of a "standard" Pascal. By the time a draft standard for Pascal evolved, several different Pascals were already firmly entrenched. Each version had its own supporters, and each offered a different set of extensions, machine-dependent features, and the inevitable compromises between the theoretical and the real.

Turbo has thrown compatibility—hard to realize under the best of conditions—out the window in favor of optimum performance and ease of use. In considering the approach this book should take, I originally thought of stressing those aspects of Turbo that have the most in common with other Pascals, but finally had to abandon this view. Because Turbo's idiosyncrasies afford unparalleled speed and ease of use, it seemed most logical to present Turbo almost as an independent language. Yet once this decision was made, I was continually reminded just how much Turbo is a "true" Pascal—absolutely faithful to the fundamental Pascal concepts.

Conceptually then, Turbo algorithms, data structures, and modules can generally be translated logically into parallel structures in any dialect of Pascal. But the details of syntax will vary widely, and the conventions of compilation, linking, and creating tasks will be radically different. In fact, it was the frustration of trying to use Turbo based on a "standard" Pascal text that drove me to write this book. While syntactical details are irrelevant to *understanding* Turbo, they can be an impediment to enjoying and using it.

Reserved Words, Identifiers, and Standard Identifiers

The most fundamental steps in learning to program in Turbo Pascal are first to learn the basic vocabulary and then to learn how to combine the words into meaningful sentences (instructions, statements, and modules).

The vocabulary of Turbo Pascal is exceptionally approachable. There are no cryptic symbols as in APL, no weird punctuation as in C. Instead, more like BASIC, Turbo Pascal uses a vocabulary specifically designed to be approachable while also providing unambiguous instructions to the computer. Certainly putting the words "begin" and "end" around several lines of instructions conveys a clear, general message to us on first glance while also providing a precise instruction to the compiler.

Turbo Pascal programs are written with a combination of *reserved words* and *standard identifiers,* whose meanings are already known to the Turbo compiler, and additional *identifiers* which are created spontaneously by the programmer. As in any natural language, there are rules of grammar and punctuation controlling the combination of these elements. However, Pascal in general and Turbo in particular allow extraordinary flexibility in the choice of user-created vocabulary. In the naming of data (variables and structures), and in the naming of processes (procedures and functions), Turbo not only allows long and informative names, it actively encourages them. We'll return to this concept, as it is one of the many ways in which the "algorithms + data structures" theory is embodied in practical programming features.

Reserved Words

A reserved word is simply one that has a special and unchangeable meaning to the Turbo compiler. These are the key words used to write a program in Turbo Pascal. Figure 2.1 lists all the reserved words in Turbo. It is not an imposing list to learn, particularly because in most cases, a word's precise meaning to the compiler is largely a subset of its everyday meaning in English. Reserved words are used to control both the logical flow and the operation of a program. They include the terms necessary to execute tests and loops,

Reserved words arranged alphabetically for reference:

ABSOLUTE	AND	ARRAY	BEGIN	CASE
CONST	DIV	DO	DOWNTO	ELSE
END	EXTERNAL	FILE	FORWARD	FOR
FUNCTION	GOTO	INLINE	IF	IN
LABEL	MOD	NIL	NOT	OVERLAY
OF	OR	PACKED	PROCEDURE	PROGRAM
RECORD	REPEAT	SET	SHL	SHR
STRING	THEN	TYPE	TO	UNTIL
VAR	WHILE	WITH	XOR	

It makes more sense to group these words by function:

Data definition and structures:

ARRAY	CONST	FILE	NIL	RECORD
SET	STRING	TYPE	VAR	

Program structure and control:

BEGIN	CASE	DO	DOWNTO	ELSE
END	EXTERNAL	FORWARD	FOR	FUNCTION
GOTO	INLINE	IF	LABEL	OVERLAY
OF	PROCEDURE	PROGRAM	REPEAT	THEN
TO	UNTIL	WHILE	WITH	

Mathematical and logical operations:

AND	DIV	IN	MOD	NOT
OR	SHL	SHR	XOR	

Memory addressing:

ABSOLUTE

Figure 2.1 – Turbo Pascal reserved words.

and to accomplish calculations and comparisons. Programmers must take care not to use a reserved word in place of a user-created variable or program name.

Unfortunately, even in this small list, there are seven words (ABSOLUTE, EXTERNAL, INLINE, SHL, SHR, XOR, and even such a common word as STRING) that have no meaning in standard Pascal and several more that have nonstandard interpretations in Turbo.

Similarly, other Pascals add their own reserved words, which have no meaning either to standard Pascal or to Turbo. Even the concept of *reserved word* differs between implementations, with some Pascals drawing a vague line between terms that can be redefined by the user and terms that cannot. Turbo is very clear on this point. User-redefinable terms are called *standard identifiers* (we'll get to them soon). When using the TLIST program, you can request that reserved words be underlined to help emphasize the program's logical structure. In this book, reserved words appear in **boldface** type in program listings.

Standard Identifiers

Standard identifiers make up the remaining vocabulary of words with predefined meanings in Turbo Pascal. They differ from reserved words in that a programmer is free to redefine the function of standard identifiers to suit unique applications.

The ability to redefine standard identifiers is just one more facet of Turbo's orientation toward the definition and solution of problems in the most natural manner possible. By *natural,* we mean that you should not have to define your data and your solution in some awkward, mechanical manner dictated by the restrictions of your computer hardware and language compiler. Your computer program should mimic, as closely as possible, your normal approach to solving everyday problems without computers.

For example, the standard syntax of the SIN function returns the trigonometric sine of a value expressed in *radians.* In a complex celestial navigation program, to be used by people accustomed to using degrees rather than radians, it might be more natural for the programmer to redefine SIN to conform to his accustomed way of thinking in degrees. Redefining the function might be easier than either changing his way of thinking or passing all data through an additional routine just to convert degrees to radians.

The danger with redefining standard identifiers is that doing so makes your programs even less standard. On the other hand, for programmers who have struggled in other languages with commands that "don't quite do exactly what I want," this option can be very powerful.

Standard identifiers cover various diverse items. They refer to constants, variables, data types, procedures, functions, and all of the machine-dependent features of Turbo. All the commands that control input and output, screen manipulation, file handling, and machine limitations are standard identifiers.

Different implementations of Pascal vary tremendously in their complements of standard identifiers. Even identical releases of Turbo implemented on different computers differ in some machine-dependent standard identifiers (for example, those used to make calls to the operating system or to modify memory directly).

Identifiers

One of the continuing joys in using Turbo Pascal is the tremendous freedom it gives the programmer in choosing obvious, informative identifiers. In our first example program, the program name PrintA-Greeting tells a great deal more than, say, GREET.BAS. Similarly, as we explore variables, we will see that Turbo can accept a variable named CardinalsTeamSeasonBattingAverage, which is certainly clearer than the one-character variable names used in FORTRAN.

Turbo accepts identifiers up to 127 characters long. More importantly, all characters are significant. All other Pascal implementations allow identifiers of varying lengths, but only read the first 8, 16, or 32 characters. Thus, in Turbo, the identifiers

NovemberProfit

and

NovemberLoss

might be used to represent two different variables, while standard Pascal would look only for the first eight characters:

November

and would think that both identifiers referred to the same memory location. Conventional texts on using other Pascals therefore caution programmers not to exploit the ability to use longer identifiers to make their programs more portable. That is like saying "Don't eat a nourishing meal because other people are starving." Using descriptive identifiers is one of the best ways to make the logic of your program apparent.

Remember, too, that whether you call a variable NumberOfTreasuresInTheCave, NumTreas, or even just N, the Turbo compiler will convert a name of any length to a single memory location. The extra characters, then, are simply to make life easier for you or anyone else who may read and need to understand your program.

You apply the same logic to naming procedures that you do to naming variables. So you tell the program simply to perform a procedure called InterpretCommand or PrintAGreeting, rather than just adding lines of code at that point in the program or, even worse, issuing a cryptic command to GOSUB a line number.

Rules For Creating Identifiers

Several rules govern the creation of identifiers. You already know that they can be up to 127 characters long. Although identifiers can contain numbers, they must start with either a letter or an underscore. Also, they cannot contain spaces. You have probably noticed that the sample names that consist of several words simply ran the words together, using a mixture of upper- and lowercase characters to make the meaning clear. We can do this because, as already mentioned, the Turbo compiler does not distinguish between upper- and lowercase letters. Some programmers prefer to use the underscore character to denote spaces. To Turbo, the underscore is just another character. Thus, some of our examples using this technique might be:

    Cardinals_Team_Season_Batting_Average

or

    Boxes_On_Hand

Use whichever system is most agreeable to you.

If you come to Turbo from languages like BASIC, you probably think only variables have names. Turbo lets you use your own names to identify many additional program elements. In fact, everything in this section about identifiers applies to naming labels, constants, data types, procedures, and functions. Thus, a Turbo program contains user-created names not just for the data being manipulated, but for the key data structures and program modules, as well. These names can contribute to the high readability of Turbo programs. Take another look at the CALC.PAS program listing to see for yourself how meaningful identifiers can make programs readable.

Symbols: Serving Two Different Purposes

Natural languages use somewhat different character sets. For example, German doesn't use the tilde (~), Spanish doesn't use the umlaut (··), and English uses neither. Turbo has its own set of characters it understands. The Turbo character set is shown in Figure 2.2.

Just as the basic letters can be combined to make up words and identifiers, other symbols can be combined to make up more complex symbols. As in BASIC, for example, > means "greater than," while < > means "not equal to." Turbo adds two special combinations of its own:

   :=

and

   (*   *)

These are the symbols for "assignment" and for setting off comments, respectively. There are also a handful of words, known as *operators,* which are treated as symbols (DIV, MOD, AND, SHL, SHR, OR, XOR, IN). We'll come back to them later.

There is no meaning in Turbo assigned to such common symbols (particularly familiar to assembly-language programmers) as the percent sign (%), the "at" sign (@), the ampersand (&) and so on. However, it is important to see that even though these symbols have no meaning to Turbo, you can still use them in programs as data.

Although you can use any pattern of bits as data input to a Turbo program—including raw binary data or the complete complement of graphics characters on some computers like the IBM PC—only certain characters are recognized by the Turbo compiler. All the instructions of a Turbo program are made up entirely of members of this character set.

Turbo recognizes all the letters of the alphabet:

abcdefghijklmnopqrstuvwxyz
ABCDEFGHIJKLMNOPQRSTUVWXYZ

Turbo recognizes all the digits:

0123456789

Turbo recognizes a collection of special symbols:

. , : ; ' # $ * / + − = < > ^ [ ] ( ) { }

These symbols individually or in combination have the following meanings:

For math calculations:

*	(multiplication)
/	(division)
+	(addition)
−	(subtraction or unary minus)
( )	(control order of operations)

For program construction:

:=	(assignment)
.	(end-of-program delimiter)
;	(end-of-statement delimiter)
#	(following characters are an ASCII code)
$	(following characters are a hexadecimal value)
(* *)	(comment or compiler directive)
{ }	(comment or compiler directive)
+	(turns compiler option on)
−	(turns compiler option off)
'	(beginning and end of character or string)

Figure 2.2 – Turbo character set (continues).

For comparisons and tests:

=	(equality)
<	(less than)
>	(greater than)
< =	(less than or equal to)
> =	(greater than or equal to)
< >	(not equal to)

For data structures:

^	(pointer, also used to keyboard control codes)
[ ]	(used to index and dimension arrays; enumerate sets)
(. .)	(alternative to [ ] brackets)
( )	(parameter lists for functions and procedures)
.	(record field delimiter; separates file name and extension)
..	(denotes range)

Turbo uses certain words as if they were characters:

For logical operations and bit manipulation:

NOT	(logical not or inversion)
AND	(logical and)
OR	(logical or)
XOR	(logical not or, sometimes called "exclusive or")
SHL	(shift left, actually a multiplication operation)
SHR	(shift right, actually a division operation)
IN	(denotes inclusion in a set)

For integer mathematics:

DIV	(integer division; returns the integer quotient)
MOD	(integer division; returns the integer remainder)

Figure 2.2 – Turbo character set (continued).

For example, Turbo will not accept an identifier called:

Sales%Gain

nor will it accept

AñoPróximo

but it will accept a statement like

WRITELN("Sales%Gain")

The Turbo compiler has been programmed to interpret and assign a special meaning to a limited range of symbols. But that does not mean that a Turbo program cannot use a much wider set of characters as data to be manipulated in some way.

This important distinction once again shows the wisdom of Pascal's strict separation of data and algorithm. Turbo can accept any ASCII code as data. On computers like the IBM PC, which uses the codes 128 through 255 for many graphics and foreign-language applications, this capability is particularly useful. Advanced programmers can even extend this concept to handling any arbitrary combination of bits. Nothing, therefore, prohibits you from writing a text processor for Spanish or a communication program that transmits "pure binary" information. In fact, once Turbo is told what range of characters you are using (as data), Turbo can sort data not just in alphabetical order but in any order you specify.

We'll come back to this topic when we explore data typing. For now, the important point is that the set of characters having meaning to the Turbo compiler is just a small subset of all the possible codes a Turbo program can process.

Control Codes and Nondecimal Numbers

Turbo provides convenient ways to accept, as data, characters that are not part of the alphanumeric character set. The familiar set of Control-key sequences (such as Control-Z to close a file, Control-G to sound the beeper, Control-J/Control-M for the line feed and carriage return combination, and so on) can be keyboarded as data by using the caret (^) for the Control key. For example, Control-J appears as ^J, and Control-Z would be ^Z.

To get the Control-G sequence (sound the bell) you would type the caret (^) and a G. A line of code to sound the beeper during the execution of a program would be typed as:

WRITELN (^G);

Any ASCII character can be processed if you precede it with the number sign (#). For example, #65 accesses the uppercase A, #126 accesses the tilde (~), and #07 accesses the beeper (like Control-G). The numbers above 127 access the full range of special characters and graphics (if they are available on your computer).

Just as the number sign tells Turbo that the following number should be interpreted as an ASCII character, a dollar sign says the following number is a value in hexadecimal. For example, $3F is a hex 3F (equal to 63 in decimal).

Line Length and Delimiters

You should be aware of two more mechanical details. First, there are no continuation ("wrap-around") lines in Turbo. That is, no single line of code can have more than 127 characters. This is more of a blessing than a restriction. Turbo offers all the constructions you will ever need to handle long text messages and complex decisions. But it does all this without using lines of codes that wrap confusingly on the screen. In this way, Turbo once again enforces program readability in spite of the programmer's worst habits.

Second, any two individual language elements must be separated by a blank space (which explains the prohibition on blanks within identifiers). Hitting the carriage return at the end of a line also serves to separate elements, as does including a comment. This is almost an academic distinction because you will generally put in blank spaces before comments to improve readability, anyhow.

Hard-core BASIC programmers who are used to "packing" lines—removing all extra spaces to conserve memory—can abandon this practice at once. Remember, the compilation process turns an optimally legible source program into an optimally compact machine-language program (that is, a program whose .COM form makes minimum demands on memory).

Incidentally, the automatic indenting feature of the Turbo editor takes care of most of the spacing and indenting that make the layout of a Turbo program so distinctive.

Comments

The use of informative identifiers goes a long way toward making your Turbo programs understandable, but in any programming language, including Turbo, the liberal use of comments also helps. Once again, you can use as many comments as you want without fear of slowing up the program or wasting memory space. The compiler strips out all comments from the executable code.

Comments in Turbo are set off by curly braces:

{This is a Turbo comment}

or by Pascal's usual parentheses and asterisks:

(* This also is a Turbo comment *)

While you cannot nest curly-brace comments within curly-brace comments, or parenthesis comments within parenthesis comments, you can nest one type of comment within the other set of symbols. This is a very effective tool in isolating program bugs. Entire sections of code—including existing comments—can be removed from execution ("commented out" in programmer's slang) simply by bracketing the entire block of code with the other set of symbols. Figure 2.3 contains a fragment of a complex procedure that has many embedded comments.

In debugging this code, you might want to eliminate one of the possible options—the user's choice between sorting alphabetically or by ZIP code. Notice the placement of the (∗ and ∗) symbols to remove the lines of code dealing with this option. If you just used the { } characters, the compiler would be confused by the braces-within-braces caused by the comments like

{ONLY TEST FOR "A"}

and

{PRESUME USER DOES NOT WANT ALPHABETIC SORT}

```
PROCEDURE InputFromExternalFile;
BEGIN
    CLRSCR; {clears the screen- -see Ch.5}
    WRITELN ('What file contains the UNalphabetized entries?  ');
    READLN (SourceFile);
    ASSIGN (InFile, SourceFile);
    WRITELN ('What file will contain the alphabetized list?' );
    READLN (TargetFile);
    ASSIGN (OutFile,TargetFile);
    RESET (InFile);
    RecNum := 0;
    AlphaOnly := FALSE;   {Presume user does not want alphabetic sort}
    (*
    WRITELN ('Type A to sort alphabetically; Z to sort by ZIP code');
    READLN (AlphaOrZip);
    IF AlphaOrZIP = 'A' THEN AlphaOnly := TRUE; {ONLY TESTS FOR "A"}
    *)
    WHILE NOT EOF (InFile) DO {loads array with last names}
       BEGIN
          READ (Infile,Customer);
          RecNum := RecNum + 1;
          Number := Customer.ZIP;
          IF AlphaOnly THEN Number := '0';
          SORT[RecNum].ZIPAndName := Number + Customer.LastName;
          SORT[RecNum].Key := RecNum;
       END;
    MaxRec := RecNum;
    CLOSE(Infile);
END;
```

Figure 2.3 – Using alternate comment delimiters.

So with just a set of the (∗ ∗) comment delimiters you could remove a combination of code and any existing comments. Once you found and corrected the problem, of course, it would be a simple matter of removing the (∗ ∗) symbols to reinstate the entire block of code and comments.

Turbo uses the comment delimiters for one additional special purpose. Special instructions to the Turbo compiler are indicated as comments, with the further provision that the comment must appear as the first character on a line. The exact syntax and procedure will be covered in the discussion of compiler options.

Turbo Program Format

By now it should be clear that Turbo is more than just a set of programming conventions. It is the embodiment of a philosophy that stresses clarity, simplicity, and intelligibility. Even the few syntactical rules you've already seen are as much a help to you in sharpening your own thinking process as they are conditions imposed by the limitations of the compiler. In Turbo, unlike many programming languages, most conventions are there not simply because the compiler is incapable of handling a different structure, but because the required command structure is probably the one that best parallels your natural ways of attacking problems.

With this in mind, the very structure of a Turbo program can be viewed as an aid to orderly thought rather than a reflection of the irritating shortcomings of the compiler. In its simplest form, Turbo demands that you declare who the players will be (data types, variables, constants, and procedures) before you begin the game.

This is no more awkward than the rule that baseball managers must hand in line-ups to the umpire before the game begins. It is no more artificial than making out a shopping list before you go to the supermarket, or laying out your clothes the night before going to an important meeting. If these procedures are common sense in everyday activities, they are also common sense in developing a Turbo Pascal program to perform some task.

In fact, before we explore the format of a Turbo program, let's think how we would build, say, a garden shed. First, we would figure out what we wanted to build and would probably draw a blueprint (an algorithm). Next we would put together a shopping list to take to the lumber yard, listing the materials needed to construct the shed. We would probably also determine which tools would be needed and among those tools, which ones we would have to buy, borrow, or rent and which ones are already on hand. Then, and only then, with a plan, materials, and tools, could we build the garden shed.

In Turbo, you follow an analogous process. Your materials list becomes the declaration part of your program—listing the kinds of data that will be used. Gathering the tools is analogous to creating the specific procedures used to manipulate the data. Finally, the main body of the program uses the tools (procedures) upon the materials (data) to build the shed (solve the programming problem).

Figure 2.4 shows the organization of a Turbo program. Not all programs have all the parts shown here, but even the most complex program can be broken down into these parts. Again, it might be good to glance at CALC.PAS to see how a very complex program conforms to this organization.

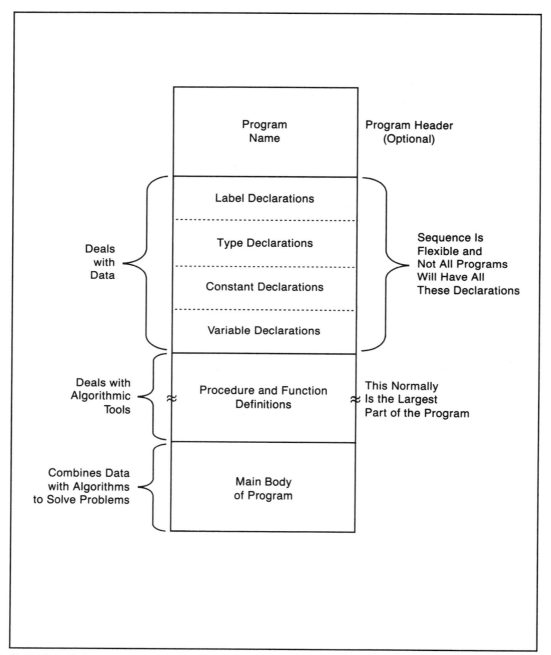

Figure 2.4 – Turbo program organization.

Figure 2.5 is a listing of a simple program that uses the number of band members and the number of "away" football games to calculate how many bus tickets will be required over the course of the entire season. Of course, you would probably find a number 2 pencil to be the most appropriate technology for solving this problem in the real world. Nonetheless, the program called BandBusTickets clearly illustrates several important points about any Turbo program.

Program Header

The first part, as you already know, is the program header; it contains the program name and, conceivably, information about files used for input and output. The program header is entirely optional in Turbo, absolutely required by standard Pascal, and treated differently by other Pascal implementations. You will almost always want to give your programs names, because a well-chosen name will remind you instantly of what the program is all about. Because the DOS file name is restricted to eight characters and a three-character extension, the amount of information you can cram into the DOS file name is limited. But the Turbo program name can really tell you what is going on. Compare these names:

DOS File Name	Turbo Program Name
SIMPLE.PAS	CalculateSimpleInterestOnSavingsAccount
COMPOUND.PAS	CalculateCompoundInterestOnSavingsAccount
SIMPLE2.PAS	Calculate_Simple_Interest_On_Car_Loan

The important point is that the Turbo program name is for your benefit. The compiler ignores it. In Figure 2.5, the program header is the program name BandBusTickets.

Declaration Section

Turbo requires that every item of data and every program module be *declared* before it is used in the execution of the program. Data declaration simply means telling the Turbo compiler what data it will have to accept while processing the program. It is necessary so that the compiler can allocate the right amount of space in memory to accomplish the task as efficiently as possible. Because some kinds of data take up more space than others (obviously, storing pi to eight decimal places—3.14159265—will take up more memory space than storing the integer 3 or the character code Q), the compiler needs to know not only what data it will be seeing but what kind of data it is. You will see that this information is required not only to allocate space, but to control the way the compiler performs different mathematical operations. Because knowing and manipulating the different data types are so critical to getting the most out of Turbo, we'll explore these topics at length in their own section.

The syntax for type declarations is very straightforward, using a colon to separate the identifier from the data type. You will see many examples of this syntax throughout the book.

Perhaps most important, though, is that the need to declare variables allows the compiler to keep you honest! In BandBusTickets, the variables we are going to use are called Band_Members, Games, and Tickets. The information that will be represented by these variables is obvious. What is less obvious, however, is that each of these variables represents a number. In a different program, the identifier Band_Members might well refer to strings of characters representing a list of names rather than a number.

Also, in this example declaration, the compiler is told that the kind of numbers to be represented by each variable will be integers. Thus, if we were to tell the program that we had 7.3 band members

```
PROGRAM BandBusTickets;

VAR
    Band_Members, Games, Tickets: INTEGER;

BEGIN
    WRITELN ('How many members are there in the band?  ');
    READLN (Band_members);
    WRITELN ('How many away games are there?  ');
    READLN (Games);
    Tickets := Games * Band_Members;
    WRITELN;
    WRITELN ('You will need ', Tickets, ' bus tickets this season.')

END
```

Figure 2.5 – A simple Turbo program.

(not an integer), the Turbo compiler would be quick to flag the error. Similarly, if we were to give a list of band members' names instead of a simple number, the compiler would not accept it. Immediately, then, the compiler acts to check the *validity* of our input. Languages with this emphasis on paying attention to data types are said to be "strongly typed."

In Defense of Strong Typing

Perhaps no other aspect of Turbo Pascal elicits as much heated debate as the necessity of declaring the type of variables. Many programmers who have become used to the freedom of BASIC see this requirement as a nuisance and conclude that Pascal is an awkward and annoying language.

It is worth pointing out the benefits of this process of declaring variables. Strong typing characterizes many of the modern languages—Pascal, C, Modula2, and Ada—because it leads to clearer thinking. And nobody needs to be reminded that clearer thinking inevitably results in programs that require less debugging and can be supported more easily in the future. Moreover, forcing the programmer to be precise in the naming and typing of data greatly simplifies the design of the compiler for a "strongly typed" language. The inherent efficiency and simplicity of its various compilers is one reason Turbo can be such a bargain and yet so powerful. Taking the larger view, it also explains why the other strongly-typed languages are becoming more popular in the world of commercial software development. They simply provide more performance with less complexity.

On a much more basic level, however, strong typing helps you avoid errors. Some of the hardest bugs to find in BASIC programs come from simple typos and misspellings. You may think you are manipulating the same variable in two different places, when you actually typed them differently, so that the program treats them as two separate variables. Your Turbo compiler will immediately flag this kind of error and tell you it doesn't recognize the typo ("undefined identifier") because it is not on the list of declared variables.

An even more insidious bug, however, crops up in large programs—and then, only when it can be the hardest to track down. You may forget that you used a variable like LIMIT or START earlier in the program and proceed to use it later. Unless you are very careful to initialize the value each time you use it, you can get unpredictable results if a single variable name is used in two different contexts. Again, Turbo immediately precludes this kind of error with a "duplicate definition" message. If only to avoid debugging hassles like these, declaring variables would be worth the minor annoyance.

Actually, declaring a variable's type along with its name is not unknown in BASIC. After all, in BASIC the last character of a string variable must be a dollar sign, string constants must be bracketed by quotation marks, and variables whose type or precision is critical to computational accuracy—or efficient utilization of memory—are ended (at least in Microsoft BASIC) with %, !, or #. These special characters serve the same purpose as type declarations in Turbo. You'll notice that when writing large, memory-hungry BASIC programs, many programmers specify that the counter variable in simple loops (e.g., FOR J% = 1 to 17) be an integer, so as not to waste the memory that the default representation (as a single-precision, real number) would require. Look at a few ambitious BASIC programs written by professionals and see how often you spot the DEFINT (define as integer) command in their programs for this very reason.

Turbo, then, encourages you to make the best use of memory by requiring you to think about the type of data you will be using. As you'll see later, an additional value of this discipline is that it also makes you think about the precision of the computations Turbo will do for you—a particularly critical concern in any program that deals with money! Yet another benefit of strong typing is that a Turbo program will immediately flag invalid input rather than compute meaningless results.

Once you have written a few programs in Turbo, declaring variables becomes second nature. And once you start working with data structures of your own creation, you will wonder why anybody would use programming languages that did not pay such close attention to data.

Constants

In addition to variables, Turbo programs expect all other data elements to be identified. Among the most common of these elements are *constants*. A constant is simply a specific value associated with a user-created identifier. Constants can be of any data type. Some examples might be:

```
Pi = 3.1416          (* real number *)
Treasures = 25       (* integer *)
Tax_Rate = 0.05      (* real number *)
RingBell = #07       (* character code *)
Message = 'I do not know that word, please try again' (* string *)
```

Constants serve two functions in Turbo. The most common is to represent a value that is constant and will not change throughout the execution of a program. An additional helpful application of the constant-declaration section is to initialize a variable, or set it equal to an initial value. This makes the starting value immediately obvious to anyone looking at the listing; it also removes the burden of adding several statements of initialization code later in the program.

The values of the constants in the example above can not be changed by the program. If we want to use the constant definition to initialize the values, we have to modify the declaration to include both the data type and the initial value:

```
Pi : REAL = 3.1416;
Treasures : INTEGER = 25;
Tax_Rate : REAL = 0.05;
RingBell : CHAR = #07;
Message : STRING [80] = 'I do not know that word, please try again';
```

Declaring Structures

We've seen that Turbo requires you to declare an identifier and data type for each element of data. You must also identify the algorithmic devices you will be using. In normal English, this means, "What are you calling the modules of code that solve the programming problem?" If you use only Turbo's own toolbox of procedures and functions, there is nothing to be declared here. Typical standard Turbo functions include the commands for all basic screen and disk I/O, all the trigonometric functions, and a host of others.

Nevertheless, all but the most trivial programs include some user-defined program modules. It is these modules—your own procedures and functions—that make up the bulk of most programs and serve as the arena for most of your programming skills.

It is now time to look at a more complex program than those you have seen already. Although it contains many features that have not been described yet, look at Figure 2.6 for a program example called Headliner.

Procedures and Functions

Most of the code in a typical Turbo program is contained in the various modules called *procedures*. You will see that *functions* are really just a specialized type of the general concept of *procedures*. A function, by definition, produces a data value and can be substituted for a data variable. Procedures may produce data, but they also do

```
PROGRAM Headliner;    {header}

VAR                    {declarations}
   NumberOfStars : INTEGER;
   Message : STRING[76];
   StartPoint : INTEGER;

PROCEDURE StarLine (Width : INTEGER);
VAR
   Counter : INTEGER;
BEGIN
   FOR Counter := 1 TO Width DO WRITE ('*');
   WRITELN;
END;

PROCEDURE GetUserMessage;
BEGIN
   WRITELN ('What is your message?  ');
   READLN (Message);
END;

BEGIN              {program execution begins here}
   GetUserMessage;
   CLRSCR;
   NumberOfStars := Length(Message) + 4;
   StarLine (NumberOfStars);
   WRITELN ('  ',Message,'  ');
   StarLine (NumberOfStars)
END.
```

Figure 2.6 – Turbo program using several procedures.

quite a few other things. Thus, they may not necessarily be substituted freely for data variables. Most of this book is concerned with creating procedures and functions.

Labels

Turbo allows you to declare *labels,* or names of places within a program to which you can jump using the familiar GOTO instruction. Although labels are normally declared before the data, at the top of a program, they are used by the system to control program flow, so it makes sense to group them—at least in your mind—with procedures and functions. Labels are used only rarely, because it is common practice to write Turbo programs without ever using a GOTO. In fact, many Turbo programmers avoid the use of GOTOs not only to improve program clarity but as a way to demonstrate their mastery of Turbo's spectacular collection of control structures. There also are some restrictions on what you can do with a GOTO in Turbo. But if you are going to use GOTOs and labels, the labels must be declared. Unlike all other forms of Pascal, Turbo applies all the same rules to labels as it does to other user-created identifiers. In addition, labels can begin with a number. Standard Pascal and most implementations restrict labels to four-digit numbers.

The Main Body of the Program

The main body of most Pascal programs tends to be the shortest part of all. Generally, the main body consists only of commands for initial and final housekeeping tasks (typically opening and closing files and perhaps printing screen messages) and then calls to the procedures, which do all the work of the program. The main body always begins with the reserved word BEGIN and ends with the reserved word END (followed by a period). Its descriptive procedure names should also immediately convey a sense of what the major elements of the program will be. Figure 2.7 shows the main body of a real mailing-list program.

Program Structures Summarized

Programs begin with an optional header, which identifies the program. Following this comes the declaration of labels and the data that will be used in the program—variables, constants, and data structures. Next come declarations concerning the program operation and flow—procedures and functions. Unlike other Pascals, Turbo is flexible in its declaration format. Variables, types, constants, and labels can be declared in any order. Also, they can be declared in more than one section, although fragmenting your declaration section serves no purpose in all but the most complex programs. In these programs, you may feel that keeping the data declarations grouped with the relevant procedures makes the program easier to follow. (Of course, by the time you are writing programs that complex, you won't need this book for advice.)

Finally, the last section of a Turbo program is the main body, which does little more than call all the predefined procedures.

Punctuation

You'll soon see that Turbo has some precise rules concerning punctuation. These rules are best learned through practice, but they can be summarized here. The major rules for punctuation of type declarations are:

- A *constant* declaration uses an equal sign and ends with a semicolon:

  Pi = 3.1416;

- A *variable* declaration uses a colon and ends with a semicolon:

  Rooms_Visited : INTEGER;

```
BEGIN        {actual program execution begins here}
   AllFinished:=FALSE;
   Initialize;
   WHILE NOT AllFinished DO
      BEGIN
         DisplayMenu;
         InterpretChoice;
      END;
END.
```

Figure 2.7 – Main body of a multipage Turbo program.

- All declarations can be joined with commas:

  Ogres_Slain, Objects_Carried, Rooms_Visited : INTEGER;

  Selling_Price, Tax_Rate : REAL;

You may wonder when to end a line with a semicolon and when not to. In Turbo, the semicolon is a *statement separator*. For the most part, this means that it appears at the end of almost every line of code. In a few control structures (IF/THEN/ELSE being the most common), the individual options are not separated by semicolons, no matter how complex they may be. Also, the last statement before the final END. of a program does not have to end with a semicolon.

Most programmers find it hard to remember the punctuation rules at first. There is nothing to worry about, though, because the Turbo compiler has several error messages to point out exactly what punctuation is wrong or misplaced. Finding and correcting these mechanical errors is a breeze in Turbo. In other Pascals, finding punctuation errors is more often like root-canal work. In Turbo, the easiest way to become familiar with punctuation is to study the punctuation used in program examples, write your own programs, and pay attention to the helpful messages from the compiler.

The correct punctuation will quickly become second nature.

Variables Revisited

So far, we've looked briefly at variables in Turbo, but without really getting beyond the meaning we already share from high-school algebra and programming in other languages. Turbo uses the term *variable* to refer to any location in the computer's memory that contains the value of some item of data. Generally, this value is either unknown during some or all of the program's execution or is likely to change at some time during the execution. Almost all programs are written to find the result of manipulating or computing some variable.

As mentioned already, Turbo is very flexible in the ways you can identify the data you are going to be using in a program. This flexibility applies to variables, constants, and entire data structures. We have also touched upon Turbo's insistence on knowing the type of data associated with any identifier. We can now explore the basic data types in Turbo. The treatment will emphasize the concepts and applications of the different data types. As with all of Turbo's rules of syntax, the best way to learn the mechanics of using data types is by writing your own code and letting Turbo's straightforward error messages serve as your line-for-line personal tutor. Most people feel that learning a large body of rules is a chore, but correcting a few specific lines of code in direct response to error messages leads to a painless assimilation of the rules. The Turbo compiler automatically positions the cursor on the erring line and prints explicit error messages like "Integer constant expected," "Invalid result type," or "Error in integer constant." Responding to such clear messages in the context of your program makes the application of the rules clear in real— rather than hypothetical—situations.

Turbo's Predefined Data Types

The predefined data types in Turbo Pascal are *integer, real, byte, character,* and *Boolean.* A predefined data type is one that is already known to the Turbo compiler. You merely have to declare a variable as belonging to one of these types, and the compiler will know what to do without any further definition on your part. By contrast, when you start defining your own data types, you will have to define them in terms of predefined data types.

One important point to remember about all data types is that they refer to both variables and constants.

Integers

Integers are simply the whole numbers. They can be positive or negative, in the range from − 32768 to 32767. The vast majority of loops and counters are controlled with integer values:

FOR X = 1 **TO** 10 **DO**

In Turbo Pascal, an integer is stored in memory using two bytes. Incidentally, never use a comma within an integer. The Turbo compiler will generate an error message, thinking that you have mixed numbers with an alphabetic character. The BCD (binary-coded decimal) option available from Borland supports extensive formatting of numerical output. If you don't have that option, and find that you need to format output with commas, it is not difficult to write your own procedure to analyze a number, determine where any commas belong, and then output the number with commas in place.

Turbo has a standard identifier, MAXINT, which is a constant equal to 32767 (the largest positive integer). Larger numbers can be accommodated, of course, but if a calculation is likely to produce a number larger than 32767, the Turbo compiler will *not* flag this integer overflow. Instead, it will complete the calculation with utterly spurious data! If your program is going to use larger numbers, there are several ways to avoid this problem, the simplest being to use real values instead.

Integers can be added, subtracted, and multiplied exactly as you would expect. In each case the result of the computation is also an integer. Division, however, can produce results that are not integers. For example, 8/2 produces the integer 4, but 4/3 produces the non-integer result 1.33333. If you want a real-number result, all well and good—Turbo will be glad to provide it. But if you are looking for integer results, Turbo has two special mathematical operators, DIV and MOD. They operate exactly as they do in BASIC. DIV returns the integer quotient of an operation, and MOD returns the remainder. For example:

```
15 DIV 3   = 5
15 DIV 2   = 7    (not 7.5, which is not an integer)
15 / 3     = 5.0 (a real number)
15 / 2     = 7.5 (a real number)
15 MOD 3 = 0    (there is no remainder; 2 divides into 10 evenly)
15 MOD 2 = 1
```

As a reminder, you can also work with integers expressed as hexadecimal numbers. This capability is particularly useful when you are exploiting Turbo's advanced commands for bit and byte manipulation, or directly manipulating memory addresses (which are always expressed in hex). Hex values are preceded with a dollar sign, so that the decimal number 2634 would be expressed as $A4B.

Byte Values

The *byte* data type refers to the *subrange* of integers with values between 0 and 255. As the name implies, a byte value takes up only one byte of memory space. Byte data items can be mixed freely with integers. You will almost never use this data type except for programs in which you have to conserve every possible byte of memory. In most other cases, you will find using the integer type to be more natural.

Real Numbers

Real numbers have two distinct applications that cannot be served by integers. The most important is that they can express fractional values. Whether you need to express 1.5 or 0.0000000285, you must use a real number. In addition, real numbers can express a much wider range of numbers (without special programming tricks) than can integers.

Because very large and very small numbers are so unwieldy (with those long strings of zeros), Turbo normally expresses real numbers using *exponential notation*. This includes a *base* (or *mantissa*) and an *exponent*. A few examples should help you recall this technique from algebra. Figure 2.8 shows a short program and the output it produces.

```
BEGIN
   WRITELN (0.12345);
   WRITELN (1.2345);
   WRITELN (12.345);
   WRITELN (0.0000000012345);
   WRITELN (12345000000.0)
END.


   1.2345000000E-01
   1.2345000000E+00
   1.2345000000E+01
   1.2345000000E-09
   1.2345000000E+10
```

Figure 2.8 – Turbo program to write a range of real numbers.

The wisdom and flexibility of using exponential notation are shown most dramatically when you examine the greatest and smallest numbers that can be represented as real values in Turbo. They are:

1E – 38 to 1E38

That is a much neater way to express the same values as these:

1 × 1/100,000,000,000,000,000,000,000,000,000,000,000,000

and

1 × 100,000,000,000,000,000,000,000,000,000,000,000,000

Although it is a clever method for expressing very large, small, or precise numbers, exponential notation is definitely awkward when expressing common numbers like $1.75, 1/2, or even 1.0. Unfortunately, Turbo, like all other Pascals, defaults to expressing real numbers in this form. For output to the screen or printer, you can always convert this representation into the more familiar decimal notation with a comprehensive set of formatting controls. This conversion will be covered in the section describing screen I/O.

A real value takes six bytes of memory.

Although the possibility of calculated values exceeding the limits of real values is much less likely than that of exceeding the bounds of integers, you should still watch out for it. If you instruct the computer to perform a calculation that produces a value larger than the limit, the program will halt rather than progress with an invalid result. As with integers, if you do use numbers outside the range, there are advanced techniques for handling them; these techniques are outside the scope of this book.

Real numbers lend themselves to performing calculations. All the basic mathematical operations use them in the way you would expect. On the other hand, real numbers do not lend themselves to most programming control structures. Specifically, they cannot be used to index arrays or to control counters and loops. There are a few other restrictions on the use of real numbers, but they are either obvious or so obscure you need not bother about them until you are writing very advanced Turbo programs.

Boolean Values

Most programmers think of Boolean values as having only the values TRUE and FALSE. For the most part, this is equally correct in Turbo. On probing more deeply, though, you will see that Turbo (like many programming languages) equates TRUE *internally* as 1 and FALSE as 0. This ability to use either a numerical value or the words TRUE and FALSE can lead to some interesting programming tricks. Boolean, or logical values, are used exclusively in conditional statements that control program flow. A Boolean value takes up only one byte of memory.

Characters

We have already mentioned that characters can be any ASCII code between 0 and 255. Even if your computer and printer do not have characters for the codes between 128 and 255, you still can use these values in Turbo programs. Turbo has several powerful tools for sorting, ordering ("alphabetizing"), and comparing characters. Remember, too, that even though Borland's documentation refers to characters as ASCII codes, your programs can manipulate them regardless of their ASCII meaning. For example, although Turbo internally accepts #11 as an ASCII code, when you output this character to an external device, it might show up as an EBCDIC character or even an "end-of-take" to an old Teletype machine. Characters become particularly useful when used in groups to form strings. A character takes up only one byte of memory.

A Note on Scalar Types

The data types mentioned so far (integer, real, byte, character, and Boolean) are referred to in some books, including the Borland documentation, as *scalar* types. Unfortunately, different sources define this term differently, and different implementations have chosen— arbitrarily it would seem—just what types to include. The term *scalar* should apply to any data type that includes a collection of discrete values. The most common definition, involving a scale with fixed intervals, implies that there is always a clear-cut predecessor or successor for any value. This definition works well for whole numbers (1, 2, 3, etc.), characters (A, B, C, etc.), and even Boolean values

(TRUE or FALSE), but it doesn't work with real numbers. What is the predecessor of 3.0? Is it 2.0 or 2.9 or 2.99999? From a programming point of view, then, the most logical definition for scalars is that they are data types that can be used to make a decision or operate a counter (choose option A, B, or C or to control the typical DO loop: FOR X=1 TO 17 DO . . .). Clearly you need a data type in which values have fixed, discrete steps.

On the other hand, some Pascals (including Turbo) lump real numbers as scalar values—and then give a catalog of restrictions on the use of reals. The reason is that real numbers can be used to control some situations (for example, "IF P > 2.75 THEN DO something"). The best thing you can do is try to ignore the confusing and contradictory concept of scalars. But remember, when establishing counters and loops and tests, that real numbers generally don't lend themselves to controlling program flow as well as the true scalar types.

User-defined Data Types

We'll come back to this topic when we explore more ambitious data structures, but you should know that the data types we have seen are all standard, predefined types. Most computer scientists class all data types as data structures, with a distinction drawn between simple structures—characters, integers, real numbers, and so on—which cannot be broken up into more fundamental units; and complex data structures—strings, arrays, records, files, and so on—which are made up by combining simple structures. This is roughly analogous to atoms and molecules. You are perfectly free to create your own data types as well as your own data structures. When you write your own text formatter program, you might need a data structure called "page," made up of several strings. Similarly, you can arrange a group of Boolean values into an array called "Answer_Key" for correcting true-and-false exams.

If these examples seem a trifle contrived, perhaps you should know that you can create a data type called "Week," made up of individual elements called "Monday," "Tuesday," "Wednesday," etc. You can create your own "alphabet" in any sequence. This capability was a tremendous help when a program had to be written to manipulate text encoded in the TTS code used on phototypesetting equipment. This code (totally unlike ASCII and EBCDIC) was designed in the era before computers. The numerical codes that represent the letters of the alphabet are determined by the order of frequency in which the characters occur in normal English, rather than in alphabetical order. Alphabetizing by character-code numbers was impossible. In Turbo, the programmer simply defined a data type called "TTSCodes" and listed the possible codes in their actual alphabetical order.

Turbo also has a powerful set of tools for combining data items of different types into coherent structures called records. All of these will be covered in time, but as you use data types in the earliest programming examples, you should be aware that you are developing habits that will enable you to transcend the limitations of earlier, albeit, slightly simpler languages.

Math Operators and the Order of Precedence

Most of Turbo's rules about mathematical operators and the order of operations are common to most programming languages, and the habits you may have acquired in BASIC or FORTRAN carry over here. Because Turbo is so strongly typed, however, it is quite sensitive to operations on unlike data types. You have to pay attention when adding real numbers and integers, or dividing integers when you want a real number result. It is easy to overlook these combinations, but once again, Turbo's clear error messages will generally point out the problem. In any case, Figure 2.9 sums up the operators in Turbo and the types of data that can be used with each. Figure 2.10 lists the order of precedence of the different operators.

When you write a program, just use common sense and refer to the tables when you run into a situation that can't be solved more quickly by trial and error, using the instant feedback from the results of your calculations or the messages from the Turbo compiler. At worst, you can try to decipher the standard Borland documentation for all the gory details.

As a rule, when integers and real numbers are permitted to be mixed in a computation, the result will be a real value.

For math calculations:		INPUT TYPES	RESULT TYPE
*	multiplication	int	int
		real	real
		int, real	real
/	division	real	real
		int	real
		int, real	real
+	addition	int	int
		real	real
		real, int	real
−	subtraction or unary minus	int	int
		real	real
		int, real	real

The following are used exclusively for integer division:

DIV (quotient)		int	int
MOD (remainder)		int	int

The following take a range of inputs but always produce Boolean results, which can be interpreted either as TRUE and FALSE or as 1 and 0:

=	equality
<	less than
>	greater than
<=	less than or equal to
>=	greater than or equal to
<>	not equal to

Figure 2.9 – Turbo operators (continues).

The following take Boolean or integer values for intput:

NOT	arithmetic not (bit inversion)	int	int
	logical not	Boolean	Boolean
AND	arithmetic and	int	int
	logical and	Boolean	Boolean
OR	arithmetic or	int	int
	logical or	Boolean	Boolean

The following are used primarily for manipulating bit patterns and producing modified bit patterns (it is assumed that the raw bit patterns are considered as integers for input and output):

XOR	arithmetic not or	int	int
XOR	logical not or	Boolean	Boolean
SHL	shift left	int	int
SHR	shift right	int	int

Figure 2.9 – Turbo operators (continued).

Operations take place from left to right. When operators are of the same precedence, the leftmost operation takes place first.

Values within parentheses are evaluated first regardless of the operator involved within or before the parentheses. With nested parentheses, the innermost parentheses are evaluated first.

The standard order of precedence in Turbo Pascal is:

Unary minus	(−)
Logical negation	(NOT)
All forms of multiplication and division	(∗, /, DIV, MOD, AND, SHL, SHR)
All forms of addition and subtraction	(+, −, OR, XOR)
All relational operators	(=, <, >, <>, <=, >=, IN)

Figure 2.10 – Operators and data types.

Expressions

You have noticed that data types do not solve problems by themselves. They have to be manipulated and combined into *expressions* to do something useful. An expression (to all but the most hard-core mathematicians) is simply a meaningful sequence of terms separated by operators. Some expressions are:

+ 2

Principle + Interest

3.14 * 208

Numbers AND Letters

7 + SQRT(144)

– Temperature (the negative of the value identified by Temperature)

A < B

An expression can consist of variables, constants, and functions. A few rules govern the use of expressions. The most important is this: All the operators used in an expression must be valid for the data types upon which they are operating.

The discussion, under the heading "Integers" of DIV and MOD illustrates this rule. The following is not a valid expression:

3.00 **DIV** 1.00

Even though you know the answer "should be" 3, the DIV operator can only work on integers. Again, the Turbo compiler helps catch and point out most of these gross errors. Somehow, seeing the errors flagged in your own programs does an excellent job of conveying the principles.

Statements

A statement is any single, clearly-defined instruction to the computer. Statements get things done. In our first program, the line:

WRITELN ('Good Morning')

was a statement. In the BandBusTickets program, other statements were:

```
WRITELN ('How many members are there in the band? ');
READLN (Band_members);
```

Statements perform input and output; they also take the result of some expression and assign it to an identifier. Here are some examples:

```
Tickets : = Games * Band_Members;
TotalPrice : = Cost + Overhead
Location : = Treasure_Room
Apples : = Oranges
SumOfTheSquares : = SQR(A) + SQR(B)
Counter : = Counter + 1
```

Notice that expressions need to be combined into statements to do any work. In the earlier example, the expression 2 + 2 is meaningless unless you do something with the result:

```
Sum : = 2 + 2
```

You have noticed the use of the *assignment operator* (: =) instead of the simple equal sign familiar from BASIC and everyday math. Turbo uses the equal sign solely to test for equality. An equal sign by itself is considered a *relational operator.* The assignment operator assigns some value to some identifier. A syntactical definition for an assignment statement is this: a variable and an expression linked by an assignment operator.

Turbo allows you to use a group of statements (a *compound statement*) whenever a single statement is legal. This freedom makes GOTO constructions unnecessary, and allows you to construct some very powerful structures. Compound statements are always bracketed by the reserved words BEGIN and END. In the program listed in Figure 2.11, all the lines between these words make up a compound statement. You don't have to bother with the details of the CASE statement yet; we will cover its operation in Chapter 3 along with the creation of procedures. What is important in Figure 2.11 is that the multiple lines of the CASE statement replace a single line calling a procedure such as ProduceLabels. Instead of a simple call to one procedure, the CASE statement—clearly a compound statement made up of eleven lines—selects any one of nine different options based on the operator input. Note that the result of the eleven lines of code—calling one procedure—is the same work done by a one-line, simple statement.

In Figure 2.12 an even more complex example demonstrates compound statements within compound statements.

```
PROCEDURE InterpretChoice;   {interprets menu selection}
BEGIN
    READLN (Option);
    CASE Option OF
        1: AcceptNewNames;
        2: AlphabetizeList;
        3: SortLabelsByZip;
        4: ProofListToScreen;
        5: ProduceLabels;
        6: CreateMailingListBook;
        7: LookUpOrChangeAnEntry;
        8: ExitProgram;
    ELSE ErrorHandler;
  END;
END;
```

Figure 2.11 – Use of compound statement.

```
PROCEDURE SortProg;
BEGIN        {SortProg}
   FOR Pass := MaxRec DOWNTO 2 DO
     BEGIN
       Swap := true;
       IF Swap THEN
       BEGIN             {while swap flag set}
         I := 1;
         Swap := false;
         WHILE  I < MaxRec DO
           BEGIN              {actual swap}
             IF Sort[I].Name > Sort [I+1].Name THEN FlipFlop;
             I := I+1;
           END;        {end swap}
       END;    {While swap flag is set}
     END;    {Each Pass . . . }
 END;  {entire SortProg}
```

Figure 2.12 – Program with compound statements within compound statements.

Although this example may seem a little intimidating at first, it can be broken down into BEGIN and END pairs. Notice the use of comments in this procedure to help identify which END goes with which BEGIN. This example also demonstrates how the consistent use of indenting helps the reader to see compound statements as logical modules.

Common
Tools and
Techniques

Chapter 3

Introduction and a
Warning of Incompatibility

All programs need to handle information coming from the outside world. A completely self-contained program is, by definition, a useless program. Most programs expect some human interaction, generally through the keyboard and screen. Many programs also send output to a line printer. More ambitious programs use the computer's other ports to manipulate data passing through a modem, accept input from joysticks, control machinery, drive a typesetter, or do some other useful work. When programmers think of input/output, these are the operations that come to mind immediately.

The other major area of I/O consists of reading and writing to files.

Standard Pascal was weak in the area of real-world I/O. Support for even the most trivially interactive use of the screen and keyboard was not available. All real-world I/O had to emulate punched cards or magnetic tape files, which can only be accessed *serially*—one item after another.

Random-access files were not part of the original Pascal world. Truly interactive screens—not to mention windows, colors, and graphics—were unheard-of. As a result of these severe restrictions, every implementation of Pascal offers some unique extensions for input/output. Turbo has an exceptional array of I/O tools, which not only surpass those of all other Pascals, but offer capabilities unequalled by any other PC-based language, and are only equalled by assembly language itself.

While many of the techniques for addressing ports and accepting interrupts are advanced topics, every program you write will include some I/O statements. You will see that Turbo is absolutely consistent in the ways it handles I/O, regardless of the devices. But once again, be warned that Turbo has chosen to offer optimal I/O and programming ease at the price of incompatibility with standard Pascal and most other Pascals as well. Almost every aspect of I/O in Turbo, from the most basic screen interaction to the transfer of huge disk files, is somehow unique to Turbo, or in some way differs from other implementations. In no other area is it quite so frustrating to follow the conventional Pascal programming books.

Interacting with You

Figure 3.1 is a listing for a program called Simple, which illustrates the most basic kind of screen I/O. Try running it on your own computer, but be sure to turn on your line printer first.

As a fast review, the program name is Simple. The declaration section contains only three identifiers (FirstInteger, SecondInteger, and Sum), which are integers. There are no procedures and functions; the body of the program comprises eight statements bracketed by the reserved words BEGIN and END.

Input to the program consist of two integers typed by the user. Output from the program includes not just the final sum, but also all the messages and prompts the program prints on the screen during the course of execution. Although you frequently think that only the last few lines of a program produce "useful" output, Turbo considers any information written by the program to be output.

Notice that in this program, output is sent to your screen and also to the line printer. Unlike some versions of BASIC, Turbo has no separate PRINT and LPRINT commands. In fact, Turbo uses one set of standard procedures to read from and write to screens, keyboards, line printers, modems, and other devices, and to text files and data files. Just as the original Pascal defined its world in terms of simple, sequential tape-like files, Turbo also defines the world of I/O as reading and writing files. The key difference, however, is that Turbo defines a file much more flexibly, to include the devices named above.

Run the Simple program, entering 5 and 9 in response to the prompts, and the computer will print out on your screen the information shown in Figure 3.2. It also prints on the line printer:

THE SUM IS: 14

The predefined procedure WRITELN takes care of this output for us. Similarly, the predefined procedure READLN took care of reading the two numbers you typed in response to the prompts and

```
PROGRAM Simple;

VAR
   FirstInteger, SecondInteger, Sum : INTEGER;

BEGIN
   WRITELN (OUTPUT, 'This program will add two integers');
   WRITELN ('What is the first number?' );
   READLN (INPUT, FirstInteger);
   WRITELN ('What is the second number?' );
   READLN (SecondInteger);
   Sum := FirstInteger + SecondInteger;
   WRITELN;
   WRITELN('The sum of your two numbers is ',Sum);
   WRITELN (1ST,'THE SUM IS: ',Sum)
END.
```

Figure 3.1 – Simple screen input and output.

```
This program will add two integers
What is the first number?  5
What is the second number? 9
The sum of your two numbers is 14
```

Figure 3.2 – Screen display produced by program Simple.

storing them in the variables FirstInteger and SecondInteger.

Take a closer look at the first statement:

WRITELN (OUTPUT, 'This program will add two integers');

All Turbo I/O follows a similar format. The command (READ, READLN, WRITE, or WRITELN) is followed by an argument in brackets. The argument specifies two things: the file you want to write to or read from, and the data involved. In this example we are writing one line to a file. The file name is OUTPUT and the data, of course, is the message between the two single quotes:

'This program will add two integers'

The single quotes, like the double quotes in a PRINT statement in BASIC, simply tell Turbo that the information is text and not an identifier (that is, a variable name). When printing out numbers, the writing commands can take additional arguments to control horizontal positioning. Specifically, you can specify how many leading spaces you want before the number begins, how wide a field the number can occupy, and, with real numbers, how many digits should appear beyond the decimal point.

In this example, OUTPUT is an identifier that refers to a predefined *standard output file.* Unless you specifically tell the system otherwise, this file will be your computer screen. Similarly, there is a predefined *standard input file,* called INPUT. Again, unless you specifically tell the system otherwise, it will be your computer keyboard. Now look at the next WRITELN statement:

WRITELN ('What is the second number?');

There appears to be something missing here, but the program still works. If no file name is given with a writing (output) statement, Turbo assumes you want output to go to the screen. Likewise, in any reading (input) statement, Turbo will assume you want to read input from your keyboard if you don't give the command a file name. Now look at the last WRITELN statement:

WRITELN (LST, 'THE SUM IS: ',Sum)

In this case, the data to be output is obviously the message (THE SUM IS:) but the file name is LST, the standard identifier for the system listing device—almost invariably the line printer.

Standard Files

With this simple format Turbo does virtually all its input and output. The data to be output can be anything: characters, numbers, variables, constants, strings, and entire records. And the files can be disk files as well as physical devices. To distinguish them, Turbo has several standard identifiers for files associated with common physical devices. They are listed in Figure 3.3. Generally, before you can read and write to files, Turbo requires a few special "housekeeping" steps: to identify the file, open it, position the file pointer at the beginning of the file, and close it when you are finished with it. Turbo takes care of all the housekeeping chores automatically when you use any of the predefined standard files shown in Figure 3.3. In effect, this means that even though physical devices are treated as files for consistency in using the READ and WRITE commands, you are spared the awkwardness that often accompanies this concept.

The most important of these files are INPUT, OUTPUT, and LST. They take care of all normal operator input and output and getting anything printed on the line printer. Turbo is simply giving *logical file names* to the data moving to and from physical devices. This means that you can write a Turbo program without regard for the physical devices that will be used on the system. Logical device names are a particularly powerful tool in writing communications programs and programs to drive external machines (punches, typesetters, stadium scoreboards, radioteletype terminal units, etc.). For example, you can write and debug a communications program using your console as the physical device, giving it the same logical name as the modem. You can look at the screen to check the output while debugging the basic code, and only assign the OUTPUT file name to the modem when you are ready to debug the "handshaking" code.

Standard Files and Logical Devices

There might be some confusion concerning the standard text files CON, TRM, and KBD (for console, terminal, and keyboard). The CON file directs output to the screen, takes input from your keyboard, and echoes the effect of your keyboard typing on your own screen. It also buffers your input, allowing you to backspace and delete characters before using the Enter key to transmit the data. Its operation is identical to the default INPUT and OUTPUT files.

Default Files Unless You Specify Other Output:

INPUT   Standard input device; assumes keyboard input. Buffers your typing so you can correct typing errors with the backspace and Escape keys. Echoes input on your screen, including all carriage returns and line feeds.

OUTPUT   Standard output device, normally your computer screen. Acts on all carriage returns and line feeds.

Used in Both Input and Output:

CON   Console device; performs both input and output, using the computer keyboard for input and the screen for output. Functions identically to using INPUT and OUTPUT.

TRM   Terminal device; performs both input and output, using the computer keyboard for input and the screen for output. Characters are echoed as they are typed but input is not buffered. Thus, your typing cannot be edited as you go along, but you do not have to hit the Enter key at the end of input.

AUX   Auxiliary device; performs both input and output. Normally used for a modem, but can refer to other devices as well, such as a paper-tape punch and reader. In fact, in CP/M implementations AUX is linked to the RDR: (reader) and PUN: (punch) logical devices. In MS-DOS it is linked to the COM1: logical device.

USR   User-defined device; performs both input and output. Used only in advanced programming projects for custom-written driver packages.

Input-Only and Output-Only Devices

KBD   Keyboard device; input only. Your typing is neither echoed to the screen nor buffered.

LST   System list device; output only. Normally the system line printer. Output is routed via the operating system, so you do not normally have to know whether the printer is serial or parallel nor into which port it is connected.

Figure 3.3 – Standard identifiers.

Although it would seem logical that merely substituting KBD for INPUT and TRM for OUTPUT would operate the same way, that is not the case. Both INPUT and CON make excellent use of keyboard buffering to make programs more tolerant of operator typing errors. As you type at the keyboard, the keystrokes are echoed on the screen, but they are not sent to the application program immediately. Instead, the are put into a temporary storage area called a buffer. You can manipulate the characters in the buffer—for example, overstriking, inserting, and deleting them. You must hit the Enter key to send the characters in the buffer to the application program. The concept is used in electronic typewriters, which have a small buffer to allow the user to correct typing errors before the characters appear on paper. Incidentally, buffering is provided by the operating system, not by the application program. KBD does not buffer input and your typing is not echoed on the screen. (This feature has its uses; passwords, for example, should not be printed on the screen.) To see the effect of using these file names, alter the program from Figure 3.1 to look like the program listed in Figure 3.4.

The two other predefined files are AUX and USR, which represent the auxiliary and "user" devices. Most often you will use AUX to refer to the RS-232 port on your computer—particularly when processing data moving to and from a modem. The USR file is generally

```
PROGRAM Simple;

VAR
   FirstInteger, SecondInteger, Sum : INTEGER;

BEGIN
   WRITELN (OUTPUT, 'This program will add two integers');
   WRITELN ('What is the first number?' );
   READLN (KBD, FirstInteger);   {How does this affect the
screen?}
   WRITELN ('What is the second number?' );
   READLN (CON, SecondInteger);   {How does this affect the
screen?}
   Sum := FirstInteger + SecondInteger;
   WRITELN;
   WRITELN ('The sum of your two numbers is ',Sum);
   WRITELN (LST,'THE SUM IS: ',Sum)
END.
```

Figure 3.4 – Program modified to demonstrate I/O to different standard files.

used in advanced I/O programs you have written to control a machine (such as a robot, plotter, or special graphics display).

Programmers familiar with CP/M and MS-DOS will find strong similarities between Turbo's standard file names and the names these operating systems give to logical devices. This similarity can be confusing, because Turbo also uses the concept of logical device names. Turbo's logical devices are listed in Figure 3.5. Most of these names are similar to the standard file identifiers, but logical devices always end with a colon. In day-to-day programming you can simply use the standard file name (such as LST) and ignore the distinction between that name and the logical device name (LST:).

In the example programs so far, you have used the functions WRITELN and READLN (for "write line" and "read line"). When you don't want to read all the information in a line (that is, up to an end-of-line delimiter), Turbo has two other commands: WRITE and READ. We'll discuss the difference between these two pairs of commands shortly, but first there are some variations on READLN and WRITELN illustrated in Figure 3.6.

Try entering and running this program. You should find that it does just about the same thing as the earlier demo program, except that for the sake of simplicity, this program doesn't print out to the line printer. There are a few minor changes, however, in the ways data is moved into and out of the program. First, the sequence in the first program:

```
WRITELN ('What is the first number?' );
READLN (INPUT, FirstInteger);
WRITELN ('What is the second number?' );
READLN (SecondInteger);
```

has been replaced with the more compact:

```
WRITELN ('Please type the two numbers you want to add. ');
READLN (FirstInteger, SecondInteger);
```

Also, a typical result of the first program might look like the following:

```
The sum of your two numbers is 278
```

All of the following devices are treated like text files for character I/O. Note that for each device name, there is a similarly named preassigned file (listed in Figure 3.3).

Devices Capable of Both Input and Output

CON: Console device; performs both input and output, using the computer keyboard for input and the screen for output. All keyboard input is echoed to the screen as it is typed. Input, however, is read from a one-line buffer, allowing the operator to edit input before it is read by the program.

TRM: Terminal device; performs both input and output, using the computer keyboard for input and the screen for output. Characters are echoed as they are typed, but input is not buffered.

AUX: Auxiliary device; performs both input and output. Normally used for a modem, but can refer to other devices as well, such as a paper-tape punch and reader. In fact, in CP/M implementations AUX is linked to the RDR: (reader) and PUN: (punch) logical device names. In MS-DOS it is linked to the COM1: logical device name.

USR: User-defined device; performs both input and output. Used only in advanced programming projects for custom-written driver packages—for example, controlling robots, driving phototypesetters, or communication with real-time data sampling devices.

Devices Restricted to Input-Only or Output-Only

KBD: Keyboard device; input only. Your typing is neither echoed to the screen nor buffered.

LST: System list device; output only. Normally the system line printer. Output is routed via the operating system, so you do not normally have to know whether the printer is serial or parallel, nor into which port it is connected.

Figure 3.5 – Logical devices.

while the result of the second program might look like this:

The sum of your two numbers is
278

These distinctions are clearly not earth-shaking in programs this trivial. When you read data from huge disk files, however, these fine points can make all the difference between having to write clumsy procedures to dissect blocks of data into its meaningful parts (name, address, city, and ZIP code, for example) and being able to zero in on the information you really want to access.

The READLN and READ commands can read as many different variables as you ask them to, as long as an end-of-line delimiter does not separate the values. You can see this in the second program, which minimizes the use of the first program's prompt–answer–read-the-answer loop. All you had to do in the second program was tell the READLN statement what identifiers to use for storing the input values. The commands are quite flexible and, if the identifiers have already been declared, one READ statement can accept a series of input values of different data types.

You will see example programs that use the commands READ and READLN apparently interchangeably. The difference between them is a particularly confusing point about Turbo. It is not intuitively obvious and is, unfortunately, buried in the standard documentation. Like all computer commands, the READ and READLN operations

```
PROGRAM WriteLines;

VAR
   FirstInteger, SecondInteger, Sum : INTEGER;

BEGIN
   WRITELN ('This program will add two integers while also showing
off some new techniques.');
   WRITELN ('Please type the two numbers you want to add. ');
   READLN (FirstInteger, SecondInteger);
   Sum := FirstInteger + SecondInteger;
   WRITELN;
   WRITELN ('The sum of your two numbers is ');
   WRITELN (Sum);
END.
```

Figure 3.6 – Program to demonstrate both line-oriented and individual value-oriented I/O.

are logical and consistent—once you understand what each is trying to do. Save yourself the aggravation of determining the difference between the two commands by bewildering trial-and-error (no helpful error messages here, because Turbo thinks it is doing exactly what you want it to). Run the series of programs and examine the screen displays listed in Figures 3.7 through 3.16. They should shed some light on what is actually a very simple operation.

Run the program in Figure 3.7. Figure 3.8 shows the results of running the program with no data input, just two carriage returns (represented by the symbol ◄┘). As you would expect, the variables are equal to their initialized value, zero.

Figure 3.9 shows the screen display with valid data input on one line only. In all these displays, individual numbers were entered separated by spaces.

```
PROGRAM Demonstrate_Read_And_Readln;

VAR
A, B, C, D : INTEGER;

PROCEDURE InitializeValues;
BEGIN
    A := 0;
    B := 0;
    C := 0;
    D := 0;
END;

PROCEDUREProofThem;
BEGIN
    WRITELN; WRITELN; {just for spacing on the screen}
    WRITELN ('A = ', A);
    WRITELN ('B = ', B);
    WRITELN ('C = ', C);
    WRITELN ('D = ', D);
END;

BEGIN
    InitializeValues;
    WRITELN ('Give me four integers: ');
    WRITELN;
    READLN (A, B);
    READ (C, D);
    ProofThem
END.
```

Figure 3.7 – Demonstration of READ and READLN.

Notice that although the program is looking for four numbers, it has only read the first two values on the line. The READLN instruction told it that once it read A and B it should ignore all other input on the line.

Figure 3.10 shows the screen display with valid data input on two lines.

Here again, the system was told to read the first two values from the first line and the first two values from the second line. (We typed more values than requested, to demonstrate exactly what will be read and what will be ignored.)

Figure 3.11 shows the same program as Figure 3.7, but with the first READLN changed to READ. This tiny change will have some startling effects. Figure 3.12 shows the screen display produced by this program.

```
     Give me four integers:

     ↵
     ↵

     A = 0
     B = 0
     C = 0
     D = 0
```

Figure 3.8 – Screen display from program in Figure 3.7, with no input values.

```
     Give me four integers:

     1   2   3   4 ↵
     ↵

     A = 1
     B = 2
     C = 0
     D = 0
```

Figure 3.9 – Screen display from program in Figure 3.7, with input values typed on just one line.

Figure 3.12 is not a typographic error! The numbers were each typed followed by a space. After the 9 a carriage return was entered, *but there was no indication of this on the screen because READ does*

```
        Give me four integers:

        1   2   3   4 ⏎
        5   6   7   8 ⏎

        A = 1
        B = 2
        C = 5
        D = 6
```

Figure 3.10 – *Screen display from program in Figure 3.7, with input values typed on two lines.*

```
        PROGRAM Demonstrate_Read_And_Readln;

        VAR
        A, B, C, D : INTEGER;

        PROCEDURE InitializeValues;
        BEGIN
           A := 0;
           B := 0;
           C := 0;
           D := 0;
        END;

        PROCEDURE ProofThem;
        BEGIN
           WRITELN; WRITELN; {just for spacing on the screen}
           WRITELN ('A = ', A);
           WRITELN ('B = ', B);
           WRITELN ('C = ', C);
           WRITELN ('D = ', D);
        END;

        BEGIN
           InitializeValues;
           WRITELN ('Give me four integers: ');
           WRITELN;
           READ (A, B);    {changed from READLN to READ}
           READ (C, D);
           ProofThem
        END.
```

Figure 3.11 – *Program modified to demonstrate READ command only.*

not look at end-of-line delimiters! But just by looking at the screen display you can tear your hair out wondering why the program seems to have skipped randomly from 2 to 10. Perhaps making the carriage return "visible" will make the pattern clearer. Figure 3.13 shows the screen with the carriage return displayed.

Figure 3.14 shows another situation, exactly as it would appear (perplexingly enough) on the screen. Figure 3.15 shows the same display with the "invisible" carriage returns marked.

```
      Give me four integers:

      1 2 3 4 5 6 7 8 9 10 11 12 13 14

      A = 1
      B = 2
      C = 10
      D = 11
```

Figure 3.12 – Screen display from modified program, with input values typed on two different lines.

```
      Give me four integers:

      1 2 3 4 5 6 7 8 9 ↵  10 11 12 13 14

      A = 1
      B = 2
      C = 10
      D = 11
```

Figure 3.13 – Screen display from Figure 3.12 with carriage return indicated.

```
      Give me four integers:

      1           2

      A = 1
      B = 0
      C = 2
      D = 0
```

Figure 3.14 – Screen display from modified program, with two input values separated by a carriage return (not displayed).

Finally, Figure 3.16 shows the program modified once again. Figure 3.17 shows the resulting screen display.

Finally, it makes sense.

Perhaps nothing in Turbo is quite so cryptically documented and unintuitive. Look at the examples again if the distinction between

```
Give me four integers:

1  ⏎       2  ⏎

A = 1
B = 0
C = 2
D = 0
```

Figure 3.15 – Screen display from Figure 3.14 with carriage returns indicated.

```
PROGRAM Demonstrate_Read_And_Readln;

VAR
A, B, C, D : INTEGER;

PROCEDURE InitializeValues;
BEGIN
   A := 0;
   B := 0;
   C := 0;
   D := 0;
END;

PROCEDURE ProofThem;
BEGIN
   WRITELN; WRITELN; {just for spacing on the screen}
   WRITELN ('A = ', A);
   WRITELN ('B = ', B);
   WRITELN ('C = ', C);
   WRITELN ('D = ', D);
END;

BEGIN
   InitializeValues;
   WRITELN ('Give me four integers: ');
   WRITELN;
   READLN (A, B, C, D);  {looking for all data on one line}
   ProofThem

END.
```

Figure 3.16 – Program modified to look for all values on just one line.

READ and READLN *in reading screen input* is still hazy. Better yet, modify the programs and experiment on your own.

To sum up the operation of these commands, in reading input from a data file, once the READLN command accepts all the values it is looking for, it ignores any other input on the same line and positions itself to do any further reading at the beginning of the next line. Conversely, once the READ command finds all the data it is looking for, it simply stops. It is positioned to do the next READ operation on the same line.

Look again at the program shown in Figure 3.1 to see how Turbo writes output. WRITELN and WRITE have different effects on the screen. WRITELN always outputs the specified information and then issues an end-of-line sequence. WRITE simply outputs information and does not "move on." Thus, a WRITELN by itself causes a blank line to print. In the version of the program shown in Figure 3.4, the value SUM was printed on a separate line because the information message

The sum of your two numbers is

was printed using the WRITELN command. Go back to this program and make the changes shown below. Change

WRITELN ('The sum of your two numbers is ');

to use WRITE:

WRITE ('The sum of your two numbers is ');

and look at the effect.

```
Give me four integers:

1 2 3 4 5 6 7 8 9 ◄┘


A = 1
B = 2
C = 3
D = 4
```

Figure 3.17 – Screen display from modified program, with input values typed all on one line.

Formatting Output

All of the programs so far have used only integers. We have avoided using real numbers up to now, because they require special handling on output for maximum legibility. Here is another well-hidden function, buried in the documentation supplied with Turbo Pascal. Turbo has some exceptionally flexible ways to format output, and they should not be buried in an obscure list of parameters as a footnote to the WRITE function. The next few programs should give you valuable practice in getting your printouts in the clearest possible format.

The program called AreaOfACircle in Figure 3.18 uses real numbers.

Enter and run the program. With a diameter of 1234.56789, the typical screen output would look like Figure 3.19. As you can see, exponential notation is not exactly the clearest way to present the output!

```
PROGRAM AreaOfACircle;

VAR
    Radius, Area: REAL;

CONST
    Pi = 3.1416;

BEGIN
    WRITELN ('What is the radius of the circle?  ');
    READLN (Radius);
    Area := Pi*Radius*Radius;
    WRITELN ('The area of a circle with a radius of',Radius, '
units is: ');
    WRITELN (Area,' square units')
END.
```

Figure 3.18 – Program that calculates with real numbers.

```
What is the radius of the circle?
1234.56789
The area of a circle with a radius of  1.2345678900E+03 units is:
    4.7882943801E+06 square units
```

Figure 3.19 – Screen display from program AreaOfACircle, demonstrating unformatted real-number input and output.

Look at Figure 3.20, which demonstrates the techniques available to you for making the output clearer. Now run the program. If you enter a radius of 1234.56789 units, the screen display should be similar to Figure 3.21.

Turbo not only lets you convert from exponential notation to conventional decimal notation painlessly, it also lets you choose how many digits you want after the decimal point, how many blank spaces you want before the number, and even if you want the entire entry left- or right-justified in a column. Best of all, it lets you do all

```
PROGRAM FormattedOutput;

VAR
    Radius, Area: REAL;

CONST
    Pi = 3.1416;

BEGIN
    WRITELN ('What is the radius of the circle?  ');
    READLN (Radius);
    WRITELN ('The radius you typed was:',Radius);
    WRITELN ('The radius you typed was:',Radius:1:1);
    WRITELN ('The radius you typed was:', Radius:7:2);
    WRITELN ('The radius you typed was:',Radius:10:3);
    WRITELN ('The radius you typed was:',Radius:12:6);
    Area := Pi * SQR(Radius);
    write ('Circle with radius of',Radius:11:5, ' units has area
of');
    WRITELN (Area:15:6,' square units');

END.
```

Figure 3.20 – Program to demonstrate options for formatting real-number output.

```
What is the radius of the circle?
1234.56789
The radius you typed was:   1.2345678900E+03
The radius you typed was:1234.6
The radius you typed was:1234.57
The radius you typed was:   1234.568
The radius you typed was: 1234.567890
Circle with radius of 1234.56789 units has area of  4788294.380100
square units
```

Figure 3.21 – Screen display from program FormattedOutput, showing different real-number formatting options.

this manipulation of the output without affecting the way the number is stored internally. So you are free to round off numbers all you want in a report, but you can still retain all the decimal places for better accuracy in later computations.

As illustrated in the format of Borland documentation, the WRITE and WRITELN commands you first looked at used the syntax:

WRITELN (FileVar, Var1, Var2, . . .)

In this notation, *FileVar* means file variable, or simply the name of a file. *Var1, Var2,* etc., refer to individual variable identifiers. They can also be constants or text. When you typed in the earlier example:

WRITELN (LST,'THE SUM IS: ',Sum)

the *FileVar* was LST, meaning the standard file that represents line printer output. The first variable was the text in quotes, and the second variable was the integer variable Sum. As you saw in Figure 3.21, you can add information to the command to say not only what you want written, but how you want it written.

When writing real numbers, use additional parameters after the variable identifier to tell Turbo how many spaces to use in printing out the number and how many digits to display after the decimal point. In the last program, you saw:

WRITELN ('The radius you typed was:',Radius:12:6);

which produced:

The radius you typed was: 1234.567890

The total number takes twelve spaces (in this example they are the ten digits, the decimal point, and the leading blank) and devotes six of these places to the decimal value (.567890). Look at the other example lines and notice how forgiving Turbo is if you specify too few nondecimal spaces. It will not truncate the most significant digits of your number, but will print all the digits before the decimal point anyhow.

Turbo also lets you control the way integers are printed out. Figure 3.22 is a simplified version of our earlier example program, modified to show the different ways of printing integers.

Figure 3.23 shows the corresponding screen display produced by running this program.

In case A, the variable was printed out without any special formatting. There is no leading blank. In case B, Turbo was told to use seven places, so it prints three leading blanks before the four digits. In case C, Turbo was told to use only one place, but it was impossible to do this, so Turbo ignored the specifier and used the default format. In case D, Turbo was told to use six places, resulting in two leading blanks.

```
PROGRAM Demonstrate_Printing_Integers;

VAR
A : INTEGER;

PROCEDURE ProofThem;
BEGIN
    WRITELN; WRITELN; {just for spacing on the screen}
    WRITELN ('A =', A);
    WRITELN ('B =', A:7);
    WRITELN ('C =', A:1);
    WRITELN ('D =', A:6);
END;

BEGIN
    WRITELN ('Give me an integer: ');
    WRITELN;
    READLN (A);
    ProofThem
END.
```

Figure 3.22 – Program to demonstrate formatting options when printing integers.

```
Give me an integer:

1234

A =1234
B =   1234
C =1234
D =  1234
```

Figure 3.23 – Screen display from program in Figure 3.22.

For screen I/O, Turbo also allows you to print output almost any-place, using the GOTOXY(x,y) command, where x is a horizontal displacement and y is a vertical displacement from the upper-left corner of the screen. The range of x and y depend on your screen display. GOTOXY is similar to the LOCATE command available in many dialects of BASIC.

For output, however, Turbo does not have a command similar to BASIC's TAB(n) function, to direct horizontal placement of a PRINT or LPRINT operation. Simply write your own procedure to do this. You can write a generic one, which outputs spaces on any screen or line printer, or a procedure specific to your own line printer, to best exploit its internal tabbing software.

The fact that Turbo does *not* contain such a function is actually one of its strengths. One reason the BASIC interpreter is such a large and slow program is that it must support a vast range of commands—many of which you seldom (if ever) use. Turbo has been pared to the bone to produce as small and efficient a program as possible. Most Turbo programmers—and almost every commercial programming operation that uses Pascal or C—create a library of special-purpose procedures that can be easily included in programs when required, or simply left out of the compilation when not needed.

Program Control Structures

An Historical Note

Most of the example programs so far have been relatively simple, with the programs following a straightforward progression from beginning to end. Although this structure is fine for doing simple calculations or trivial screen displays, it does not lend itself to doing much more useful work than a pocket calculator.

Turbo offers a variety of structures that vastly increase the capability of a program to do useful work. Statements can be executed in order; they can also be repeated. Right here Turbo takes a quantum leap from simple calculators. But the clearest way in which Turbo exploits the power of your computer is its ability to test a condition and choose an alternative course of action based on the test.

Although these capabilities unlock the power of your computer, they are all quite straightforward and almost intuitively obvious. In the early days, when computers were programmed only in assembly language, programmers used the buzzwords "control structures" almost as an incantation. Like all jargon, the phrase was meant to intimidate the uninitiated, by implying that only superior beings could possibly understand such complex concepts (and thus write programs to put computers through their paces). While that was an exaggeration, for most programmers the hardest part of mastering assembly language—and thus all computer programming—was learning how to control program flow.

Programmers were responsible for loading specific values into different registers and going through comparisons. They constantly had to read and mask a set of status flags to figure out the results of a comparison before telling the computer what to do in light of which flags were set. Often it took several discrete comparisons to make a single decision, and it always involved saving and restoring data before and after the tests. It was, in short, a nuisance. Today we still have a legacy of thinking of program-control structures as difficult, bewildering, tedious, and somehow separating the sheep from the goats.

Fortunately, Turbo offers a set of control structures that are flexible, immensely powerful, and best of all, can be understood by anyone, almost intuitively. More sophisticated and complicated decisions can be coded by combining or nesting structures to mind-boggling levels of complexity.

In addition, for anyone who finds one of those obscure applications in which even combinations of Turbo's regular structures don't quite do the job (I am still looking for such an application, incidentally), Turbo also offers an array of bit-level tests and masks matched only by assembly language.

Before we explore Turbo's specific structures, it is important to remember that, within a control structure, Turbo always allows you to use a compound statement interchangeably with a simple, one-line statement. You will see that this ability multiplies the flexibility of every control structure.

Repetition

The REPEAT/UNTIL Structure

The simplest control structure, REPEAT/UNTIL simply tells the computer to execute a statement repeatedly. It is illustrated in the procedure listed in Figure 3.24.

Notice that between the reserved words REPEAT and UNTIL, we could have any number of statements. In addition, the phrasing and syntax are similar to everyday English. Each iteration of the process is followed by a test to see if the process should be repeated. Thus, a REPEAT/UNTIL structure always ends with a test. It can be an obvious Boolean test (such as "UNTIL AllFinished = TRUE" or simply, "UNTIL AllFinished") or a not-so-obvious Boolean test, as in Figure 3.24. In this example the computer is evaluating whether the phrase "Stars = 5" is true, rather than testing the value of Stars. The distinction is of interest mainly to writers of compilers, but I mention it only to make the point that this structure, like so many others, is controlled by the results of a Boolean test, as opposed to "stepping" by a counter.

Nothing says that the test has to be for simple equality, of course. You could test for other conditions, such as these:

UNTIL Stars > 5;
UNTIL Stars > = 5;
UNTIL Stars = Limit;
UNTIL Stars > (Limit − 3);

But the test has got to make sense. If you ask for

UNTIL Stars < Limit;

```
PROCEDURE SimpleRepeat;
BEGIN
   Stars := 0;
   REPEAT
      WRITE ('* ');
      Stars := Stars + 1;
   UNTIL Stars = 5;
END;
```

Figure 3.24 – Program demonstrating simple repetition.

and Stars is already greater than Limit, your program will repeat endlessly. This, of course, would not be a bug in Turbo, but a programming error.

The WHILE/DO Loop

Another method of accomplishing simple repetition is shown in Figure 3.25.

This structure uses the reserved words WHILE and DO. Notice that *after* these reserved words we could have any number of statements. Once again the phrasing and syntax are similar to those of everyday English. Each iteration of the process is preceded by a test to see if the process should be repeated. Thus, a WHILE/DO structure always begins with a test. It can be an obvious Boolean test (such as "WHILE AllFinished = FALSE") or a not-so-obvious Boolean test, as in Figure 3.25.

Comparing Structures for Repetition

You are probably wondering when it is best to use the REPEAT/ UNTIL structure and when to use the WHILE/DO structure. The program shown in Figure 3.26 combines slightly modified versions of the procedures used in Figures 3.24 and 3.25; it shows how both structures react to the same data input.

Figure 3.27 shows the screen display produced by the program. Zero is entered as the starting value of each repetition. Notice that each procedure identifies itself when called ('Simple Repeat' and 'Simple While'), just to let you know which structure is being demonstrated. In this series of examples, we are asking for stars to be

```
PROCEDURE SimpleWhile;
BEGIN
    Stars := 0;
    WHILE Stars < 5 DO
    BEGIN
        WRITE('* ');
        Stars := Stars + 1;
    END;
END;
```

Figure 3.25 – Program using WHILE/DO control structure.

```
PROGRAM Demonstrate_Control_Structures;

CONST
   Limit = 5;

VAR
   Stars, StartingPoint : INTEGER;

PROCEDURE SimpleWhile;
BEGIN
   WRITELN ('Simple While');
   Stars := StartingPoint;
   WHILE Stars < Limit DO
   BEGIN
      WRITE (' * ');
      Stars := Stars + 1;
   END;
   WRITELN;
END;

PROCEDURE SimpleRepeat;
BEGIN
   Stars := StartingPoint;
   WRITELN ('Simple Repeat');
   REPEAT
      WRITE (' * ');
      Stars := Stars + 1;
   UNTIL Stars > Limit;
   WRITELN;
END;

BEGIN
   WRITELN ('How many stars are we starting with? ');
   READLN (StartingPoint);
      SimpleWhile;
      SimpleRepeat;
END.
```

Figure 3.26 – Program contrasting REPEAT and WHILE structures.

```
How many stars are we starting with?
0
Simple While
 *   *   *   *   *
Simple Repeat
 *   *   *   *   *   *
```

Figure 3.27 – Screen display from program in Figure 3.26.

printed out. The maximum number of stars is set by the constant Limit, which is set to a value of 5.

Notice that the WHILE structure prints out five stars, while the REPEAT structure prints out six. You would have to change the test if you wanted to get five stars. In that case the procedure would have to be modified as shown in Figure 3.28.

But to continue with the original program, Figure 3.29 shows the screen display with different input.

So far, the result is what you would expect. But now look at Figure 3.30, in which we ask for 5 as both the starting value and the limiting value of the test.

```
PROCEDURE SimpleRepeat;
BEGIN
    Stars := StartingPoint;
    WRITELN ('Simple Repeat');
    REPEAT
        WRITE (' * ');
        Stars := Stars + 1;
    UNTIL Stars > Limit - 1;   {just change to 'Limit - 1'}
    WRITELN;
END;
```

Figure 3.28 – Program of Figure 3.24 modified to print exactly like the WHILE structure.

```
How many stars are we starting with?
4
Simple While
 *
Simple Repeat
 *   *
```

Figure 3.29 – Screen display from program in Figure 3.26, with a starting value of four stars.

```
How many stars are we starting with?
5
Simple While

Simple Repeat
 *
```

Figure 3.30 – Screen display from program in Figure 3.26, with a starting value that equals the five-star limit.

Here you see that the WHILE/DO structure does what we would expect; it prints no stars at all. But the REPEAT/UNTIL structure prints out one star. Look at Figure 3.31, in which the starting point is well in excess of the limit.

You still get one star printing out from the REPEAT/UNTIL loop. Once again, this is not a bug, but a strength of Turbo. It offers you two simple repetition control structures; one will always execute the loop at least once, while the other will execute only if the test conditions are satisfied.

This option is a fundamental tool of Turbo, and you will see many examples of it throughout the book. The distinction, like so much of Turbo, will quickly become automatic.

Incidentally, to increase your understanding of these two structures, change the REPEAT/UNTIL procedure to look like Figure 3.32 and run the program with the same sets of data used in the other example.

Once again, this last exercise should emphasize that you have to use common sense in defining the test used in a repetition structure.

```
How many stars are we starting with?
20
Simple While

Simple Repeat
   *
```

Figure 3.31 – Screen display from program in Figure 3.26, with a starting value that exceeds the five-star limit.

```
PROCEDURE SimpleRepeat;
BEGIN
   Stars := StartingPoint;
   WRITELN ('Simple Repeat');
   REPEAT
      WRITE (' * ');
      Stars := Stars + 1;
   UNTIL Stars = Limit;
   WRITELN;
END;
```

Figure 3.32 – Program to demonstrate the effect of forgetting to set a limit on a repetitive control structure.

But aside from that, there is nothing particularly complex or obscure about these structures for repetition.

FOR/TO/DO Loops

Notice in the previous examples that you had to include a line in the compound statement to increment the Stars counter:

Stars : = Stars + 1

Incremental repetition is such a common occurrence that Turbo has a structure which both repeats the instruction(s) and automatically increases a counter. It is similar to the FOR/TO/STEP command in BASIC. Figure 3.33 shows our existing example modified to use the FOR/TO/DO structure.

Run the program in Figure 3.33, using starting values of 0, 1, 3, 5, 20, and – 12 to get an idea of how the structure works. Notice that this structure does not test for a condition. You simply tell it what the limits are, and it executes the command the specified number of times.

```
PROGRAM Demonstrate_Control_Structures;

CONST
  Limit : INTEGER = 5;

VAR
  Stars, StartingPoint : INTEGER;

PROCEDURE ForDo;
BEGIN
  WRITELN ('Simple FOR/DO loop');
  Stars := StartingPoint;
  FOR Stars := StartingPoint TO Limit DO
  BEGIN
    WRITE (' * ');
  END;
  WRITELN;
END;

BEGIN
  WRITELN ('How many stars are we starting with? ');
  READLN (StartingPoint);
    ForDo;
END.
```

Figure 3.33 – Program to demonstrate FOR/TO/DO loops.

FOR/TO/DO works equally well substituting DOWNTO in place of TO. Moreover, you can use any scalar type (except, once again, real numbers) to control the loop. For an example of characters as control variables, run the program in Figure 3.34.

Run the program in Figure 3.34 with different beginning and ending characters. Look up the table of ASCII character codes as a guide to the sequence of characters that will be displayed.

Each of these structures for repetition has its uses and its restrictions. As you read Turbo programs in this book and elsewhere, pay attention to which structure has been chosen. In most cases it is simply a matter of the programmer's preference, but there are cases in which the number of repetitions should be controlled by a computation taking place within the loop. In a case like that the FOR structure is useless, because you have to dictate the number of iterations before the loop begins. On the other hand, it makes no sense to have extra tests or statements in a program in which you know exactly how many iterations you want (for example, printing a line of stars at the top of a report).

```
PROGRAM Characters_As_Control_Variables;

VAR
   Character, Firstchar, LastChar : CHAR;

PROCEDURE ForDo;
BEGIN
   FOR Character := FirstChar TO LastChar DO
   BEGIN
      WRITE (Character);
   END;
   WRITELN;
END;

BEGIN
   WRITELN ('What is the first character in your alphabet? ');
   READLN (FirstChar);
   WRITELN ('What is the last character in your alphabet? ');
   READLN (LastChar);
   ForDo;
END.
```

Figure 3.34 – Program to demonstrate loop controlled by characters rather than integers.

Conditional Statements

Repetition is useful, but an even more powerful capability is the ability not just to choose whether to repeat something or not, but to do one operation if a condition is true and an entirely different operation if the condition is false. Still more powerful is the ability to choose one of several alternative activities based on the result of a test. Turbo supports all these capabilities with a set of straightforward, no-nonsense program structures. Like those for repetition, these structures have an understandable syntax, resembling everyday English.

Two-Way Selection: IF/THEN/ELSE

Perhaps IF/THEN/ELSE is the most intuitive of all Turbo control structures, because it directly reflects the type of decisions we are constantly making in daily life. The syntax is very simple:

IF Today : = PayDay **THEN** WRITELN ('Want to Boogie?');

In this case we will take an action only if today is payday. If it is not, we simply move on to the next statement. We can add a specific alternative action if we desire:

IF Today : = PayDay **THEN** WRITELN ('Want to Boogie?')
   ELSE WRITELN ('Can you lend me five bucks?');

Remember that these simple actions can be replaced with compound statements. A fragment from a program to print a mailing list is shown in Figure 3.35. While some of its details might still be a little obscure, the principle of using multiline, compound statements should be clear.

As mentioned earlier, tests can be nested. This technique is particularly handy in filtering invalid input from a program. In Figure 3.36, the program won't let you ask for anything other than a lowercase alphabet (or subset of it). Although this program uses some compound tests as well, you should be able to see what is going on just by reading it.

Notice that the GetInput routine was capable of calling itself all over again when it received invalid input. Try running the program with both valid and invalid input to see how it behaves. Then modify the tests (for example, change the >= to >) and check the behavior again.

Multiple Alternatives: CASE

When a decision could result in more than a simple either-or choice, Turbo offers the CASE/OF structure. This tremendously powerful structure lends itself to many operations, the most obvious of which is taking input from a menu and accessing the chosen option. Figure 3.37 shows a typical example of this use. Once a menu is displayed the user types a number, which is read as the variable Option. Depending on the value of Option, eight different routines can be chosen. And if an invalid number is entered, the CASE structure lets you use ELSE to handle all other input values.

The test variable (Option in this example) can be any nonreal scalar value. Boolean, integer, and character data are all valid. You may have as many different choices as you wish in a CASE statement.

The program in Figure 3.38 shows one technique for getting discrete integer steps with real-number input. Try running the program entering real numbers that come very close to the limits and observe the operation. In addition to demonstrating the use of the CASE

```
PROCEDURE Print_Crew_List;
  BEGIN
  IF LinesDone < 58 THEN   {While not a full page, print names}
    BEGIN
      READ (OutFile,CrewMember);
      WRITELN (1st, CrewMember.Name);
      WRITELN (1st, CrewMember.Street);
      WRITELN (1st,CrewMember.City,' ',CrewMember.StateAndZip);
      LinesDone := LinesDone + 1;
    END
    ELSE                   {This is the alternative action}
    BEGIN
      LinesDone := 7;
      WRITELN (LST,#12);
              {prints form-feed to begin report page header}
      WRITELN (LST,'           CREW  LIST  H.M.S.  PINAFORE');
      WRITELN (LST,                    APRIL  24,  1880');
      WRITELN; WRITELN; WRITELN;
      LinesDone := 4;
    END;
  END;
```

Figure 3.35 – Program fragment demonstrating multiline, compound statements.

```
PROGRAM Demonstrate_Compound;

VAR
   Character, Firstchar, LastChar : CHAR;

PROCEDURE GetInput;
BEGIN
   WRITELN;
   WRITELN ('This is the Get Input routine.');
   WRITELN;
   WRITELN ('What is the first character in your alphabet? ');
   READLN (FirstChar);
   WRITELN ('What is the last character in your alphabet? ');
   READLN (LastChar);
   IF (FirstChar >= 'a') AND (FirstChar <= 'z') THEN
      IF (LastChar <= 'z') AND (LastChar >= FirstChar ) THEN
WRITELN' ('I will process your valid input!')
         ELSE GetInput
   ELSE GetInput
END;

PROCEDURE ForDo;
BEGIN
    FOR Character := FirstChar TO LastChar DO
      WRITE (Character);
   WRITELN;
END;

BEGIN
   GetInput;
   ForDo;
END.
```

Figure 3.36 – Program to demonstrate nested IF/THEN structures.

```
PROCEDURE InterpretChoice;   {interprets menu selection}
BEGIN
   READLN (Option);
   CASE Option OF
      1: AcceptNewNames;
      2: AlphabetizeList;
      3: SortLabelsByZip;
      4: ProofListToScreen;
      5: ProduceLabels;
      6: CreateMailingListBook;
      7: LookUpOrChangeAnEntry;
      8: ExitProgram;
   ELSE ErrorHandler;
  END;
END;
```

Figure 3.37 – Program to demonstrate use of CASE structure.

structure, this program also illustrates how real numbers are rounded and evaluated by Turbo.

The GOTO/LABEL Structure

Turbo also supports an *unconditional* branch, for programming situations in which you always want to divert program flow from the next sequential instruction. This structure, GOTO/LABEL, does not test a condition or counter, but always proceeds to the program line prefaced with the appropriate label. Turbo makes minimal use of GOTO and, in fact, puts severe limits on how far you can jump with it. Still, it can be useful as a "safety valve" to escape a loop or to terminate a program cleanly under an error condition. Many Turbo programmers, however, take (perhaps undue) pride in never using this command. With Turbo's range of control structures, you should be able to program for every contingency without using any unconditional branches. Nonetheless, the goal of programming is to solve problems as easily as possible. If you find it more convenient to use a

```
PROGRAM Demonstrate_Case;

VAR
  A  : REAL;
  B  : INTEGER;

PROCEDURE DoIt;
BEGIN
   WRITELN ('Give me a number, please. ');
    READLN (A);
    IF (A <= 2) THEN B := 2;
    IF (A > 2) AND (A < 4) THEN B := 4;
    IF (A >= 4) AND (A <= 6) THEN B := 6;
    IF (A > 6) THEN B := 7;
    CASE B OF
      2: WRITELN ('two or less ');
      4:  WRITELN ('two to four');
      6: WRITELN ('four to six');
    ELSE
      WRITELN ('Over six');
    END;
    DoIt;
END;

BEGIN
  DoIt;
  END.
```

Figure 3.38 – Program to demonstrate use of CASE structure, using real-number input.

GOTO than a cleverly-devised WHILE, just do what is most natural. Sooner or later, though, you will think in terms of Turbo's control structures and find yourself abandoning GOTO.

Labels must be declared before being used. However, the declaration format is not like those of other variables. A label has no type and uses no colons, equal signs, or assignment operators. The following program fragment shows how labels are declared and used:

```
PROCEDURE ShowLabel
LABEL
    SampleLabel;
BEGIN
    WRITELN ('Good Morning');
    SampleLabel:
        WRITELN ('This is the first line to be executed when Turbo sees the
statement GOTO SampleLabel');
    .
    .
    .
    GOTO SampleLabel;
END;
```

Also keep in mind that GOTOs work only within the same block. You cannot jump into or out of a procedure or function with a GOTO. Look at the more ambitious sample programs in this book and you will see that when you need to jump from one procedure to another, you simply call for the next procedure by name. The most common use of GOTO in languages like BASIC—jumping into subprograms—is handled in Turbo by calling procedures by name. If you have chosen informative identifiers for your procedures, this technique makes the flow of the program obvious to the reader.

Because you cannot jump out of a module with a GOTO, label definitions are normally included with the procedure-declaration section.

GOTO is sometimes used to exit from a procedure or a program. Turbo also offers two standard procedures, HALT and EXIT, precisely for these purposes. Regardless of where it occurs in a program, the HALT procedure terminates the program. If the file has been compiled, it returns you to the operating-system prompt. If the task is running within the Turbo environment, it returns you to the Turbo prompt but does not exit from Turbo.

EXIT is more conditional. If EXIT occurs in the main body of the program, it operates exactly like HALT. If EXIT occurs within a procedure or a function, it exits from just that module; program execution continues with the next line of the module or main body of code that called the procedure. Thus, EXIT can be used as a safety valve within an error-handler procedure; it will not abort the entire program.

Procedures and Functions: Turbo's Tools

You have probably noticed that the programming examples in this book use many calls to separate procedures rather than long modules of sequential lines of code. By now you should have a good sense of the appearance and overall organization of a Turbo Pascal program. The idea that a short module of code at the end of the entire program listing calls all the previously-defined procedures should seem natural by now, and the earlier analogy of assembling your tools before building your garden shed should make more sense. It is about time, then, to explore more deeply the concepts of procedures and functions and some of the ways you can use them. You will see that organizing a Turbo program into procedures is a powerful aid in writing programs that work—and work with an absolute minimum of debugging.

First, let's differentiate between procedures and functions. They are quite similar—both resemble the subroutines and subprograms of other programming languages. In Turbo programming, you know that you can always use a compound statement in place of a simple statement. Similarly, you can always use a procedure in place of a statement. Look back through the sample programs you have run so far and confirm that (syntactically, at least) any time we have used a procedure name, we could just as well have used a single or compound statement. In this way calls to procedures are simply ways to access blocks of code more conveniently, more clearly, or more naturally than by inserting the lines of code at that point in the program. It is often suggested that for optimum intelligibility, no one program module should be longer than can be fit into one screen. Thus, calls to separate procedures to perform specific tasks (get input, convert characters, print a menu, process an option, and so on) make the overall program clearer. Clarity and intelligibility are important not just when you go back to look at a program you wrote a long time ago. Breaking up a large programming task into separately coded and separately debugged modules is one of the keys to developing bug-free programs quickly.

Functions always return a value to the calling program. Just as you use a variable identifier in a program when you need to manipulate the value it represents, you use functions in a program when you need to manipulate the values they produce. For example, there are standard functions to take a number and return its square, and to take a number and return its square root. Others take a value and return one of the trigonometric functions of that value. The following statements are exactly equivalent:

```
Area : = Side * Side
Area : = Sqr (Side) {Uses the Sqr—square—function.}
```

If X is a real number equal to 7.525, and DaysInTheWeek is an integer equal to 7, the following statements are all equivalent:

```
WholePart : = Trunc (X);
WholePart : = Trunc (7.525);
WholePart : = 7;
WholePart : = 4 + 3;
WholePart : = DaysInTheWeek;
```

User-defined functions are used to perform operations that are not available from Turbo's collection of standard procedures and functions. There is no standard Turbo command to cube a number, or to figure what balance will be produced after some amount is invested at a given interest rate for X years. If your program needs to calculate such a value *more than once,* a function is the way to do it. You would write a function that would take an initial value and period of time, and would produce and return to the calling program the ending balance.

An extension of this concept is commonly found in commercial program-development labs, where entire libraries of standard functions specifically designed for the type of work being done at that lab are developed and made available to all programmers working there. A business-oriented shop might have a library of amortization tables; a scientific shop might have functions to return the wavelength or antenna dimensions for any input frequency. Thus it is easy to customize Turbo for your specific applications.

For most of your everyday programming, however, you will find that Turbo has between 40 and 60 (depending on your version of Turbo and your operating system and computer) predefined functions, which cover a staggering array of applications. Figure 3.39 is a table of the predefined functions available in release 3.0 of Turbo for the IBM PC.

User-Created Procedures

As a quick review, procedures are subprograms used to make a larger program clearer, more readable, and easier to test and debug. They can be long or short, but they all begin with the reserved word PROCEDURE and terminate with END; (the semicolon *must* be there). All the statements between these reserved words are collectively called the *scope* of the procedure. Any declarations made at the beginning of the entire program are in effect within all the individual procedures of that program. Looking back at some of the earlier program examples, you will see that variables calculated or input in one procedure can be further manipulated in other procedures. When a value is input outside of a procedure, but is read and acted upon by another procedure, the value is called a *parameter,* and the process of transferring the value is called *passing a parameter* to the procedure. In all the sample programs so far, parameter passing was done simply by using variables that were common to the entire program. If you have programmed in BASIC, this is exactly the way you are used to using variables.

Another Historical Note

Don't be intimidated by the terms *parameter* and *parameter passing.* Like the buzzword *control structures* discussed earlier, these terms evoke an unfortunate image left over from the days of assembly-language programming: frazzled programmers emerging

In this table the following abbreviations are used to represent the arguments of the various functions:

B	Boolean
C	character
E	either integer or real-number value
F	file variable
FUNC	operating system BIOS or BDOS function number
I	integer
POS	position within a string
PTR	pointer variable
R	real
SC	any scalar value
ST	string
SUB	substring
V	any variable
X	special value explained in chart

Unless otherwise noted, the result of a procedure or function will be of the same data type as the input value. Some functions and procedures appear under more than one heading.

Arithmetic Functions and Procedures

ABS (*E*)	Returns the absolute value of *E*.
EXP (*E*)	Returns the exponential of *E*.
FRAC (*E*)	Returns the fractional part of *E*; result is always real.
INT (*E*)	Returns the integer part of *E*. Note, however, that the result is always real.

Figure 3.39 – Predefined functions (continues).

LN (*E*)	Returns the natural logarithm of *E;* result is always real.
RANDOM	Returns a random number greater than or equal to zero and less than one; result is always real.
RANDOM (*I*)	Returns a random number greater than or equal to zero and less than *I;* result is always an integer.
ROUND (*R*)	Returns *R* rounded up or down to nearest integer; result is always an integer.
SQR (*E*)	Returns the square of *E* (*E* ∗ *E*).
SQRT (*E*)	Returns the square root of *E;* result is always real.
TRUNC (*R*)	Returns the greatest integer less than or equal to *R;* result is always an integer.

Conversion, Translation, and Transfer Functions

CHR (*I*)	Returns the ASCII character with ordinal value *I.*
HI (*I*)	Returns, in the low-order byte of the result, the high-order byte of the value *I.* The high-order byte of the result is zero. Result is always an integer.
LO (*I*)	Returns the low-order byte of the value *I.* The high-order byte of the result is zero. Result is always an integer.
ORD (*SC*)	Returns the ordinal value of *SC* within its defined data type; result is always an integer and *SC* cannot be real. Note that ORD operates very differently with pointers (see below).
ROUND (*R*)	Returns *R* rounded up or down to nearest integer. Result is always an integer.
STR (, *ST*)	Converts the numeric value of *E* into string *ST.* *E* must be expressed as a WRITE parameter.

Figure 3.39 – Predefined functions (continues).

SWAP (*I*)	Returns a value with the high- and low-order bytes of *I* swapped. Result is always an integer.
TRUNC (*R*)	Returns the greatest integer less than or equal to *R*; result is always an integer.
UPCASE (*C*)	Returns uppercase equivalent of *C*.
VAL (*ST, E, I*)	Converts the string expression *ST* to either a real or integer value *E*. If an error occurs, *I* is set to the position of the character causing the error.

Functions and Procedures Used Only with CP/M or CP/M-86

ADDR (*V*)	Returns the absolute address in memory of the first byte of the variable *V* under the CP/M-86 operating system. The address is returned as a 32-bit pointer made up of both a segment address and an offset.
ADDR (*X*)	Returns the absolute address in memory of the first byte of the variable, array, record, procedure, or function *X* under the CP/M operating system. The address of individual array elements and record elements can also be obtained by using the appropriate index. The address returned is always an integer.
BDOS (*FUNC, I*)	Procedure; invokes the CP/M operating system BDOS call indicated by the integer *FUNC*. *I* is an optional integer value loaded into the DE registers prior to the call. A call to address 5 invokes the function.
BDOS	Function; returns the integer value loaded into the A register by the CP/M BDOS invoked with the BDOS or BDOSHL procedures.
BDOSHL (*FUNC, I*)	Procedure; invokes the CP/M operating system BDOS call indicated by the integer *FUNC*. *I* is an optional integer value loaded into the HL registers prior to the call. A call to address 5 invokes the function.

Figure 3.39 – Predefined functions (continues).

BDOS (X)	Function; performs a CP/M-86 operating system BDOS call. X is a record made up of the values to be loaded into the relevant system registers. Results of the call (changed flags and register values) are also returned in this record. Note that the desired BDOS function code is included in register pair CL and not as a separate parameter as is the case with an MS-DOS call.
BIOS (*FUNC, I*)	Procedure; invokes the CP/M operating system BIOS call indicated by the integer *FUNC. I* is an optional integer value loaded into the BC registers prior to the call.
BIOS	Function; returns the integer value loaded into the A register by the CP/M BIOS invoked with the BIOS or BIOSHL procedures.
BIOSHL (*FUNC, I*)	Procedure; invokes the CP/M operating system BIOS call indicated by the integer *FUNC. I* is an optional integer value loaded into the HL registers prior to the call.
OVRDRIVE (*I*)	Procedure; directs system to look on the drive indicated by integer *I* (0 = logged drive, 1 = drive A, 2 = drive B, etc.) for overlay files.
ADDR (*V*)	Returns the absolute address in memory of the first byte of the variable *V* under the CP/M-86 operating system. The address is returned as a 32-bit pointer made up of both a segment address and an offset.
ADDR	(CP/M)

Functions and Procedures Used with MS-DOS and PC-DOS Only

ADDR (*V*)	Returns the absolute address in memory of the first byte of the variable *V* under the MS-DOS or PC-DOS operating systems. The address is returned as a 32-bit pointer made up of both a segment address and an offset.

Figure 3.39 – Predefined functions (continues).

APPEND (*F*)	Procedure; opens disk file *F* (like REWRITE) , but the file pointer points to the end of the file. Elements can only be added to the file (not read from it). MS-DOS only.
CHDIR (*ST*)	Procedure; changes current directory to the path described by *ST.*
GETDIR (*I, ST*)	Function; returns in *ST* the current directory identifier of the drive corresponding to *I* (with drive A represented by 0, B by 1, etc.). Note that *ST* includes only a directory identifier, not a directory list of files.
INTR (*I, X*)	Procedure; makes software interrupt number *I* once it has loaded values into (or initialized) the system registers. *X* is a record made up of the values to be loaded into all the registers and flags.
MEMAVAIL	Function; returns number of paragraphs (16 bytes) of free space on heap. MS-DOS only. Result is always an integer.
MKDIR (*ST*)	Procedure; creates a new subdirectory as described by *ST.*
MSDOS (*X*)	Performs DOS system call. *X* is a record made up of the values to be loaded into all the registers and flags. Unlike INTR, MSDOS does not use a separate parameter to indicate the appropriate value(s) into the variables constituting the record *X*. Most commonly, this involves loading a value in the high-order byte of the AX register; but other registers are used by some system calls.
OVRPATH (*ST*)	Procedure; directs system to access overlay files from the directory path included in string *ST.*
RMDIR (*ST*)	Procedure; removes the subdirectory described by *ST.*

Figure 3.39 – Predefined functions (continues).

File-Handling Functions

APPEND (*F*)   Opens disk file *F* (like REWRITE), but the file pointer points to the end of the file. Elements can be added to the file, but not read from it. MS-DOS only.

ASSIGN (*F, ST*)   Assigns the valid file name included in the string *ST* to the file variable *F*.

CLOSE (*F*)   Instructs the operating system to close disk file *F* and to perform all related housekeeping and directory updates.

EOF (*F*)   Returns Boolean TRUE if file pointer points beyond the last component of disk file *F*.

EOLN (*F*)   Returns Boolean TRUE if file pointer points at a carriage-return character within text file *F*. Note that in a text file, if EOF (*F*) is true, then EOLN (*F*) must also be true.

ERASE (*F*)   Disk file *F* is erased.

FILEPOS (*F*)   Returns current position of the file pointer in file *F*; result is always an integer. Does not work on text files.

FILESIZE (*F*)   Returns the size of disk file *F*, measured in its constituent components (e.g., a file of records is counted in the number of records); result is always an integer. Does not work on text files.

FLUSH (*F*)   Empties internal sector buffer of disk file *F* in non–MS-DOS implementations. Normally this operation is done automatically, and this function is rarely invoked by the program. Does not work on text files. In MS-DOS it works only on text files, in which case it empties the text-file buffer.

RENAME (*F, ST*)   Renames disk file *F* with the valid file name contained in string *ST*.

Figure 3.39 – Predefined functions (continues).

REWRITE (F)   Prepares file F for writing. Will erase existing file F or will create a new one. File pointer points to the beginning of the file.

RESET (F)   Prepares file F for reading. File pointer points to the beginning of the file. Cannot create a file if one does not exist.

SEEK (F, I)   Moves file pointer to point to component number I of disk file F. Does not work on text files.

SEEKEOF (F)   Returns Boolean TRUE if file pointer points beyond the last component of disk file F. Unlike EOF, SEEKEOF skips blanks, tab stops, and carriage returns before it tests for the end-of-file marker.

SEEKEOLN (F)   Returns Boolean TRUE if file pointer points at a carriage-return character within text file F. Unlike EOLN, SEEKEOLN skips blanks and tab stops before it tests for the carriage return. Note that, in a text file, if EOF (F) is true, then SEEKEOLN (F) must also be true.

Heap and Pointer-Related Functions

DISPOSE (PTR)   Reclaims heap space of variable PTR.

FREEMEM (PTR, I)   Reclaims I bytes of heap space previously allocated with GETMEM.

GETMEM (PTR, I)   Allocates I bytes of heap space to pointer variable PTR.

MARK (PTR)   Procedure; assigns heap pointer to PTR.

MAXAVAIL   Returns the size of the largest consecutive block of free space on the heap. Result is always an integer but may need further interpretation if larger than MAXINT.

MEMAVAIL   Returns number of paragraphs (16 bytes) of free space on heap. MS-DOS only. Result is always an integer.

NEW (PTR)   Creates pointer variable PTR.

Figure 3.39 – Predefined functions (continues).

ORD (*PTR*)	Returns the address contained in pointer *PTR*. Result is always an integer. Note that ORD works entirely differently with a scalar argument.
PTR (*I*)	Function; converts integer value *I* to a pointer.
RELEASE (*PTR*)	Sets heap pointer to *PTR* (previously marked by the MARK procedure) in order to free dynamically allocated heap space from the specified pointer variable upwards.

Input and Output Functions

BLOCKREAD (*F, V, I*)	Reads *I* number of 128-byte blocks from untyped disk file *F* and puts them in variable *V*.
BLOCKWRITE (*F, V, I*)	Writes *I* number of 128-byte blocks from variable *V* into untyped disk file *F*.
IORESULT	Returns a value corresponding to the I/O error code whenever an I/O error has taken place. A call to IORESULT following an I/O error resets the system error-trapping routine, and thus allows continued program operation in spite of the error.

Most I/O is done with the following four procedures. The sections on I/O and files list the various parameters and options available with these procedures to deal with all types of data. Those sections also describe the use of these procedures for input and output to all forms of files, logical devices, standard files, and user-created files.

READ (*F, V..V*)

READLN (*F, V..V*)

WRITE (*F, V..V*)

WRITELN (*F, V..V*)

Figure 3.39 – Predefined functions (continues).

Scalar Functions

ODD (*I*)   Returns Boolean TRUE if *I* is odd.

PRED (*SC*)   Returns predecessor of *SC* if one exists.

SUCC (*SC*)   Returns successor of *SC* if one exists.

Screen and Keyboard Procedures and Functions:

CLREOL   Clears all screen characters from cursor position to the end of the current line without changing the cursor position.

CLRSCR   Clears the screen and then repositions the cursor to the upper-left corner of the screen.

CRTINIT   Sends the terminal initialization string to the screen. Used very rarely.

CRTEXIT   Sends the terminal reset string to the screen. Used very rarely.

DELLINE   Deletes the line upon which the cursor is presently positioned. Moves all lines below the cursor position up one line-space.

FILLCHAR   Fills *I* number of bytes of memory starting with the first
(*V, I, VAL*)   byte of variable *V. VAL* (either a character or byte data type) defines the value that will be used to fill the bytes. Primarily used for initializing image planes for graphics, but applicable to initializing data structures as well.

GOTOXY (*X, Y*)   Moves the cursor to the screen coordinates *X, Y. X* is a horizontal position and *Y* is a vertical position. Both are integer values measured from the upper-left corner of the screen. *X* and *Y* must both be integers.

HIGHVIDEO   Sets screen display for high (usually bold) video as defined in terminal installation procedure.

INSLINE   Inserts a blank line at the cursor position.

Figure 3.39 – Predefined functions (continues).

KEYPRESSED	Returns Boolean TRUE if a key has been pressed on the keyboard.
LOWVIDEO	Sets screen display for low video as defined in terminal installation procedure.
MOVE (*V1, V2, I*)	Does a block-copy within memory of *I* bytes, beginning with the first byte of variable *V1* and moving them to the portion of memory beginning with the first byte of variable *V2*. Primarily used to swap screen images for high-speed graphics ("image planes").
NORMVIDEO	Sets screen display for normal video as defined in terminal installation procedure.

String-Handling Routines:

CONCAT (*ST..ST*)	Concatenates any number of string expressions separated by commas; result is always a string. Note that the same function can be accomplished using plus signs as concatenation operators.
COPY (*ST, POS, I*)	Returns a substring from *ST, I* characters long and beginning at position *POS*; result is always a string.
DELETE (*ST, POS, I*)	Removes a substring from *ST, I* characters long and beginning at position *POS*; result is always a string.
INSERT (*SU, ST, POS*)	Inserts string *SU* into *ST* at position *POS*.
LENGTH (*ST*)	Returns the number of characters in *ST*; result is always an integer.
POS (*ST1, ST2*)	Returns the position number at which string *ST1* begins within string *ST2*; result is always an integer.
STR (*E, ST*)	Converts the numeric value of *E* into string *ST*. *E* must be expressed as a WRITE parameter.
VAL (*ST, E, I*)	Converts the string expression *ST* to either a real or integer value *E*. If an error occurs, *I* is set to the position of the character causing the error.

Figure 3.39 – Predefined functions (continues).

Trigonometric Functions

All angles are expressed in radians.

ARCTAN (*E*)	Arctangent; returns angle whose tangent is *E*.
COS (*E*)	Cosine; returns real cosine for angle *E*.
SIN (*E*)	Sine; returns real sine for angle *E*.

Miscellaneous Functions

DELAY (*I*)	Executes a delay loop for approximately *I* milliseconds.
EXIT	If called from a program module (procedure or function), jumps to the calling program. If called from the main body of a program, causes the program to terminate.
FILLCHAR (*V, I, VAL*)	Fills *I* bytes of memory starting with the first byte of variable *V. VAL* (either a character or byte data type) defines the value that will be used to fill the bytes. Primarily used for initializing image planes for graphics, but applicable to initializing data structures as well.
HALT	Stops program execution. Returns operation to the operating-system prompt.
MOVE (*V1, V2, I*)	Does a block-copy within memory of *I* bytes beginning with the first byte of variable *V1* and moving them to the portion of memory beginning with the first byte of variable *V2*. Primarily used to swap screen images for high-speed graphics ("image planes") but can be used anyplace in memory.
PARAMCOUNT	Returns number of parameters passed to the program in the command-line buffer. Result is always an integer.
PARAMSTR (*I*)	Returns parameter number *I* from the command-line buffer.
SIZEOF (*X*)	Returns number of memory bytes taken up by variable or type identifier *X*; result is always an integer.

Figure 3.39 – Predefined functions (continued).

from an all-night programming session, mumbling about registers, stacks, and—the most arcane of all—parameter passing. Mere mortals were supposed to be in awe of anyone who could understand what was so obviously an obscure, obtuse, and perplexing concept.

Once again, this just isn't so any more. Certainly, these programming pioneers had to keep track of what values were properly loaded into individual registers while cleverly protecting the data that was not to be manipulated. Parameter passing did, at one time, demand a thorough understanding of the internal working of the computer, in particular its stack and registers. Today, in Turbo, parameter passing is the equivalent of knowing that you have to put the quarter in the jukebox for the tunes to come out. It is simply a matter of knowing exactly what information you must put into a procedure in order to get the desired result.

In everyday life it does not take a master chef to know that to put together breakfast you have to get out the milk, Cheerios, and sugar. These are the "parameters" of the breakfast "procedure." It is not much more complex than that. To eat breakfast, you don't need to understand how General Mills gets the holes in the middle of each Cheerio nor how the dairy pasteurizes the milk. So don't be intimidated by old computer hands mumbling about parameter passing. (Of course, if you want to sound like a grizzled old computer hand yourself, you can go to users' group meetings and start mumbling about passing parameters. You may impress the neophytes, but as more people use Turbo, you will impress fewer and fewer people with this approach.)

With that in mind, let's get back to exploring procedures, and get some practice in parameter passing. You recall that Turbo does not have a command that performs horizontal tabbing. You have to write your own command to do this. The procedure in Figure 3.40 performs simple tabbing. You supply a string and a field width, and the procedure will center the string within the field.

Enter the program and run it. Notice that we use the identifiers Phrase and Field in the main body of the program; once we assign values to them we call the Tab procedure, which operates on the same variables. This process works and is very straightforward. Phrase and Field are analogous to the Cheerios and milk in our breakfast procedure. They are the input values required to achieve the result: the placement of the phrase where we want it on the page.

The procedure in Figure 3.40 is workable, but it can be a little tedious if you are doing a great deal of tabbing. For each phrase you want centered, you need one statement to assign a value to the variable (Phrase), another statement to assign a value to the variable Field, and then a third statement, to call the Tab procedure. For a quick-and-dirty, one-time solution in one program this operation is acceptable, but to create a general-purpose tabbing tool, you want something more elegant. You want to do the same tabbing task using only one statement, which calls the Tab procedure and tells it the phrase and the field width. In addition, it would be nice to choose whether the text should be centered, right-aligned, or left-aligned.

The program in Figure 3.41 uses a Tab procedure that does all of these things. In all the tabbing programs in this book, the function generates hyphens in place of spaces, so you can see more clearly

```pascal
PROGRAM Demonstrate_Tabbing_Command;

VAR
LSpaces, RSpaces, Phrase : STRING[80];
A, I, Field, LeftSideSpaces, RightSideSpaces, SpaceOnLine :
INTEGER;

PROCEDURE Tab;    {does horizontal tabbing with centered text}
BEGIN
   LSpaces := '';
   RSpaces := '';
   SpaceOnLine := Field - Length (Phrase);
   LeftSideSpaces := SpaceOnLine DIV 2;
   RightSideSpaces := (SpaceOnLine DIV 2) + (SpaceOnLine) MOD 2;
   FOR I := 1 TO LeftSideSpaces DO LSpaces := LSpaces + ' ';
   FOR I := 1 TO RightSideSpaces DO RSpaces := RSpaces + ' ';
   WRITE (LST, LSpaces, Phrase, RSpaces);
END;

BEGIN
   FOR A := 1 TO 3 DO    {sets up for three-column test}
     BEGIN
       WRITELN ('What is the phrase?');
       READLN (Phrase);
       WRITELN ('How wide a column?');
       READLN (Field);
       Tab;
       WRITELN (LST);                    {very important!}
     END;
END
```

Figure 3.40 – A user-created procedure to do simple tabbing.

```
PROGRAM Demonstrate_Functions;
   {tabs horizontally using passed parameters}

TYPE
  Words = STRING[80];

VAR
InputPhrase : Words;
A, Width : INTEGER;
Position : CHAR;

PROCEDURE Tab (Phrase : Words; Field : INTEGER; Pos : CHAR);
VAR
  LSpaces, RSpaces : STRING[80];
  I, LeftSideSpaces, RightSideSpaces, SpaceOnLine : INTEGER;
BEGIN
  LSpaces := '';
  RSpaces := '';
  SpaceOnLine := Field - Length (Phrase);

  IF (Pos = 'C') OR (Pos = 'c') THEN        {centering}
  BEGIN
    LeftSideSpaces := SpaceOnLine DIV 2;
    RightSideSpaces := (SpaceOnLine DIV 2) + (SpaceOnLine) MOD 2;
    FOR I := 1 TO LeftSideSpaces DO LSpaces :=  LSpaces + '-';
    FOR I := 1 TO RightSideSpaces DO RSpaces := RSpaces + '-';
  END;

  IF (Pos = 'R') OR (Pos = 'r') THEN      {flush right}
  BEGIN
    LeftSideSpaces := SpaceOnLine;
    FOR I := 1 TO LeftSideSpaces DO LSpaces :=  LSpaces + '-';
  END;

  IF (Pos = 'L') OR (Pos = 'l') THEN      {flush left}
  BEGIN
    RightSideSpaces := SpaceOnLine;
    FOR I := 1 TO RightSideSpaces DO RSpaces :=  RSpaces + '-';
  END;

  WRITE (LST, LSpaces, Phrase, RSpaces);
END;

BEGIN
  FOR A := 1 TO 3 DO
  BEGIN   {demonstration of Tab procedure}
    WRITELN ('What is the phrase?');
    READLN (InputPhrase);
    WRITELN ('How wide a column?');
    READLN (Width);
    WRITELN ('Left, Right, or Centered?');
    READLN (Position);
    Tab (InputPhrase, Width, Position); {call to Tab procedure}
    WRITELN (LST);
    END;
  END.
```

Figure 3.41 – Program from Figure 3.40 modified to accept passed parameters.

how the function positions the text. Once you understand the operation of the function, you can substitute a space within quotes (' ') wherever the program uses a hyphen within quotes ('-').

The program in Figure 3.41 does a nice job. Notice that the Tab procedure is called with the single statement:

Tab (InputPhrase, Width, Position)

For example, the Tab function with these input values:

Tab (GreetingPhrase, 80, C)

centers the words "Good Morning"—the value assigned to the string variable GreetingPhrase—across 80 columns. This version:

Tab (CustomerName, 40, L)

prints the variable identified by CustomerName, in a field 40 characters wide. Extra spaces appear to the right of the name.

In a real application program, this procedure would be used as follows:

```
{The program would first access a data file to get the necessary
information.}

Tab (MonthlyTotals, 40, C);
WRITELN (LST);

{Here a loop would read successive customer records.}
Tab (CustomerName, 25, L);
Tab (CustomerBalance, 10, R);
WRITELN (LST);

{The program would continue.}
```

This program fragment might produce something like the sample shown in Figure 3.42.

It should be obvious that the second approach is much neater than the first. It avoids the hassle of assigning the variables used in the body of the program to those used in the Tab procedure. For example, in the customer-record program you don't have to assign the identifier CustomerName to the identifier Phrase, the name the Tab procedure in Figure 3.40 is looking for.

Notice in Figure 3.41 that within the Tab procedure you have a declaration section. The variables and identifiers declared within a procedure are defined only for that procedure. If you tried to use LSpaces, RSpaces, LeftSideSpaces, RightSideSpaces, or SpaceOnLine anyplace else in the program, Turbo would be quick to give you the familiar "Unknown identifier" or "syntax error" message.

What do you gain by using these *local* variables? For one thing, doing so allows you to put a group of common procedures and functions in a separate library file. You can combine (in Turbo jargon, "include") this file with any other program at compilation time without bothering to extract all the declaration information from your library procedures and putting it at the top of the main program. The internal (local) declaration for each of the procedures is perfectly sufficient. In this way you get the best of Turbo's strict typing within your main program, but without restrictions on the library routines you can access.

Another advantage of local declarations is that once you have debugged a procedure and know that it works well, you can simply use it as if it were a predefined function. You only have to remember the syntax to access it, without having to be concerned with what is happening inside the procedure. You have created a "black box."

In fact, many of the commands you have been using, like WRITELN and READLN, are simply predefined procedures, to which you pass parameters and which do some work for you. They are effectively black boxes you use in every program.

Not only do procedures and functions accept input (parameters), but they frequently produce output. Figure 3.43 shows the earlier program modified to create the phrase-plus-spacing information and pass it back to the calling program, rather than printing it out itself. This modification would be desirable, for example, if you wanted the

```
------------------12,246----------------
Joseph Porter----------------245.47
Ralph Rackstraw--------------445.00
Reginal Bunthorne------------2.25
Archibald Grosvenor---------1378.03
```

Figure 3.42 – Sample printer output running program in Figure 3.41.

calling program to have the option of directing the tabbed information to a line printer, disk file, or screen. In this case, notice that the variable Phrase is passed to the Tab procedure without spaces, and is returned by the procedure with the strings of spaces concatenated to it. Notice also that we have passed information back and forth to the procedure *without* ever having to declare the same identifiers for both the main body and the procedure.

To clarify the usage of variables to move data to and from the function, note that in Figure 3.40, the procedure as well as the main body used the identifiers Phrase and Field, while our universal Tab procedure in Figure 3.41 was totally self-contained; it could be used with any program because it did not need to know the identifiers used by the host program. This program could not send information back to the host, because there was no identifier understood by both this foreign procedure and the calling program. Figure 3.43 solves this problem. It shows the technique whereby a self-contained procedure can communicate both ways with the calling program. The main program uses the identifier InputPhrase as the input phrase (without spaces) and also uses this identifier for the modified (text and spaces) phrase as well. But the Tab procedure never uses this identifier. The last line of the Tab procedure, in fact, seems to use its own *locally defined identifier* (Phrase) to contain this output information.

Somehow, we have built a link between Phrase, known only to the Tab procedure, and InputPhrase, known to the calling program. This feat of legerdemain was achieved simply by adding the reserved word VAR to the first line of the Tab procedure.

When we use the reserved word VAR, Turbo equated Phrase (known only to the Tab procedure) and InputPhrase (known only to the calling program). We did not have to duplicate definitions in both places or explicitly write the line

    Phrase : = InputPhrase;

Any calling program, using any variable which had been declared to be an 80-character string, could use this Tab procedure. The Turbo compiler takes care of equating the input string with the string the Tab procedure uses for internal manipulation. Similarly, Turbo will take Phrase after it has been modified by the Tab procedure and equate it with the same variable identifier originally used by the calling program to pass the information to the Tab procedure.

```
PROGRAM Demonstrate_Functions;
   {does horizontal tabs using passed parameters}
   {passes parameters back and forth}
TYPE
  Words = STRING[80];

VAR
InputPhrase : Words;
A, Width : INTEGER;
Position : CHAR;

PROCEDURE Tab (VAR Phrase : Words; Field : INTEGER; Pos : CHAR);
     {This is the only modified line.}
VAR
  LSpaces, RSpaces : STRING[80];
  I, LeftSideSpaces, RightSideSpaces, SpaceOnLine : INTEGER;
BEGIN
   LSpaces := '';
   RSpaces := '';
   SpaceOnLine := Field - Length (Phrase);

   IF (Pos = 'C') OR (Pos = 'c') THEN         {centering}
   BEGIN
     LeftSideSpaces := SpaceOnLine DIV 2;
     RightSideSpaces := (SpaceOnLine DIV 2) + (SpaceOnLine) MOD 2;
     FOR I := 1 TO LeftSideSpaces DO LSpaces :=  LSpaces + '-';
     FOR I := 1 TO RightSideSpaces DO RSpaces := RSpaces + '-';
   END;

   IF (Pos = 'R') OR (Pos = 'r') THEN       {flush right}
   BEGIN
     LeftSideSpaces := SpaceOnLine;
     FOR I := 1 TO LeftSideSpaces DO LSpaces :=  LSpaces + '.';
   END;

   IF (Pos = 'L') OR (Pos = 'l') THEN       {flush left}
   BEGIN
     RightSideSpaces := SpaceOnLine;
     FOR I := 1 TO RightSideSpaces DO RSpaces :=  RSpaces + '_';
   END;

   Phrase := LSpaces + Phrase + RSpaces;
END;

BEGIN
  BEGIN
     WRITELN ('What is the phrase?');
     READLN (InputPhrase);
     WRITELN ('How wide a column?');
     READLN (Width);
     WRITELN ('Left, Right, or Centered?');
     READLN (Position);
     Tab (InputPhrase, Width, Position);
     END;
     WRITELN (InputPhrase);
  END.
```

Figure 3.43 – Program from Figure 3.40, further modified for even more flexible parameter passing.

Run the program in Figure 3.43. Notice that it sends output to the screen, simply for ease of debugging and demonstration. To make it print on the line printer, merely change the final WRITELN to:

WRITELN (LST, InputPhrase);

Of course, you could have it write to a file as well, or even send output once to the screen and once to the line printer. You have a much more flexible procedure now. We have told the Tab procedure what to expect as input. It (the Tab procedure) would see first something it was going to call Phrase, second something it was going to call Field, and finally something it was going to call Pos. It neither knew nor cared *what identifiers the calling program might use for the same information.* Indeed, in different parts of the calling program you could use many different phrase identifiers, or even none at all, and the Tab procedure would work equally well. The following input would be processed properly by the Tab procedure:

Tab (NumberOfTickets, 20, R);

You could even print out the information from one of our earliest sample programs:

Tab (CrewMemberName, ColumnWidth, L);

Here both CrewMemberName and ColumnWidth are obviously identifiers unique to the calling program. However, the following will *not* work:

Tab ('SECTION 3: COMMON TECHNIQUES', 80, C);

The calling program is using a string directly, rather than a string variable. That is, there is no identifier connected with the phrase. To Turbo—which considers an identifier merely an address in memory—the Tab procedure does not know where to look for the string.

To recap, we told the Tab procedure that the first value it sees would be a string of up to 80 characters, which it was to call Phrase. Next it would see an integer, which it would call Field, and finally it would find a lone character, which it was to call Pos. By adding the reserved word VAR to this list of expected input data specifications, we further told the procedure that it was allowed to modify this input information and not just read it. Once the Tab procedure has added all the spaces to the original characters, Turbo assigns the value of Phrase from within the Tab procedure to InputPhrase in the calling program. This is the opposite, but equally automatic, process to the assignment of the value of InputPhrase to Phrase at the beginning of the Tab procedure. The Tab procedure simply takes its input values and modifies one of them (Phrase).

In the original program, shown in Figure 3.40, you used only one set of memory locations to store the string called Phrase. In the program in 3.41, you used up two sets of memory locations to store copies of the same string. One memory location is used to store InputPhrase. The Tab procedure can read this information, but is prohibited from modifying it. The Tab procedure has to use an additional memory location, into which it copies the contents of InputPhrase. The Tab procedure operates on this copy of the input data. This process protects the original input from modification, but it wastes memory, requiring that every variable passed to the function exist in memory in two places. When we use the variable parameters in the program in Figure 3.43, however, we are back to using only one memory location, which contains a variable (containing the input phrase) but also serves as the storage place for the output from the procedure. When passing simple numbers and short phrases to and from a procedure this is a minor point, of interest only to nit-pickers. But when we are passing huge data arrays to a procedure, using a variable parameter saves all the memory space that would have to be devoted to creating an additional "working copy" of the array for the procedure. Needless to say, this not only conserves working space, it also results in faster program execution.

Being able to exploit procedures and functions is the key to making Turbo do just about anything you want it to do. As you gain experience in programming, you will develop your own groups of functions that do common jobs for you—processing text, formatting pages, solving standard navigation problems, or whatever your day-to-day applications may be. It only takes a little extra work to develop a one-of-a-kind program into a general-purpose procedure, so that you never have to "reinvent the wheel" when you need to do the same job in a different program. It is almost like writing your own programming language without having to spend years learning compiler theory and design.

IMPORTANT NOTE [Warning: Thin Ice!]

There is a potentially perplexing idiosyncrasy in Turbo's handling of strings passed to a procedure. If the string passed from the host program is not defined to have *exactly the same length as the string in the procedure,* Turbo will think they have violated its scheme of strict typing and will generate an error message. Fortunately, Turbo provides a neat way around the problem. A compiler directive ({$V-}) can be included in the program to tell Turbo to ignore this situation. Incidentally, Borland acknowledges that this problem ranks among the most often asked questions received by their user hotline.

User-Created Functions

Virtually everything that has been said about procedures can be said about functions as well. Functions also can contain local variables. But unlike procedures, which may or may not return information to the calling program, functions by definition must return some value or values to the calling program. A quick glance at the list of predefined functions in Figure 3.39 should illustrate the point. You call the function and give it an argument, and it returns the absolute value of the argument. Similarly, you call the function and give it an argument, and it returns the square root of the number.

Functions are among the most powerful of Turbo's features. As mentioned earlier, you can even redefine and customize these predefined functions for special applications. But more often, you might want to create your own function to solve a common problem. In Figure 3.44, the demonstration program calls a function to figure interest—compounded daily—on any dollar amount, invested for any number of years, invested at any interest rate. It is an example of the type of coding you do not want to have to rewrite for every financial program you ever write.

Run the program a few times with different values. Figure 3.45 shows the screen display from a sample run of the program.

The calling program does not need to waste any memory locations nor require any declarations for information being passed directly to a function, unless (as with A, B, and C) you have a legitimate reason to store this information (in this case, getting the interactive screen responses) in the host program. Once you understand this point, you can modify the demo program so as to not print the "canned" demonstration. Notice that the result of the function named Interest can be treated just like a value stored in the identifier named Interest.

Incidentally, the Interest function used a standard predefined function, the exponential function EXP.

Also note that in the final WRITELN statement of the procedure, there is a good example of a function being used in place of a variable.

```
PROGRAM
Demonstrate_Function_To_Compute_Continually_Compounded_Interest;

VAR
    A, B, C, Amount : REAL;

FUNCTION Interest (Principal, Term, Rate : REAL) : REAL;
VAR
    OneYearMultiplier, MultiYearMultiplier, PercentInterest : REAL;
BEGIN
    PercentInterest := Rate / 100.0;
    OneYearMultiplier := PercentInterest + 1.0;
    MultiYearMultiplier := EXP (Term * PercentInterest);
    Interest := Principal * MultiYearMultiplier;
  END;    {end of Interest function}

BEGIN         {Main demo program begins here.}
    WRITELN;
    WRITELN (Interest (1000, 3, 7.5):5:2);
    WRITELN ('The demo program asked for $1000 at 7.5% interest
        for 3 years.');
    WRITELN ('Notice that the calling program used no identifiers
        at all');
    WRITELN ('to get this information computed.');
    WRITELN; WRITELN;
    WRITELN ('The second example prompts for input and prints the
        results.');

        {Notice that variables A, B, and C are never used by the
        function!!}

    WRITELN ('Principal amount?');
    READLN (A);
    WRITELN ('Term in years?');
    READLN (B);
    WRITELN ('Interest rate?');
    READLN (C);
    WRITELN ('The result is:');
    WRITELN (Interest (A, B, C):6:2);
  END.
```

Figure 3.44 – Program to demonstrate function to calculate interest.

Assuming that Money has been declared as a real variable, and using the values shown in Figure 3.45, then the following two program fragments are equivalent and will produce identical output:

WRITELN (Interest (A, B, C):6:2);

Money : = 81337.92;
WRITELN (Money:6:2);

More on Parameters

You can use all forms of data as parameters, including complex structures as well as your your own user-created data types. Unlike standard Pascal, however, Turbo does not allow you to pass a procedure or function to another procedure or function as a parameter. While some old-time Pascal programmers consider this a weakness in Turbo, the language still offers so much flexibility that you can always program your way around those rare instances in which you might miss this capability. It is hardly an everyday occurrence.

Also, you must declare procedures and functions before you call them. In the sample programs, you defined all the code for Tab and Interest before using them. Sometimes you don't want to clutter up the beginning of a program with procedures you will use later on. More commonly, you find the need for an extra procedure you had not originally planned on. In these cases Turbo allows you to put the procedure wherever you like. However, someplace before the module in which the procedure is called, you have to include a *forward*

```
1252.32
The demo program asked for $1000 at 7.5% interest for 3 years.
Notice that the calling program used no identifiers at all to get
this information computed.

The second example prompts for input and prints the results.
Principal amount?
3000
Term in years?
20
Interest rate?
16.5
The result is:
81337.92
```

Figure 3.45 – *Screen display from the program in Figure 3.44.*

reference, which merely tells Turbo to look through the entire program for the procedure code.

Modify Figure 3.44 to look like the listing in Figure 3.46. In this case we have the main program calling the demonstration procedure, which in turn calls the Interest function. Although a bit contrived for a simple program, this example reflects the order in which you are likely to be doing things in an ambitious real-world program. You will get an error message when you try to compile this program, but that is the point I want to illustrate. It is to avoid this common (but potentially perplexing) error that you use the forward reference.

The problem in trying to compile the program in Figure 3.46 is that the DoDemo procedure cannot find the Interest function; it has

```
PROGRAM
Demonstrate_Function_To_Compute_Continually_Compounded_Interest;

VAR
    A, B, C, Amount : REAL;
    Iterations : INTEGER;

PROCEDURE DoDemo;
BEGIN
    WRITELN ('Principal amount?');
    READLN (A);
    WRITELN ('Term in years?');
    READLN (B);
    WRITELN ('Interest rate?');
    READLN (C);
    WRITELN ('The result is:');
    WRITELN (Interest (A, B, C):6:2);

END;

FUNCTION Interest (Principal, Term, Rate : REAL) : REAL;
VAR
    OneYearMultiplier, MultiYearMultiplier, PercentInterest : REAL;
BEGIN
    PercentInterest := Rate / 100.0;
    OneYearMultiplier := PercentInterest + 1.0;
    MultiYearMultiplier := EXP (Term * PercentInterest);
    Interest := Principal * MultiYearMultiplier;
  END;    {end of Interest function}

BEGIN         {Main demo program begins here.}
  FOR Iterations := 1 TO 3 DO DoDemo;
END.
```

Figure 3.46 – Program to demonstrate erroneous calling sequence.

not yet been declared. Modify the program to resemble the listing in Figure 3.47, and it should run perfectly.

You will find many situations in which you want to link programs together and in which it is easier to type a number of forward references than to move blocks of code around.

There is one final detail about which you may eventually want to know when you are an experienced Turbo programmer. You can create subprograms in assembly language and call them into your Turbo program during compilation. These programs are called *external procedures*. There are many restrictions on this process, and it is a genuinely advanced topic. Even more importantly, Turbo

```
PROGRAM
Demonstrate_Function_To_Compute_Continually_Compounded_Interest;

VAR
    A, B, C, Amount : REAL;
    Iterations : INTEGER;
{Here is the forward reference}

PROCEDURE DoDemo;
BEGIN
    WRITELN ('Principal amount?');
    READLN (A);
    WRITELN ('Term in years?');
    READLN (B);
    WRITELN ('Interest rate?');
    READLN (C);
    WRITELN ('The result is:');
    WRITELN (Interest (A, B, C):6:2);

END;

FUNCTION Interest;
VAR
    OneYearMultiplier, MultiYearMultiplier, PercentInterest : REAL;
BEGIN
    PercentInterest := Rate / 100.0;
    OneYearMultiplier := PercentInterest + 1.0;
    MultiYearMultiplier := EXP (Term * PercentInterest);
    Interest := Principal * MultiYearMultiplier;
  END;    {End of Interest function.}

  BEGIN           {Main demo program begins here.}
    FOR Iterations := 1 TO 3 DO DoDemo;
  END.
```

Figure 3.47 – Program to demonstrate correct sequence of declaring and calling functions.

offers speed and a set of capabilities normally available only with assembly language. Standard Turbo procedures and functions include the ability to generate and intercept system interrupts, alter specific memory locations, make calls to the BDOS (basic disk operating system) and BIOS (basic input-output system), communicate with the operating system's error handler, and send data to the CPU's ports. Most of these features are used only by advanced programmers. Yet even the most experienced programmer will have to search hard for an application that cannot be addressed by Turbo and absolutely requires recourse to assembly language.

Advanced
Data
Structures

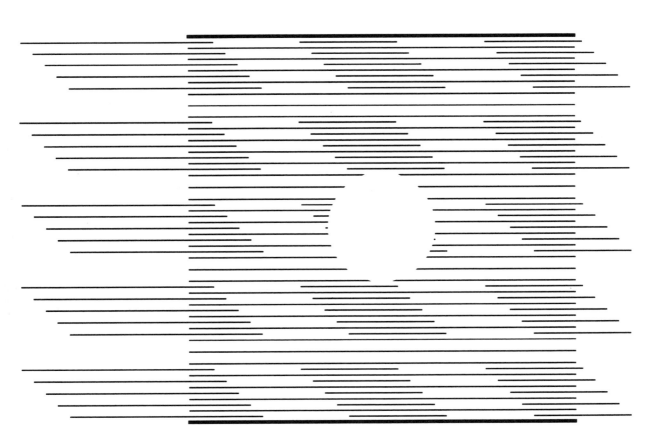

Chapter 4

Overview

Earlier you learned about Niklaus Wirth's conception of programming, and the philosophy behind Turbo Pascal. Briefly, Wirth believes that programming is the art of combining algorithms and data structures. Most of this book has dealt with the development of algorithms—procedures, functions, and the control of program flow with tests and control structures. So far you have used predefined data types—characters, integers, real numbers, and an occasional Boolean value. These data types handled input, output, and the control of loops and tests. Everything you have done with data could have been done fairly well in languages like BASIC. You have adjusted to Turbo's strong typing and been rewarded with much easier debugging. Now it is time to explore Turbo's tools to really give you control over the data you will be manipulating.

The representation and organization of data is not something to be done indiscriminately, just to get the information into the program. Representing data in its most natural form is

half the task of programming. Moreover, if the task of programming is defined as solving real-world problems, then the programming techniques that lend themselves to defining problems in
the most natural and intuitive manner are the ones most likely to
produce efficient, user-friendly programs that work. Turbo offers a
complement of powerful yet intuitive data types and structures to
speed the translation of real-world information into data that can be
processed by computer.

Turbo's data structures—arrays, records, and files—all complement each other. When you tackle most ambitious programming
tasks, you will use several of the structures in the same program. You
will notice that almost all the example programs in this chapter do
real work and use some features that have not yet been covered.
You can ignore the new features while concentrating on the aspects
being examined and then, as you learn the other techniques, return
to these program examples to see how the different structures and
techniques work together.

Arrays

In Turbo, as in BASIC, an array is a collection of *similar data elements.* You might have arrays of integers, arrays of strings, and arrays
of real numbers, representing, say, test scores, names, and prices,
respectively. The array is a natural structure, one that reflects the kinds
of lists we make in everyday life—clothes to pack (all are garments),
bills to pay (all are dollar amounts), people to whom we owe thank-
you notes (all are people), and so on. An array must be declared with
an identifier, the data type to which its individual elements belong,
and the number of both the first and the last element in the array.
Some typical declarations might be:

```
NameList         : ARRAY[1 . . 30] OF Name;
TestScores       : ARRAY[1 . . 10] OF REAL;
RoomsVisited     : ARRAY[CaveEntrance . . TreasureRoom] OF Rooms;
Conditions       : ARRAY[1 . . 8] OF BOOLEAN;
InputCharacters : ARRAY[a . . z] OF CHAR;
WorkDays         : ARRAY[Monday . . Friday] OF Days;
```

In the first, third, and sixth examples, the data types Name, Rooms, and Days would each have to have been declared earlier, as they are not predefined. Unlike BASIC, which asks you to dimension an array with only its maximum size, Turbo asks for a starting and ending value. It thus avoids the frustrations many programmers experience in working with BASIC arrays, which start so irritatingly and unintuitively with 0 instead of 1. In fact, arrays can be declared in the most natural terms for the programming situation. If you are dealing with a user-created data type called Days, why not dimension the array as having elements called Monday–Friday instead of 1–5? Or if you have created an array called Rooms, for an adventure game that begins with the room called CaveEntrance and ends with TreasureRoom, isn't it natural to define the array the same way?

An individual element of an array can be accessed by its index, exactly as in BASIC. Remember, too, that arrays can be passed to procedures as parameters—a technique used frequently in general-purpose sorting and generic code-conversion procedures. The manipulation of arrays is quite straightforward, as Turbo's strict type-checking prevents you from storing meaningless data in the array. If you try to store a value in an array that is not of the declared type, or if you try to access an element outside the declared minimum and maximum index values, Turbo will flag the error immediately. Similarly, if you calculate an index value using real numbers and try to access an array element with the calculated index of, say, 1.99999999, Turbo will flag the error; it also checks indices to be certain that they are true scalar values (having a discrete predecessor and successor).

Standard Pascal does not allow strings of characters, but it does allow arrays of characters. Thus, in many books on Pascal you will find an unusual emphasis on arrays, as they offer the only convenient way to manipulate text (especially screen prompts). Turbo not only allows you to use character strings, it has a collection of special procedures and functions to manipulate them. Thus the one-dimensional array, while still one of the workhorses of Turbo Pascal, is not quite the Swiss army knife of programming techniques it seems to be in more limited versions of the language.

Arrays are data structures stored entirely in memory, so operations on arrays are not slowed by the mechanics of disk access. Thus, arrays are often the optimal—both the fastest and the simplest—data structures for sorting, maintaining directories, and converting codes. The program in Figure 4.1 uses a simple array to do a fast Shell sort. This program appears in hundreds of programming books in one form or another.

Enter the program and run it. Not only does this program demonstrate the declaration and optimal use of arrays, it also demonstrates, to even the most skeptical critics, how fast Turbo Pascal is. In fact, you can modify the program to sort a thousand or more random numbers. Then tackle the same program in BASIC or any other language. Get out your stop watch and run it again. Now you know how Turbo got its name.

Although it is beyond the scope of this book to examine sorting algorithms, you should be able to adapt this example to do fast sorts in your own application programs. You will see many arrays used in the programming examples in the rest of this book. Figure 4.2 is the bubble-sort version of Figure 4.1. While it is not as fast as the Shell sort, the operation of this bubble sort is still faster than the same process done in any other language. It also makes the same optimal use of simple arrays. A bubble sort of under 100 values in Turbo combines impressive speed with simplicity. Try it using several different values for MaxElement. Like the Shell sort, the bubble sort is one of the primary applications for simple arrays.

Multidimensional Arrays

Arrays can also have more than one dimension. In this respect, Turbo is very much like BASIC. Remember, however, that all elements of an array must be of the same data type. Because BASIC has such a limited range of data structures, many programmers have developed the habit of declaring most of their arrays to be arrays of strings and storing even numerical values as strings. The classic programming example of a two-dimensional array is a teacher's class list, containing names and test scores. In BASIC, such an array would require that both name *and* test score be stored as strings, in a string array. Turbo offers the much more flexible *record* structure, for storing items that are logically related but of different data types together. *Arrays of records* are often used in Turbo. Records are discussed in a later section of this chapter.

```
      PROGRAM ShellSort;
            {Demonstrates Shell sort of 500 random numbers.}
      CONST
        MaxElement = 500;
      VAR
        Nums : ARRAY[1..500] OF INTEGER;
        Temp, I, J, Pass, Gap : INTEGER;

      PROCEDURE GenerateInput;
      BEGIN
        RANDOMIZE;
        FOR I := 1 TO MaxElement DO
           BEGIN
           Nums[I] := RANDOM (1000);
           END;
      END;

      PROCEDURE PrintOut;
      BEGIN
        FOR I := 1 TO MaxElement DO
        BEGIN
        WRITE (Nums[I]);
        WRITE (´   ´);
        END;
        WRITELN; WRITELN; WRITELN;
      END;

      PROCEDURE FlipFlop;
      BEGIN
        Temp := Nums[J];
        Nums[J] := Nums[J+Gap];
        Nums[J+Gap] := Temp;
      END;

      PROCEDURE Sort;
      BEGIN
         Gap := MaxElement DIV 2;
         WHILE Gap > 0 DO
         BEGIN
          FOR  I := (Gap + 1) TO MaxElement DO
             BEGIN
                 J := I-Gap;
                 WHILE J > 0 DO
                     BEGIN
                       IF Nums[J] > Nums[J+Gap] THEN
                       BEGIN
                         FlipFlop;
                         J := J-Gap;
                       END
                       ELSE J := 0;
                     END;                {end WHILE}
             END;                   {swap flag set}
             Gap := Gap DIV 2;
          END;            {WHILE Gap > 0 }
      END;          {Sort}
```

Figure 4.1 – Use of one-dimensional array in a Shell sort (continues).

```
BEGIN
   WRITELN ('Turbo Shell sort program begins now.');
   GenerateInput;
   WRITELN ('Array of ', MaxElement, ' values is all loaded and
the sort is about to begin.');
   Sort;
   WRITELN ('The sort is completed.  Here are the ', MaxElement, '
values in order:');
   PrintOut
END.
```

Figure 4.1 – Use of one-dimensional array in a Shell sort (continued).

One common valid use for multidimensional arrays is to store "look-up" tables in an array. Frequently it is simpler and faster to look up a value in an array than to compute the same value (particularly if you can organize the table so that the most frequently needed values are found first). How many times have you seen store clerks look up sales tax on a chart rather than figure the amount—even with a calculator? It can also be faster for the computer to do the same thing. Moreover, some tables do not lend themselves to straightforward calculations. I have written several programs for newspaper publishers to automate the billing of classified advertising. Most small newspapers have a capricious pricing structure for their ads, which combines the number of lines, number of consecutive insertions, total number of lines ordered to date, and (presumably) the publisher's lucky number. It is almost always easier to construct a table—at least to cover the most frequently accessed values—than to compute the same prices over and over again.

A two- (or more) dimensional array is normally pictured as a grid. (For example, Figure 4.5 is a representation of the two-dimensional array created in the program listed in Figure 4.3.) Each element of a two-dimensional array is uniquely identified by two indices—one referring to the row and one to the column. The syntax to declare

```
PROGRAM BubbleSort;
  {Demonstrates bubble sort of 500 random numbers.}
CONST
  MaxElement = 500;
VAR
  Nums : ARRAY[1..500] OF INTEGER;
  Element : INTEGER;
  Temp, I, J, Pass : INTEGER;
  Swap : BOOLEAN;

PROCEDURE GenerateInput;
BEGIN
  RANDOMIZE;
  FOR I := 1 TO MaxElement DO
     BEGIN
     Nums[I] := RANDOM (1000);
     END;
END;

PROCEDURE PrintOut;
BEGIN
  FOR I := 1 TO MaxElement DO
  BEGIN
  WRITE (Nums[I]);
  WRITE (´   ´);
  END;
  WRITELN; WRITELN; WRITELN;
END;

PROCEDURE FlipFlop;
BEGIN
  Temp := Nums[J];
  Nums[J] := Nums[J+1];
  Nums[J+1] := Temp;
  Swap := True;
END;

PROCEDURE Sort;
BEGIN
  FOR  I := 2 TO MaxElement DO
     BEGIN
          J := I-1;
          WHILE J > 0 DO
             BEGIN
               IF Nums[J] > Nums[J+1] THEN
               BEGIN
                 FlipFlop;
                 J := J-1;
               END
               ELSE J := 0;
             END;  {End WHILE.}
        END;  {Swap flag set.}
     END; {pass}
```

Figure 4.2 – Use of one-dimensional array in a bubble sort (continues).

```
BEGIN
  WRITELN ('Turbo bubble sort program begins now.');
  GenerateInput;
  WRITELN ('Array of ', MaxElement, ' values is all loaded and
the sort is about to begin.');
  Sort;
  WRITELN ('The sort is completed.  Here are the ', MaxElement,
values in order:');
  PrintOut
END.
```

Figure 4.2 – Use of one-dimensional array in a bubble sort (continued).

and dimension an array containing 21 elements stored as three rows of seven elements would be:

VAR
    Schedule : **ARRAY** [1 . . 3, 1 . . 7] **OF** INTEGER;

To identify one specific element of this two-dimensional array would require two indices:

WeekendRate : = RateChart [12, 25];
MetrolinerArrival : = TrainArray [3, 4]

One application for a two-dimensional array is the computer representation of a train schedule. Here you have many columns of numbers representing different trains—locals, expresses, and specials—and it is impossible to calculate the actual arrival and departure times of the trains, because there are too many variables for each run. But it is a trivial process to look up any particular time for any train in a multidimensional array. The program in Figure 4.3 demonstrates the rudiments of this process.

Incidentally, Turbo supports arrays of even more than two dimensions, although they are not used often. Unfortunately, unlike most Turbo data structures, arrays of more than two dimensions are not a simple reflection of the way information is arranged in the "natural" world. They are often used in some adventure games to represent complex—but certainly not realistic—structures such as maze locations that may simultaneously contain treasures, special hazards, monsters, and the player.

```
PROGRAM Train_Schedule;
CONST
  Limit = 7;  {Maximum number of trains in this table.}
TYPE
  Trains = STRING[10];
VAR
  TrainArray  : ARRAY[1..3, 1..7] OF Trains; {Array is 3 columns
by 7 rows.}
  Row, Column : INTEGER;

PROCEDURE LoadArray;
CONST

{All the information for the train schedule is contained in these three}
{strings. The strings are read ten characters at a time, with each group}
{of ten characters being assigned to one entry in the array. Because the}
{process is looking for a fixed number of characters, we have manually}
{padded out the raw data strings with spaces so that every array entry}
{will have a total of ten characters counting the spaces and the useful}
{information.}

   RawDataTrains = 'MetrolinerCardinal   MontrealerBankers
Palmetto  Patriot   Potomac   ';
   RawDataDep    = '08:00     09:15     10:03     14:37     20:00
21:18     23:55     ';
   RawDataArv    = '08:13     09:30     10:24     14:52     20:12
21:31     00:07     ';
VAR
   FirstChar : INTEGER;
BEGIN
   FirstChar := 1;
   Column := 1;
   FOR Row := 1 TO Limit DO
   BEGIN
      TrainArray [Column, Row] := COPY (RawDataTrains, FirstChar, 10);
      FirstChar := FirstChar + 10;
   END;
   Column := 2;
   FirstChar := 1;
   FOR Row := 1 TO Limit DO
   BEGIN
      TrainArray [Column, Row] := COPY (RawDataDep, FirstChar, 10);
      FirstChar := FirstChar + 10;
   END;
   FirstChar := 1;
   Column := 3;
   FOR Row := 1 TO Limit DO
   BEGIN
      TrainArray [Column, Row] := COPY (RawDataArv, FirstChar, 10);
      FirstChar := FirstChar + 10;
   END;
END;
```

Figure 4.3 – Program to demonstrate use of a multidimensional array.

```
PROCEDURE DisplaySchedule;
BEGIN
   CLRSCR;
   WRITELN ('   TRAIN       DEPARTS       ARRIVES ');
   WRITELN ('_____');
   FOR Row := 1 TO Limit DO
   BEGIN
     WRITE (TrainArray [1, Row],'    ');
     WRITE (TrainArray [2, Row],'    ');
     WRITELN (TrainArray [3, Row]);
   END;
END;

PROCEDURE SeekInfo;
VAR
  NotDone : BOOLEAN;
  WhichColumn, WhichRow : INTEGER;
BEGIN
  NotDone := TRUE;
  WRITELN;
  WRITELN ('Demonstration of simple data access from an array.');
  WHILE NotDone DO
  BEGIN
    WRITELN;
    WRITELN ('There are seven trains listed in this timetable.');
    WRITELN ('To get either the train name, departure time or
arrival time');
    WRITELN ('please type two numbers separated by a space:');
    WRITELN;
    WRITELN ('The first number says what information you want:');
    WRITELN ('1-Name of the train, 2-Departure Time, 3-Arrival
Time');
    WRITELN ('And the second number selects which of the seven
trains you care about.');
    READLN  (WhichColumn, WhichRow);
    WRITELN;
    WRITELN (TrainArray [WhichColumn, WhichRow]);
  END;
END;

BEGIN
   LoadArray;
   DisplaySchedule;
   SeekInfo;
END.
```

Figure 4.3 – Program to demonstrate use of a multidimensional array (continued).

There are several string-manipulation procedures used in Figure 4.3 to load the array. You can ignore them for now, but come back and look at this example after reading about strings. Figure 4.4 shows the screen display produced by running the program.

The primary intention of this program is to illustrate an application of arrays to the storage of data that lends itself to a tabular format. In a finished program, you would probably load the information into the array from an external data file, or you might use a more sophisticated procedure—perhaps using nested loops—than the obvious but less elegant LoadArray procedure here. Printing the entire train

```
    TRAIN        DEPARTS        ARRIVES

    -------------------------------------
    Metroliner   08:00          08:13
    Cardinal     09:15          09:30
    Montrealer   10:03          10:24
    Bankers      14:37          14:52
    Palmetto     20:00          20:12
    Patriot      21:18          21:31
    Potomac      23:55          00:07

Demonstration of simple data access from an array.

There are seven trains listed in this timetable.
To get either the train name, departure time or arrival time
please type two numbers separated by a space:

The first number says what information you want:
1-Name of the train, 2-Departure Time, 3-Arrival Time
And the second number selects which of the seven trains you care about:
1 3

Montrealer

There are seven trains listed in this timetable.
To get either the train name, departure time or arrival time
please type two numbers separated by a space:

The first number says what information you want:
1-Name of the train, 2-Departure Time, 3-Arrival Time
And the second number selects which of the seven trains you care about:
3 6

21:31
```

Figure 4.4 – Screen display produced by program in Figure 4.3.

schedule as we do here demonstrates what the array "looks like," by displaying it in tabular form.

You can see from the program that multidimensional arrays do not lend themselves to interactive interrogation, because of all the massaging that must be done to convert the user's screen reponses into data that can be used to index one particular value in an array. Notice how complex and explicit the prompts had to be to guide the user's two-number input. This is not to say that you cannot use multidimensional arrays for interactive input; merely that their use often demands cumbersome programming, involving a series of elaborate, specific prompts. The program must verify that it has received valid integer responses to all the prompts and must then combine the responses in the right order to index a value.

Nonetheless, the multidimensional array is an excellent structure for accessing information within a program. Thus, in this demo program when you are asked for two numbers, you are simulating some procedure that would generate the numbers to be passed to the SeekInfo procedure.

Figure 4.5 is a diagram of the data array used in Figures 4.3 and 4.4. Try different input data until you understand how the data is stored.

Strings and Characters

It is hard to find a part of any programming language that is simply as much fun to use as the string-manipulation commands. Among the hackers at any computer user's group meeting, conversation sooner or later turns to writing compilers and parsers. While compilers remain the test of the best programmers, it seems that everyone sooner or later has to write a parser. *Parsers* are programs or routines that take command input and interpret it. If you have ever played an adventure game and typed responses like GO NORTH, or simply NORTH, or even N, it was a parser that converted this keyboard input into data from which the program could then determine your new location.

The task of a parser can be as simple as converting a one-digit menu choice or as complex as interpreting a command like "PUT

	Column 1	**Column 2**	**Column 3**
Row 1 (Array Index) Location	Metroliner 1,1 Col 1, Row 1	08:00 2,1 Col 2, Row 1	08:13 3,1 Col 3, Row 1
Row 2	Cardinal 1,2 Col 1, Row 2	09:15 2,2 Col 2, Row 2	09:30 3,2 Col 3, Row 2
Row 3	Montrealer 1,3 Col 1, Row 3	08:00 2,3 Col 2, Row 3	08:13 3,3 Col 3, Row 3
Row 4	Bankers 1,4 Col 1, Row 4	14:37 2,4 Col 2, Row 4	14:52 3,4 Col 3, Row 4
Row 5	Palmetto 1,4 Col 1, Row 4	20:00 2,4 Col 2, Row 4	20:12 3,4 Col 3, Row 4
Row 6	Patriot 1,5 Col 1, Row 5	21:18 2,5 Col 2, Row 5	21:31 3,5 Col 3, Row 5
Row 7	Potomac 1,7 Col 1, Row 7	23:55 2,7 Col 2, Row 7	00:07 3,7 Col 3, Row 7

Figure 4.5 – *Pictorial representation of the multidimensional array created by the program in Figure 4.3.*

THE DIAMOND AND EGG IN THE TROPHY CASE." What all parsers have in common is that they must analyze and test strings. Writing parsers is fun because it allows you to show off your cleverness;
it is also an area in which you can make your programs friendly, as
they accept a flexible range of inputs rather than a rigid list of arbitrary codes.

In addition to developing parsers, string commands lend themselves to writing communication programs, text processors, and a
host of utility programs for data conversion. As mentioned, strings
do not exist in standard Pascal, and their absence has long been considered one of Pascal's most glaring weaknesses. Turbo recognizes
the need to support string handling and offers some useful procedures and functions in this area.

We have already seen examples of strings in the train-schedule
program and the tabbing programs of Chapter 3. Now it's time for a
formal definition. A *string* is a sequential list of characters. In Turbo it
is a predefined data type, with a maximum length of 255 characters.
But note that strings are a *structured* (or *complex*) data type, because
they are made up of a more fundamental data type—characters.
Strings must be declared like all other data. Each must have an identifier and a maximum size. Typical declarations might be:

```
TYPE
    Name = STRING[20];

VAR
    Buffer : = STRING[127];
```

Note that strings can be declared as both a data type (using the
equal sign) and a variable (using the assignment operator). In fact,
because you can only assign values to variables and not to types, if
you do declare a string as a data type, you must also declare at least
one variable of that type to hold any values. A typical declaration
might be:

```
TYPE
    MessageBuffer = STRING [132];
VAR
    ModemInput, ModemOutput : = MessageBuffer;
```

In this case ModemInput and ModemOutput are variables, which can hold data. They are both strings with a maximum value of 132 characters.

Most often, strings are used as variables. Anything you can do with a one-dimensional array of characters you can do with a string, because that is what it is. Note, too, that although you must declare a maximum size for a string variable, it can contain shorter strings; Turbo will automatically pad out the extra spaces. Specific commands allow you to determine the length of a string (only the characters, *not* the padding spaces), to extract substrings of any length beginning at any position, to concatenate strings, convert them to their numerical value, compare them, and quite a bit more. And because strings are arrays of characters, Turbo allows you to manipulate and access individual characters just as you would manipulate elements of an array.

Turbo's string-handling procedures and functions are listed in Figure 4.6.

Figure 4.7 lists a short program that simply demonstrates the basic string-manipulation commands. Its operation is documented in the WRITELN statement. Try substituting different parameters in the commands and different strings. Try using bogus parameters, which exceed the length of the string, and try looking for nonexistent strings.

Recall the LoadArray procedure from the train-schedule program. A simplified version is repeated in Figure 4.8, in which one string is broken into individual parts to be stored in a one-dimensional array. The input data has been changed to identical digits (11:11 for the first, 22:22 for the second, etc.) to make the input and output clearer. The screen display generated by the program in Figure 4.8 is shown in Figure 4.9.

The program in Figure 4.8 uses the COPY procedure. COPY extracts a substring of any length from another string beginning at a specific starting point. The syntax of the COPY procedure is identical to that used by the DELETE procedure. To use either procedure, you must give Turbo the name of a "target" string as well as the length and starting position of a substring within that target. The procedure will either copy this substring into some other string or delete the substring entirely. A closely related procedure, INSERT, will insert one string at the indicated position within the target string. This operation is not to be confused with concatenation, which appends one string to the end of another.

In this figure the following abbreviations are used to represent the arguments of the functions and procedures:

C	character
E	either integer or real-number value
I ·	integer
POS	position within a string
ST1, ST2	strings
SUB	substring

Procedures and Functions

CONCAT (*ST . . ST*)	Concatenates any number of string expressions separated by commas; result is always a string. Note that the same function can be accomplished using plus signs instead (e.g., ST4 := ST1 + ST2 + ST3).
COPY (*ST, POS, I*)	Returns, from string ST, a substring that is *I* characters long and begins at position *POS*; result is always a string.
DELETE (*ST, POS, I*)	Removes, from string ST, a substring that is *I* characters long and begins at position *POS*; result is always a string.
INSERT (*SUB, ST, POS*)	Inserts substring *SUB* into string *ST* at position *POS*.
LENGTH (*ST*)	Returns the number of characters in string *ST*. Note that this is not the same value as the declared maximum length of the string; it ignores spaces and counts only the number of characters in the string. Result is always an integer.
POS (*ST1, ST2*)	Returns the position number at which string *ST1* begins within string *ST2*; result is always an integer.
STR (*E, ST*)	Converts the numeric value of *E* into string *ST*. *E* can be either an integer or real number, but it should be expressed in a WRITE-parameter form (such as Age:5 for an integer or Dollars:5:2 for a real number).

Figure 4.6 – String-handling procedures and functions in Turbo Pascal (continues).

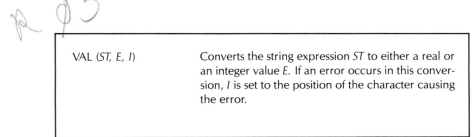

| VAL (*ST, E, I*) | Converts the string expression *ST* to either a real or an integer value *E*. If an error occurs in this conversion, *I* is set to the position of the character causing the error. |

Figure 4.6 – String-handling procedures and functions in Turbo Pascal (continued).

```
PROGRAM DemonstrateStringCommands;
CONST
  Phrase1 = 'Gilbert & Sullivan';
  Phrase2 = ' present H.M.S. PINAFORE';
  Phrase3 = 'Sullivan';
  Date = '1885';
VAR
  Number, Size, Place, ErrorCode : INTEGER;
  RealNumber : REAL;
  SubPhrase : STRING[18];

BEGIN
  WRITELN ('Phrase1 = ',Phrase1);
  WRITELN ('Date = ',Date);
  WRITELN;
  Size := LENGTH (Phrase1);
  WRITELN ('The length of the phrase is ', Size);
  WRITELN;
  Place := POS ('&', Phrase1);
  WRITELN ('The ampersand is in position ',Place,' in the phrase: ', Phrase1);
  Place := POS ('G', Phrase1);
  WRITELN ('The G is in position ', Place,' in the phrase: ',
Phrase1);
  WRITELN;
  SubPhrase := COPY (Phrase1, 11, 8);
  WRITELN ('The subphrase stretching from the 11th to the 18th
position is: ', SubPhrase);
  WRITELN;
  WRITELN ('Phrase1 = ',Phrase1);
  WRITELN ('Phrase2 = ',Phrase2);
  WRITELN (CONCAT (Phrase1, Phrase2));
  WRITELN (Phrase1 + Phrase2);  {simpler than the line above!}
  WRITELN;
  WRITELN ('The date is stored as a string: ', Date);
  WRITELN ('Remember that you cannot do math operations on a string!');
  VAL (Date, Number, ErrorCode);
  VAL (Date, RealNumber, ErrorCode);
  WRITELN ('The date converted to an integer: ', Number);
  WRITELN ('The date converted to a real number: ', RealNumber);
  WRITELN ('The date plus 25 is: ', Number + 25);
END.
```

Figure 4.7 – Program to demonstrate basic string-manipulation routines.

```
PROGRAM StringManipulation;
CONST
  Limit = 5;
TYPE
  Trains = STRING[5];
VAR
  Index : INTEGER;
  TrainArray : ARRAY[1..5] OF Trains;

PROCEDURE LoadArray;
CONST
  RawData = '11:1122:2233:3344:4455:5566:6677:77';
VAR
  FirstChar : INTEGER;
BEGIN
  FirstChar := 1;
  FOR Index := 1 TO Limit DO
      BEGIN
          TrainArray [Index] := COPY (RawData, FirstChar, 5);
          FirstChar := FirstChar + 5;
      END;
END;

PROCEDURE PrintArray;
BEGIN
    FOR Index := 1 TO Limit DO
    WRITELN ('TrainArray[', Index, '] = ', TrainArray[Index]);
END;

BEGIN
  LoadArray;
  PrintArray
END.
```

Figure 4.8 – Program to demonstrate use of string procedures to load an array.

```
TrainArray[1]  =  11:11
TrainArray[2]  =  22:22
TrainArray[3]  =  33:33
TrainArray[4]  =  44:44
TrainArray[5]  =  55:55
```

Figure 4.9 – Screen display produced by the program in Figure 4.8.

In the example below, the 32-character string InputPhrase is assigned the value

FORTRAN, BASIC, and Turbo Pascal

We use the COPY procedure to parse out (extract) the phrase

Turbo Pascal

and assign the parsed phrase to a string variable called BestLanguage. To do this, we tell the COPY procedure the identifier of the target string, the position within the target of the first character to be extracted, and the length of the string to be extracted:

```
VAR
    InputPhrase   : STRING [32];
    BestLanguage : STRING [12];
BEGIN
    InputPhrase   : = 'FORTRAN, BASIC, and Turbo Pascal';
    BestLanguage : = COPY (InputPhrase, 21, 12);
END.
```

In most cases, however, the starting point and string length need to be calculated using other procedures.

In the program shown in Figure 4.8, the "target" string is called RawData, the starting point is called FirstChar, and the length of the string to be extracted is given by the constant 5. To get a sense of how string manipulation works, modify the RawData string as well as FirstChar and the constant 5.

Our next example is a program written to solve a common problem—conversion between different data formats. It will also serve as an introduction to files, which are discussed later in this chapter. We had a long mailing-list data file, which had been created using MicroSoft BASICA on the IBM PC. Figure 4.10 shows a sample of the list in the format created by BASIC.

Notice how BASIC adds extraneous quotes and commas to separate the individual strings. We wanted to convert the entire file of a thousand names into a Turbo data file, made up of records. Figure 4.11 lists this "one-shot" conversion program. Like most utility programs it is far from elegant, but there was little reason to hone the tests, prune extraneous lines of code, and develop a friendly user interface when the program was intended to be used just once.

Professional programmers might quake at some of the constructions used in this program, but it was written quickly and debugged
even more quickly, and it did the job. More importantly, this program illustrates a real application rather than a contrived example.
We had to deal with a complex pattern of quotes, sometimes preceded by commas and sometimes not.

```
"Stivison","H.","67 Emerson Street","Clifton","NJ","07013"
"Stivison","Mr. M.","399 Downen Place","Hayward","CA","94544"
"St. Pierre","Mr. Rodney","757 New
Street","Uniondale","NY","11553"
"Eigen","Mrs. D.","227 Lakeview Avenue","Passaic","NJ","07055"
"Gustafson","Mrs. K.","Rte. 7 Box 1123","Fairview","NC","28730"
"Viemeister","Mr. Ian","46 Elm Street","Nutley","NJ","07110"
```

Figure 4.10 – Sample of data file created by Microsoft BASICA on an IBM PC.

```
PROGRAM ConvertBasicDataFilesToTurbo;
TYPE
  CustomerRecord =  RECORD
       LastName : STRING[13];
       FirstName : STRING[15];
       Street : STRING[30];
       Town : STRING[19];
       State : STRING[2];
       Zip : STRING[5];
     END;
VAR
  OutFile : FILE OF CustomerRecord;
  Customer : CustomerRecord;
  OneChar: CHAR;
  InFile:  FILE OF CHAR;
  Inzie,Outzie: STRING[14];    {stores file names}
  Remainder, Buffer, Information: STRING[110];
  FirstQuote, Index, NextQuote, Counter, LengthBuf : INTEGER;

PROCEDURE Initialize;
BEGIN
    WRITE ('What is the old BASIC file with all the names?  ');
    READLN (Inzie);
    ASSIGN (InFile,Inzie);
    RESET (InFile);
    WRITELN ('What is the new Turbo data file to be called?  ');
    READLN (Outzie);
```

Figure 4.11 – Program to convert Microsoft BASICA data file into Turbo data file format (continues).

```
        ASSIGN (OutFile,Outzie);
        REWRITE (OutFile);
        Buffer :=´´;
END;            {Initialize}

PROCEDURE ProcessBuffer;
BEGIN
    LengthBuf := 2;
    Index := 1;
    WHILE LengthBuf > 1 DO
      BEGIN
        FirstQuote := POS (´"´, Buffer);
        LengthBuf := LENGTH (Buffer);
        Remainder := COPY (Buffer, FirstQuote + 1, LengthBuf);
        NextQuote := POS (´"´,Remainder);
        Information := COPY (Remainder, 1, NextQuote - 1);
        IF LENGTH (Information) <> 1 THEN
            BEGIN
                CASE Index OF
                    1 : Customer.LastName :=  Information;
                    2 : Customer.FirstName := Information;
                    3 : Customer.Street := Information;
                    4 : Customer.Town := Information;
                    5 : Customer.State := Information;
                    6 : Customer.Zip := Information;
                END;

            Index := Index + 1;
            END;
        Buffer := Remainder;
      END;
Buffer := ´´;
WRITE (OutFile, Customer);
END;

PROCEDURE Stripper;
BEGIN
    WHILE NOT EOF (Infile) DO
        BEGIN
            READ (Infile,OneChar);
            Buffer := Buffer + OneChar;
            IF OneChar = #13 THEN ProcessBuffer;
        END;
END;                    {Stripper}

BEGIN                   {Main program begins here.}
    Initialize;
    Stripper;
    CLOSE (Infile); {CLOSE is described in the section on files.}
    CLOSE (OutFile);
    WRITELN (´File processed successfully´)
END.
```

Figure 4.11 – Program to convert Microsoft BASICA data file into Turbo data file format (continued).

The ProcessBuffer procedure not only uses the COPY procedure to extract a string, it also uses the LENGTH function to determine the length of a string (in characters, not including spaces added for padding) and the POS (position) function. The POS function searches a string for the first occurrence of a specific character and returns the position (the index in an array) of that character in the target string. As in this example, you seldom use POS by itself, but rather as a test to find a value that is used in turn by some other command, such as COPY. Specifically, in ProcessBuffer we use POS to find the double quotes that separate the individual strings in the BASIC file. We then use the COPY procedure to copy the next group of text characters (equal to the distance to the next quotes, less one space taken up by the quote character):

```
Information : = COPY(Remainder,1,NextQuote – 1)
```

When you have mastered Turbo files, come back to this program. Make a short test file like Figure 4.10 and exercise this program with output to the screen to see what is happening step by step. Modify the ProcessBuffer procedure as illustrated in Figure 4.12 to print out the variables every step of the way onto your screen. Notice the

```
DELAY(400)
```

line. DELAY is a predefined Turbo procedure that merely waits for the specified number of milliseconds. It is a great help in debugging programs, as it gives you time to make sense of a fleeting screen display.

Figure 4.13 shows the beginning screen display produced by running the program in Figure 4.12. The source file, HOLMES.LST, is the BASIC file shown in Figure 4.10.

If you compare the listing of the original and the modified program (Figures 4.11 and 4.12) with their output, you should get a good understanding of Turbo's string-handling techniques.

A few other standard procedures and functions are useful in converting between strings and other data types. Although the fact is almost totally undocumented, Turbo prohibits direct keyboard input of Boolean or user-created data types. Therefore, most keyboard input operations take string or numeric data and convert it to some other form. We have all used tests like the one shown in Figure 4.14, to assign a value to a variable based on some operator input. Notice, in this example, that we are assigning *strings* to the string variable Ticket.

Another common way of processing user input is the familiar CASE structure, shown in Figure 4.15. It seems to be everybody's favorite way of implementing menus.

Incidentally, a technique that is also poorly documented simulates the INKEY$ function in BASIC, in which a keystroke is read and acted upon without the ENTER key being pressed. It makes use of the KBD predeclared input file. An example is shown in Figure 4.16. This technique works only with input of a single keystroke.

```
PROCEDURE ProcessBuffer;
BEGIN
    LengthBuf := 2;
    Index := 1;
    WHILE LengthBuf > 1 DO
      BEGIN
         FirstQuote := POS ('"', Buffer);
            WRITELN ('FirstQuote = ', FirstQuote);
         LengthBuf := length(Buffer);
            WRITELN ('LengthBuf = ',LengthBuf);
         Remainder := COPY (Buffer, FirstQuote + 1, LengthBuf);
            WRITELN ('Remainder = ', Remainder);
         NextQuote := POS ('"', Remainder);
            WRITELN ('NextQuote = ', NextQuote);
         Information := COPY (Remainder, 1, NextQuote - 1);
         IF LENGTH (Information) <> 1 THEN
            BEGIN
               WRITELN;
               WRITELN ('Information = ', Information);
               DELAY (400);
               CASE Index OF
                  1 : Customer.LastName :=  Information;
                  2 : Customer.FirstName := Information;
                  3 : Customer.Street := Information;
                  4 : Customer.Town := Information;
                  5 : Customer.State := Information;
                  6 : Customer.Zip := Information;
               END;
            Index := Index + 1;
            END;
          Buffer := Remainder;
      END;
  Buffer := '';
  WRITE (OutFile, Customer);
  END;
```

Figure 4.12 – Program from Figure 4.11, modified to display the effects of string-manipulation procedures.

```
What is the old BASIC file with all the names?  HOLMES.LST
What is the new TURBO data file to be called?
HOLMES.TBO
FirstQuote = 1
LengthBuf = 59
Remainder = Stivison","H.","67 Emerson Street","Clifton","NJ","07013"
NextQuote = 9

Information = Stivison
FirstQuote = 9
LengthBuf = 58
Remainder = ,"H.","67 Emerson Street","Clifton","NJ","07013"
NextQuote = 2
FirstQuote = 2
LengthBuf = 49
Remainder = H.","67 Emerson Street","Clifton","NJ","07013"
NextQuote = 3

Information = H.
FirstQuote = 3
LengthBuf = 47
Remainder = ,"67 Emerson Street","Clifton","NJ","07013"
NextQuote = 2
FirstQuote = 2
LengthBuf = 44
Remainder = 67 Emerson Street","Clifton","NJ","07013"
NextQuote = 18

Information = 67 Emerson Street
FirstQuote = 18
LengthBuf = 42
Remainder = ,"Clifton","NJ","07013"
NextQuote = 2
FirstQuote = 2
LengthBuf = 24
Remainder = Clifton","NJ","07013"
NextQuote = 8

Information = Clifton
FirstQuote = 8
LengthBuf = 22
Remainder = ,"NJ","07013"
NextQuote = 2
FirstQuote = 2
LengthBuf = 14
Remainder = NJ","07013"
NextQuote = 3

Information = NJ
FirstQuote = 3
LengthBuf = 12
Remainder = ,"07013"
NextQuote = 2
```

Figure 4.13 – Screen display produced by program in Figure 4.12 (continues).

```
FirstQuote = 2
LengthBuf = 9
Remainder = 07013"
NextQuote = 6

Information = 07013
FirstQuote = 6
LengthBuf = 7
Remainder =
NextQuote = 0

Information =
FirstQuote = 0
LengthBuf = 1
Remainder =
NextQuote = 0

Information =
FirstQuote = 2
LengthBuf = 63
Remainder = Stivison","Mr. M.","399 Downen Place","Hayward","CA","94544"
NextQuote = 9
```

Figure 4.13 – *Screen display produced by program in Figure 4.12 (continued).*

```
{Ticket has been declared as STRING[10] earlier}

        WRITELN ('License: (N)Novice, (T)Technician, (G)General,
(A)Advanced, (E)Extra');
        READLN (Class);
        IF (Class = 'N') OR (Class = 'n') THEN Ticket := 'Novice';
        IF (Class = 'T') OR (Class = 't') THEN Ticket := 'Technician';
        IF (Class = 'G') OR (Class = 'g') THEN Ticket := 'General';
        IF (Class = 'A') OR (Class = 'a') THEN Ticket := 'Advanced';
        IF (Class = 'E') OR (Class = 'e') THEN Ticket := 'Extra';
```

Figure 4.14 – *Program fragment assigning strings to a string variable using multiple IF/THEN statements.*

User-Defined Data Types

How many computer forms have you filled out in which you had to put your date of birth in the MM-DD-YY format, using two digits to represent the month, day, and year? How many forms where you had to look up the two-digit code for eye color, hair color, race, or height? We have become so used to this imposition that we have almost forgotten that birth dates can be expressed as April 24, 1981

```
{Option has been declared as an integer}

    READLN (Option);
    CASE Option OF
        1: AcceptNewNames;
        2: LookUpOneName;
        3: AlphabetizeList;
        4: ProofListToScreen;
        5: ProduceLabels;
        6: CreateMailingListBook;
        7: GetDirectory;
        8: ExitProgram;
    ELSE ErrorHandler;
```

Figure 4.15 – Program fragment assigning strings to a string variable using CASE.

```
{Option has already been declared as a character.}

    READ (KBD, Option);
    CASE Option OF
        A: AcceptNewNames;
        B: LookUpOneName;
        C: AlphabetizeList;
        D: ProofListToScreen;
        E: ProduceLabels;
        F: CreateMailingListBook;
        G: GetDirectory;
        H: ExitProgram;
    ELSE ErrorHandler;
```

Figure 4.16 – Program fragment demonstrating Turbo simulation of INKEY$ function in BASIC.

and eye color described as blue or hair as brown. For internal manipulation at least, Turbo allows you to create your own data types, using everyday names, and even to put them in whatever sequence you think reflects their order in the real world.

This is very convenient, but don't forget that Turbo does not allow any I/O operations on user-defined data types. You cannot, for example, define a data type called Months and input a date simply as "May." In Turbo, as in BASIC, you might type "May" on the screen, but your program would need a procedure to analyze the string you typed and correlate it with a variable of the data type Month. Superficially, then, Turbo's method has no advantage over a BASIC program, in which you would type the month and a BASIC subroutine would parse the input into a number.

However, while user-declared enumerated scalar types (to use the formal name) may not ease direct user input, they are a valuable tool for tracking individual bits of data within larger structures. They certainly make your programs easier to read and understand. In the ham club program you'll be examining in the next few pages, you'll see data types called Grade and PrimaryInterests. They are declared like any data type at the start of the program. Look at Figure 4.17 for some fragments of the program listing, which demonstrate a user-created data type. The complete program will be presented in Figure 4.19.

We have defined a data type called Grade. In addition, we enumerated (listed) all the members of that data type (Novice, Technician, General, Advanced, Extra). Turbo must know what are the members of a data type—both user-defined and predefined. The programmers who created the Turbo compiler had to enumerate the numbers of predefined data types as well. Within the compiler program, the byte data type has been defined as comprising the values 0 through 255, and the Boolean data type as TRUE and FALSE. Notice that once we have defined the type, we can go ahead and declare all kinds of variable identifiers to be of this type. License and Ticket are both identifiers of the type Grade. Thus, they can take on the values Novice, Technician, General, Advanced, and Extra.

In this program fragment, the ASCII character typed by the operator in response to the first WRITELN command is loaded into the character variable Class. Depending on the value of Class, the variable Ticket takes on one of the possible values. From that point on,

Ticket can be manipulated like any scalar variable. The following would all be valid operations using variables, like Ticket, of our data type, Grade:

FOR Ticket : = Novice **TO** Advanced **DO** . . .
IF (Ticket < Technician) **OR** (Ticket > Advanced) **THEN** . . .
WHILE Ticket < General **DO** . . .

```
{Remember, this is not a working program- -just some excerpts.}

PROGRAM DemonstrateRecords;
TYPE
 Grade = (Novice, Technician, General, Advanced, Extra);

 HamOpRecord = RECORD
    Handle : STRING[30];
    CallSign : STRING[8];
    PaidUp : BOOLEAN;
    DuesOwed : REAL;
    License : Grade;
  END;

VAR
  Name : STRING[30];
  Call : STRING[8];
  GoodStanding : BOOLEAN;
  Dues : REAL;
  Class : CHAR;
  Ticket : Grade;
  HamOp : HamOpRecord;
  .
  .
  .
BEGIN
  .
  .
  .
     WRITELN ('License:  (N)Novice,  (T)Technician,  (G)General,
(A)Advanced, (E)Extra');
     READLN (Class); {Notice that the input is an ASCII character.}
     IF (Class = 'N') THEN Ticket := Novice;
     IF (Class = 'T') THEN Ticket := Technician;
     IF (Class = 'G') THEN Ticket := General;
     IF (Class = 'A') THEN Ticket := Advanced;
     IF (Class = 'E') THEN Ticket := Extra;
     HamOp.License := Ticket;
     WRITE (OutFile, HamOp);
  END;
```

Figure 4.17 – Program fragments to illustrate use of user-created data types.

Even more impressively, variables of type Grade can be sorted! The order of sorting is the order in which they were defined. In this case, Novice would come before Technician, which would come before General, and so on. To determine the *ordinality* of a variable within a user-created data type, Turbo offers the ORD function. It is used in the ham program in the process of reading records. The example in Figure 4.18 combines the case structure with the ORD function. The expression

ORD (License)

returns 0 if License has the value Novice, 1 if it has the value Technician, and so forth. In turn, the CASE structure selects the string to print based on the integer returned by the ORD function. ORD has other uses than determining the ordinality of user-created data types. It is often applied to ASCII characters, for example, to determine if they are within the ranges of the alphanumeric characters (normally ASCII 48–57, 65–90, 97–122).

You will see user-created data types used frequently in ambitious Turbo programs. As mentioned earlier, they are particularly appropriate in adventure-game programming, in which data types like Monsters, Treasures, Rooms, Ogres, and so forth are the order of the day. Most of these data types create the adventure "environment" and would be used internally by the program. However, there

```
PROCEDURE ReadExistingFile;
BEGIN
     READ (Infile, HamOp);...
     WITH HamOp DO
        BEGIN
          CASE ORD (License) OF
             0 : WRITELN ('Novice');
             1 : WRITELN ('Technician');-
             2 : WRITELN ('General');
             3 : WRITELN ('Advanced');
             4 : WRITELN ('Extra');
          END;...
     END;
```

Figure 4.18 – *Program fragment to illustrate use of ORD function with a user-created data type.*

would be no need to use them for direct screen I/O, because the game's parser automatically converts player responses (always defined as strings) into a form that can be used by the program.

Records

Records are among the most flexible data structures in Turbo. Arrays of records can be manipulated in memory for high-speed processing, and huge files of records can be easily stored, read, written, and accessed on disk. This flexibility alone would be exciting, but records offer an even greater asset. By using records, you can manipulate a collection of unlike individual data elements as if it were one object.

Every element of an array, by contrast, must be of the same data type. In a string array, every element is a string; in an integer array every element must be an integer. This often means that when you want to keep track of, say, a name and price combination, you are forced to store all the numbers as strings and constantly convert them back and forth to their numerical values when you need to do calculations.

A Turbo record reflects the structure of many standard business records. An ordinary sales slip normally includes a name, address, telephone number, date, product numbers, quantities, prices, and so on. To keep computerized records of these sales slips, we need a data structure that can link all the diverse data types and elements into a unit equivalent to the sales slip. This unit is the record.

The program in Figure 4.19 was developed to generate a roster of the members of a ham radio club. The complete program was a bit more complex than shown here, including addresses, telephone numbers, and other information. They have been removed to reduce the listing to a more manageable size. Nonetheless, the program uses quite a few related data structures and new procedures, and it demonstrates Turbo's ability to address everyday business problems with efficiency and grace.

You see that the program in Figure 4.19 uses both an array of records (HamClub) and two files of records (InFile and OutFile). In addition, it uses a user-created, enumerated data type (Grade), and converts legal screen I/O (characters, integers, and real numbers)

```
PROGRAM DemonstrateRecords;
TYPE
 Grade = (Novice, Technician, General, Advanced, Extra);

 HamOpRecord = RECORD
     Handle : STRING[30];
     CallSign : STRING[8];
     PaidUp : BOOLEAN;
     DuesOwed : REAL;
     License : Grade;
   END;

VAR
   Name : STRING[30];
   Call : STRING[8];
   GoodStanding : BOOLEAN;
   Dues : REAL;
   Class : CHAR;
   Ticket : Grade;
   HamOp : HamOpRecord;
   HamClub : ARRAY[1..73] OF HamOpRecord;
   InFile, OutFile : FILE OF HamOpRecord;
   Response : STRING[30];
   AllDone  : BOOLEAN;

PROCEDURE LoadArray;
VAR
   Amount : STRING[6];
   Result : INTEGER;
BEGIN
     AllDone := FALSE;
     WRITELN ('What file will contain all the names?');
     READLN (Response);
     ASSIGN (OutFile, Response);
     REWRITE (OutFile);
     WHILE NOT AllDone DO
     BEGIN
       WRITELN ('Name?');
       READLN (Name);
       HamOp.Handle := Name;
       WRITELN ('Call?');
       READLN (Call);
       HamOp.CallSign := Call;
       HamOp.PaidUp := GoodStanding;

       WRITELN ('How much does he owe in dues? ');
       READLN (Amount);
       VAL (Amount, Dues, Result);
       IF Dues < 0.01 THEN GoodStanding := TRUE ELSE GoodStanding
:= FALSE;
       HamOp.PaidUp := GoodStanding;
       HamOp.DuesOwed := Dues;
       WRITELN ('License: (N)Novice, (T)Technician, (G)General,
(A)Advanced, (E)Extra');
```

Figure 4.19 – Program to demonstrate use of records (continues).

```
            READLN (Class);
            IF (Class = 'N') OR (Class = 'n') THEN Ticket := Novice;
            IF (Class = 'T') OR (Class = 't') THEN Ticket := Technician;
            IF (Class = 'G') OR (Class = 'g') THEN Ticket := General;
            IF (Class = 'A') OR (Class = 'a') THEN Ticket := Advanced;
            IF (Class = 'E') OR (Class = 'e') THEN Ticket := Extra;
            HamOp.License := Ticket;
            WRITE (OutFile, HamOp);
            WRITELN ('If you are done type an asterisk (*), otherwise
    just hit Enter');
            READLN (Response);
            IF Response = '*' THEN AllDone := TRUE;
        END;
        CLOSE (OutFile);
    END;

    PROCEDURE ReadExistingFile;
    BEGIN
      WRITELN ('What file contains all the ham club records?');
      READLN (Response);
      ASSIGN (InFile, Response);
      RESET (InFile);
      WHILE NOT EOF (InFile) DO
      BEGIN
          READ (Infile, HamOp);
          WITH HamOp DO
              BEGIN
                  WRITE (Handle,' - - - ');
                  WRITELN (CallSign);
                  CASE ORD (License) OF
                      0 : WRITELN ('Novice');
                      1 : WRITELN ('Technician');
                      2 : WRITELN ('General');
                      3 : WRITELN ('Advanced');
                      4 : WRITELN ('Extra');
                  END;
                  IF PaidUp THEN WRITELN ('Member in good standing')
                  ELSE WRITELN ('Owes ', DuesOwed:5:2);
                  WRITELN;
              END;
      END;
      CLOSE (InFile);
      END;

    BEGIN
      WRITELN; {just for blank line on screen};
      WRITELN ('Do you just want to print the old file?');
      READLN (Response);
      IF Response = 'Y' THEN ReadExistingFile ELSE LoadArray;
    END.
```

Figure 4.19 – Program to demonstrate use of records (continued).

into the Boolean and user-created data types that can be manipulated internally but cannot be used for direct I/O. It also uses the VAL function. Each of these features will be covered in this chapter, so don't let their unfamiliarity deter you from examining the program at hand.

The program solicits information about club members and for each member creates a record (called HamOpRecord) of the diverse data elements that describe the member. We chose an example that not only uses characters and integers, but also makes good use of a user-created data type (Grade, to track the member's class of amateur radio operator's license), along with real numbers (to keep track of an amount of money), and perhaps most interestingly of all, a Boolean value (PaidUp, to keep track of a yes/no status). The ability to put a Boolean data element into a record can be a powerful capability for tracking a critical status—active or inactive, member or nonmember, contract customer or cash-only, citizen or alien, and so on.

Like all variables in Turbo, a record must be declared with an identifier and data type. You must also declare the individual elements of the record. Note the syntax carefully, because it is unusual. The declaration begins with the reserved word RECORD and ends with the reserved word END. Records, incidentally, can include other records among their elements.

Many Pascal programmers become confused by the distinction between declaring a data type and declaring a variable identifier. Somehow, any misunderstanding in this area surfaces when they are dealing with records. You would never think of writing statements like these:

```
REAL : = 0.05;
CHAR : = 'A';
```

using reserved words—REAL and CHAR—as if they were variables, when you actually meant:

```
TaxRate : = 0.05;
ExcellentGrade : = 'A';
```

In this correct example, the identifiers TaxRate and ExcellentGrade have already been declared to be of the types real and character. A common mistake, however, is to think of the particular record as being a variable rather than a data type. In the example program, HamOpRecord is a data type, not a variable. Thus, you cannot assign values to it. On the other hand, in the variable-declaration section you see these entries:

```
VAR
HamOp : HamOpRecord;
HamClub : ARRAY[1..73] OF HamOpRecord;
InFile, OutFile : FILE OF HamOpRecord;
```

HamOp is a variable identifier, which can—and will—have values assigned to it. It is simply common sense to use similar names for a record type and the variables that are associated with it (such as HamOpRecord and HamOp in this example).

Look at the record declaration again:

```
TYPE
   HamOpRecord = RECORD
      Handle : STRING[30];
      CallSign : STRING[8];
      PaidUp : BOOLEAN;
      DuesOwed : REAL;
      License : Grade;
   END;
```

Within the record, each data element has its own identifier. In the variable HamOp (not the data type HamOpRecord), the individual elements are called:

```
HamOp.Handle
HamOp.CallSign
HamOp.PaidUp
HamOp.DuesOwed
HamOp.License
```

Taken together, these elements make up the record variable HamOp. To repeat the introductory point, records allow you to handle as one entity a group of related elements of different data types. You can access, read, write, file, sort, and array records as if they were simple data types (like individual characters, for example), while still being able to access any individual part of any record.

The example program solicits information from the user in order to create a file. Once a data file is created, of course, it can be manipulated, added to, deleted from, and sorted by a program without keyboard interaction. Later examples will show how these operations are done.

The program uses a "quick-and-dirty" technique for signalling the end of input by entering an asterisk. There are much more elegant ways of doing this, but the method used is easy to program and functions well.

The program in Figure 4.19 prompts for information about a member. It then converts string and real-number keyboard input into the Boolean and user-defined data types that are needed internally (license and member status) and stores the individual responses in a group of variables. These variables and their data types are listed below.

Variable Name	Data Type
Name	STRING[30]
Call	STRING[8]
GoodStanding	BOOLEAN
Dues	REAL
Class	CHAR
Ticket	Grade

These variables are in turn assigned to their respective elements with the individual HamOp record:

Record Element	Data Type
HamOp.Handle	STRING[30];
HamOp.CallSign	STRING[8];
HamOp.PaidUp	BOOLEAN;
HamOp.DuesOwed	REAL;
HamOp.License	Grade;

The type declarations are listed here for two reasons: to stress the ability of records to store unlike data elements, and to help you see that for every element in a record declaration, you generally need a variable of the same type to hold information that is being written to, read from, or assigned to the record element. This point is not one of the more obvious lessons to be gleaned from the Borland documentation.

The license classes have a precise ranking or ordinality (Novice is ranked 0, Technician is 1, etc.), which is used in the CASE statement. Ranking also allows searches and tests, for example, of all licenses General class and lower as targets for a series of license-upgrade lectures. Think of your own applications for this built-in capability. The standard function ORD returns the ordinality of any scalar variable (except real numbers, of course). You will see it used several times throughout this book. In using ORD, remember that the first element always has the rank of 0 rather than 1.

Once you have assigned values to all the elements of a record, you generally use some form of indexing to move on to the next record. In the example program, each complete record is written to the output file with the simple and ubiquitous WRITE command:

    WRITE (OutFile, HamOp);

After a record is written, you can choose either to input the next record or to stop input and close the file. Figure 4.20 shows part of an interactive session accepting input.

The second option in the demonstration program reads an existing data file and then does something with it—a very common programming task. In this case, the program prints the file on the screen. Complete records are read and manipulated; the manipulation includes converting the user-created data types back into a more readable form. Other possible tasks might have included totaling back dues owed to the club or sorting the list by name, call sign, or class of license. Figure 4.21 shows part of the screen display when the display option was selected.

This program is a particularly good example of the use of data structures, because it combines records with arrays and files. Besides just reading records, the program could have loaded them into an array for sorting. Appendix B lists a mailing-list program that

```
Do you just want to print the old file?
N
What file will contain all the names?
HAMCLUB.LST
Name?
Bud Stevens
Call?
WN2MYU
How much does he owe in dues?
3.50
License: (N)Novice, (T)Technician, (G)General, (A)Advanced, (E)Extra
N
If you are done type an asterisk (*), otherwise just hit Enter

Name?
Emil F. Grumman
Call?
WB2ISA
How much does he owe in dues?
(carriage return)
License: (N)Novice, (T)Technician, (G)General, (A)Advanced, (E)Extra
T
```

Figure 4.20 – Screen display showing the file-creation option of the program in Figure 4.19.

```
Do you just want to print the old file?
Y
What file contains all the ham club records?
HAMCLUB.LST
Bud Stevens - - - WN2MYU
Novice
Owes  3.50

Emil F. Grumman - - - WB2ISA
Technician
Member in good standing

Doug Stivison - - - WA1KWJ
General
Member in good standing
```

Figure 4.21 – Screen display showing the file-display option of the program in Figure 4.19.

applies the Shell sort of Figure 4.1 to the sorting of an array of customer records. That program can sort (order) alphabetically as well as by ZIP code and even sort alphabetically within each ZIP code.

If ordinary records are not flexible enough, Turbo also features an even more flexible data structure, called *variant records.* These records not only differ one from another in the actual data stored in each element, but can have different combinations of data elements. They are a particularly useful structure for organizing data in a way that makes sense to people.

Unfortunately, they are also one of the most poorly documented features of Turbo. Even the basic Pascal books seem to gloss over this feature, perhaps because the only way to show how variant records work is to develop fairly ambitious programs and devote quite a bit of space to demonstrating how a real-life program makes use of them. That is exactly what Figures 4.22 through 4.24 will do.

Figure 4.22 shows the radio-club program extended to use variant records. The program now keeps track of the members' different interests. Members are segregated into operators and experimenters. Once this distinction is made, the file will contain two different records, each containing different items of information.

Variant records lend themselves to business programs in which some information will be common to all clients, but you also want to record different additional information for different kinds of customers (for example, contract customers, wholesale customers, and cash customers). Another application might be in a personnel office that needs to keep track of salaried, hourly, and temporary workers. Everyone has a name, address, and Social Security number, but benefits, overtime pay rate, vacation records, and salary review schedule would not apply to all employees. The capabilities and application of variant records are only limited by the ingenuity and imagination of the programmer.

The variant records can be of any data type. In the example, the experimenters' variant records both contain Boolean elements, but the operators' records include an integer value and a Boolean value. We could have used any type of data (characters, real numbers, etc.). Moreover, you can even have records within records.

While this version of the program is more complex than the earlier one, it offers greater capabilities. For example, you can generate selective reports of just experimenters or just operators.

```
PROGRAM DemonstrateVariantRecords;

TYPE
  Grade = (Novice, Technician, General, Advanced, Extra);
  PrimaryInterests = (Operator, Experimenter);

  HamOpRecord = RECORD
    Handle : STRING[30];
    CallSign : STRING[8];
    PaidUp : BOOLEAN;
    DuesOwed : REAL;
    License : Grade;
    TypeOfOp : PrimaryInterests;
    CASE OpInterest : PrimaryInterests OF   {Must come at end of
record declaration.}
        Operator:
            (NumBands : INTEGER;       {Use of parenthesis is critical.}
            Traffic : BOOLEAN);
        Experimenter:
            (VHF : BOOLEAN;
            Computer : BOOLEAN);
  END;

VAR
  Name : STRING[30];
  Call : STRING[8];
  GoodStanding : BOOLEAN;
  Dues : REAL;
  Class : CHAR;
  Ticket : Grade;
  HamOp : HamOpRecord;
  HamClub : ARRAY[1..73] OF HamOpRecord;
  InFile, OutFile : FILE OF HamOpRecord;
  Response : STRING[30];
  AllDone : BOOLEAN;
  OpInterest : PrimaryInterests;

PROCEDURE LoadArray;
VAR
  Amount : STRING[6];
  Index, Result, NumberOfBands : INTEGER;
  InterestEO, TrafficYN, VHFYN, ComputerYN : CHAR;

BEGIN
    AllDone := FALSE;
    Index := 1;
    WRITELN ('What file will contain all the names?');
    READLN (Response);
    ASSIGN (OutFile, Response);
    REWRITE (OutFile);
    WHILE NOT AllDone DO
    BEGIN
      WRITELN ('Name?');
```

Figure 4.22 – Program from Figure 4.19 modified to demonstrate use of variant records (continues).

```
        READLN (Name);
        HamOp.Handle := Name;
        WRITELN ('Call?');
        READLN (Call);
        HamOp.CallSign := Call;
        HamOp.PaidUp := GoodStanding;
        WRITELN ('How much does he owe in dues? ');
        READLN (Amount);
        VAL (Amount, Dues, Result);
        IF Dues < 0.01 THEN GoodStanding := TRUE ELSE GoodStanding
:= FALSE;
        HamOp.PaidUp := GoodStanding;
        HamOp.DuesOwed := Dues;
        WRITELN ('License: (N)Novice, (T)Technician, (G)General,
(A)Advanced, (E)Extra');
        READLN (Class);
        Class := UPCASE (Class)
        IF Class = 'N' THEN Ticket := Novice;
        IF Class = 'T' THEN Ticket := Technician;
        IF Class = 'G' THEN Ticket := General;
        IF Class = 'A' THEN Ticket := Advanced;
        IF Class = 'E' THEN Ticket := Extra;
        HamOp.License := Ticket;
        WRITELN ('Is this an (E)Experimenter or an (O)operator?');
        READLN (InterestEO);
        IF (InterestEO = 'E') OR (InterestEO = 'e') THEN OpInterest
:= Experimenter;
        IF (InterestEO = 'O') OR (InterestEO = 'o') THEN OpInterest
:= Operator;
        HamOp.TypeOfOp := OpInterest;
        IF OpInterest = Operator THEN
        BEGIN
          WRITELN ('How many bands does he work?');
          READLN (NumberOfBands);
          HamOp.NumBands := NumberOfBands;
          WRITELN ('Does he participate in traffic nets?  Y/N');
          READLN (TrafficYN);
          IF (TrafficYN = 'Y') OR (TrafficYN = 'y') THEN
HamOp.Traffic := TRUE
             ELSE HamOp.Traffic := FALSE;
        END;
        IF OpInterest = Experimenter THEN
        BEGIN
          WRITELN ('Is he interested in VHF?  (Y/N)');
          READLN (VHFYN);
          VHFYN := UPCASE (VHFYN);
          IF VHFYN = 'Y' THEN HamOp.VHF := TRUE
             ELSE HamOp.VHF := FALSE;
          WRITELN ('Is he interested in computers?  (Y/N)');
          READLN (ComputerYN);
          IF (ComputerYN = 'Y') OR (ComputerYN = 'y') THEN
HamOp.Computer := TRUE
             ELSE HamOp.Computer := FALSE;
        END;
```

Figure 4.22 – Program from Figure 4.19 modified to demonstrate use of variant records (continues).

```
        WRITE (OutFile, HamOp);
        Index := Index + 1;
        WRITELN ('If you are done type an asterisk (*), otherwise
just hit Enter');
        READLN (Response);
        IF Response = '*' THEN AllDone := TRUE;
     END;
     CLOSE (OutFile);
END;

PROCEDURE ReadExistingFile;
BEGIN
  WRITELN ('What file contains all the ham club records?');
  READLN (Response);
  ASSIGN (InFile, Response);
  RESET (InFile);
  WHILE NOT EOF (InFile) DO
  BEGIN
     READ (Infile, HamOp);
     WITH HamOp DO
        BEGIN
           WRITE (Handle,' - - - ');
           WRITELN (CallSign);
           CASE ORD (License) OF
              0 : WRITELN ('Novice');
              1 : WRITELN ('Technician');
              2 : WRITELN ('General');
              3 : WRITELN ('Advanced');
              4 : WRITELN ('Extra');
           END;
           IF PaidUp THEN WRITELN ('Member in good standing')
           ELSE WRITELN ('Owes ', DuesOwed:5:2);
           IF TypeOfOp = Operator THEN
           BEGIN
              WRITELN ('Interested primarily in operating');
              WRITELN ('Operates on ',NumBands,' bands');
              IF Traffic THEN WRITELN ('Interested in traffic-
handling') ELSE
                 WRITELN ('Not interested in traffic-handling');
           END;

           IF TypeOfOp = Experimenter THEN
           BEGIN
              WRITELN ('Interested primarily in experimentation');
              IF VHF THEN WRITELN ('Interested in VHF work') ELSE
                 WRITELN ('Interested in high-frequency bands only');
              IF Computer THEN WRITELN ('Dedicated hacker') ELSE
                 WRITELN ('Hopelessly old fashioned: never
progressed past vacuum tubes!');
           END;
           WRITELN;
        END;
  END;
  CLOSE (InFile);
  END;
```

Figure 4.22 – Program from Figure 4.19 modified to demonstrate use of variant records (continues).

A programming shortcut useful with records is illustrated in this listing—the WITH construction. This is simply a convenient way to save keystrokes in developing a program and does not affect program execution speed. Although records are normally manipulated as a unit, all Pascal implementations have this provision for "breaking down" a record to use the data stored in the constituent data elements. Each element is uniquely identified with the combination of the record name and the data element name. In the fragment below, the individual data elements are HamOp.Handle, HamOp.CallSign, and HamOp.License:

```
WRITE (HamOp.Handle,' - - - ');
    WRITELN (HamOp.CallSign);
        CASE ORD (HamOp.License) OF
            0 : WRITELN ('Novice');
    .
    .
    .
    .
```

Using WITH, you do not have to type the record identifier (HamOp) every time. Instead, you begin the block of code with a line to tell Turbo that, between the WITH and END reserved words,

```
BEGIN
  WRITELN;  {just for blank line on screen};
  WRITELN ('Do you just want to print the old file?');
  READLN (Response);
  IF (Response = 'Y') OR (Response = 'y') THEN ReadExistingFile
ELSE LoadArray;
END.
```

Figure 4.22 – Program from Figure 4.19 modified to demonstrate use of variant records (continued).

all the variables are part of the record HamOp. This method is shown in the program fragment below:

```
WITH HamOp DO
    BEGIN
        WRITE (Handle,' - - - ');
        WRITELN (CallSign);
        CASE Ord (License) OF
            0 : WRITELN ('Novice');
    .
    .
    .
    END;
```

Some languages might have required operators to type arbitrary codes for the license class or in other ways adapt to an awkward input method, simply because it is most convenient for the computer. Turbo lends itself to common-sense data input, allowing you to prompt for words, integers, or simple yes/no answers as appropriate. Even more important than this inclination towards user-friendliness is that the program is easiest for the programmer to develop, debug, and support. The programmer does not constantly have to keep track of arbitrary codes and what they stand for.

We could have tracked the members' license grades in any programming language. But it is much clearer for a programmer to work with a data type called Grade, with scalar values called Novice and Technician, than to use a cryptic 0 or 1. It is little wonder that Turbo is finding an increasing following in commercial software development.

The mechanics of implementing variant records take some getting used to. You have to establish a data type, and declare a variable of this type, that Turbo can use to select the appropriate alternative record. In the example, we created a data type called Primary-Interests, which was defined as consisting of the the elements Operator and Experimenter. In turn, we declared a variable called OpInterest of the type PrimaryInterests. When the program is run, the variable OpInterest holds the value that indicates whether the club member is an operator or an experimenter. In turn, the CASE structure—an integral part of the operation of all variant records—chooses different record variations based on the value of the Op-Interest variable. These variations are appended to the basic record common to all club members.

The punctuation and syntax used to declare variant records are critical (and poorly documented in the manual). All the record elements connected with each of the CASE options (NumBands and Traffic for Operator, and VHF and Computer for Experimenter) must be contained within parentheses. Even the syntax of the CASE statement is not a simple "CASE VariableName OF" construction, but uses a combination of a variable name and a data type, as shown below:

```
TYPE
    PrimaryInterests = (Operator, Experimenter);

    HamOpRecord = RECORD
        Handle    : STRING[30];
        CallSign  : STRING[8];
        TypeOfOp : PrimaryInterests;

    {In the line below, OpInterest is a variable of the type PrimaryInterest.
    OpInterest contains the data solicited from the operator and in turn, will
    be used to select which of the two varieties of records should be used
    for this member's record.}

    CASE OpInterest : PrimaryInterests OF
        Operator:
        (NumBands : INTEGER;   {Notice opening parentheses . . .}
            Traffic : BOOLEAN); { . . . and the closing parentheses.}
        Experimenter
                (VHF : BOOLEAN;  {Notice opening parentheses . . . }
        Computer : BOOLEAN); { . . . and the closing parentheses.}
    END;
```

A more generic illustration follows. Remember that there can be any number of variant records (not just two or three), that different variations can have different numbers of data elements, and that the data elements can be any combination of data types.

```
TYPE
    Selection = (Choice1, Choice 2, Choice 3);
    TotalRecord = RECORD
        StandardItem1 : STRING[30]; {Could be any data type.}
        StandardItem2 : STRING[8];
```

```
    CASE TestVariable : Selection OF
      Choice1:
        (OptionalElement1 : INTEGER; {Could be any data type.}
         OptionalElement2 : INTEGER;
         OptionalElement3 : INTEGER;)
      Choice2:
        (OptionalElementA : INTEGER; {Could be any data type.}
         OptionalElementB : INTEGER;
      Choice3:
        (OptionalElementX : INTEGER; {Could be any data type.}
         OptionalElementY : INTEGER;)
    END;
  VAR
    TestVariable : Selection; {Test variable is of the type Selection}
```

Of course, Turbo will issue the usual error messages if you forget the parentheses, but the punctuation is unusual enough that you might not recognize the error.

In the input phase of the program, you have to let Turbo know which variety of record you want. The example program gets this information with the question:

```
WRITELN ('Is this an (E)experimenter or an (O)operator?');
```

but any internal test would do the job as well. In fact, if you look at the output part of the program, you will see that an internal test (as opposed to one in which the user makes an interactive choice through the keyboard) chooses which record information to print out. It does this by testing the TypeOfOp field in each record. In a business application, such a test might choose whether or not a dunning notice should be generated or some similar action.

Figure 4.23 shows the screen display from the latest version of the program, soliciting new input and creating a new file called MEMBERS.LST.

Figure 4.24 shows the screen display from a second run of the program, this time displaying the file MEMBERS.LST, which had been created in the session shown in Figure 4.23.

Although the response to the question "Is he interested in computers?" was stored as a Boolean value (Figure 4.23), on output (Figure 4.24) we used the value not just to print a simple yes or no but to trigger slightly more imaginative responses. We could have

```
Do you just want to print the old file?
N
What file will contain all the names?
MEMBERS.LST
Name?
ED WEBSTER
Call?
WA2YEO
How much does he owe in dues?
5.00
License: (N)Novice, (T)Technician, (G)General, (A)Advanced, (E)Extra
T
Is this an (E)Experimenter or an (O)operator?
E
Is he interested in VHF?  (Y/N)
Y
Is he interested in computers?  (Y/N)
Y
If you are done type an asterisk (*), otherwise just hit Enter

Name?
EMIL F. GRUMMAN
Call?
WB2ISA
How much does he owe in dues?
←┘
License: (N)Novice, (T)Technician, (G)General, (A)Advanced,
(E)Extra
A
Is this an (E)Experimenter or an (O)operator?
O
How many bands does he work?
5
Does he participate in traffic nets?  Y/N
N
If you are done type an asterisk (*), otherwise just hit Enter

Name?
DOUG STIVISON
Call?
WA1KWJ
How much does he owe in dues?
←┘
License: (N)Novice, (T)Technician, (G)General, (A)Advanced, (E)Extra
G
Is this an (E)Experimenter or an (O)operator?
E
Is he interested in VHF?  (Y/N)
N
Is he interested in computers?  (Y/N)
N
If you are done type an asterisk (*), otherwise just hit Enter
*
```

Figure 4.23 – Screen display of a file-creation session using the program in Figure 4.22.

called a procedure to do almost anything based on this simple Boolean value.

Entire books could be written on the use of records, but the information presented here should be enough to help you write programs that work. It is helpful to be able to store different records within a file or in an array. These records can optimally describe the full range of different subjects (customers, club members, etc.) rather than forcing a Hobson's choice between using a comprehensive record that is profligate of space and has many fields not applicable to individual records, and using a bare-bones, one-size-fits-all record that really doesn't include all the information you need for special cases.

If you hope to do any serious Turbo programming, you owe it to yourself to explore standard and variant records. The more you use them, the more possibilities will occur to you in future programming situations.

```
Do you just want to print the old file?
Y
What file contains all the ham club records?
MEMBERS.LST

ED WEBSTER - - - WA2YEO
Technician
Owes  5.00
Interested primarily in experimentation
Interested in VHF work
Dedicated hacker

EMIL F. GRUMMAN - - - WB2ISA
Advanced
Member in good standing
Interested primarily in operating
Operates on 5 bands
Not interested in traffic-handling

DOUG STIVISON - - - WA1KWJ
General
Member in good standing
Interested primarily in experimentation
Interested in high-frequency bands only
Hopelessly old fashioned: never progressed past vacuum tubes!
```

Figure 4.24 – Screen display showing the file-display option of the program in Figure 4.22.

Files

Overview

Most programmers concede that adroit file handling is the surest test of programming skill. Most programs written for practical applications need to manipulate files that are external to the program itself. Writing and reading external files are the largest steps in separating the occasional programmer from the serious programmer. (You, of course, are a serious programmer.)

Turbo offers an unmatched collection of file-handling capabilities, surpassing those of any other Pascal we have seen. Computer scientists point out that file handling has always been one of the weakest points of standard Pascal. Once again, Turbo has overcome Pascal's shortcomings by sacrificing compatibility for astonishing capability. As a result of these innovations and extensions, conventional books on Pascal are little help in doing even the most elementary file I/O in Turbo. Even more importantly, the example programs in the documentation packed with the Turbo diskette range from the cryptic to the absolutely hopeless. To make matters worse, the Turbo error messages in the area of file-handling are not as helpful as elsewhere. Borland even acknowledges this problem, in the section of the manual listing the questions most often asked about Turbo. The fundamentals of file handling ranked high in the list!

This section will show you how to read and write all kinds of Turbo files, including the most perplexing and idiosyncratic of all, Turbo text files. Once you see how easy it is, you can turn to other books for additional ideas. But give yourself a fighting chance and read this section first.

External Files

Some programs must operate on external data. The most common reason for this is convenience—because there is a limit on the size a program can be (64K before you have to use special techniques called chaining and overlays). Turbo lets you access a separate 64K of data as well. Thus, whenever program and data need more than 64K of memory, it makes sense to use separate data files. Programs that use a mailing list, telephone directory, or employee records lend themselves to storing the data in a separate file. Even more importantly, these external data files exist when the creating or manipulating program is not being run. Thus, a data file can be copied, archived, and even sold as a separate entity.

Word processors, almost by definition, work on external files. Unlike programs, external files are simply collections of data in a form usable to a Turbo program and terminated by a valid end-of-file delimiter. The data may be stored as simple text, possibly with end-of-line markers, or as a collection of rigidly structured records. Individual elements of a file can be accessed either sequentially or randomly. Files are also dynamic. While you must specify the fields in a record, the number of elements in an array, and the number of characters in a string, files have no predetermined size! This means that you can make data files larger or smaller as need be.

Files are not limited by the memory of your computer the way data structures held in memory (such as arrays) are. In theory, if you have a 10-MB "Winchester" disk drive, you could have a data file almost that big even if you only had 128K of memory. You could write a Turbo application program to take care of the task of manipulating this monstrous data file in usable chunks. All in all, files are among the most flexible and powerful concepts available to the programmer.

Notes on File Types

Binary and ASCII Files

Once files are created by Turbo, they are actually managed by the computer's operating system—CP/M, CP/M-86, MS-DOS, or PC-DOS. The operating system stores and accesses files, generates directories, provides copying, renaming, and concatenation facilities, and moves files between disk, memory, and the I/O devices (modem and printer). Once you create a file with Turbo Pascal, you can use all your operating system's utilities to manipulate it.

Anyone who has tried to open up a .COM, .CMD, or .EXE file (or tried to download binary files from a bulletin-board system) knows that some files are stored in a form that does not use the readable ASCII codes and end-of-line conventions we expect when we open up a text file or untokenized BASIC file. In DOS, for example, there are binary files (.EXE and .COM), batch files (.BAT), system configuration files (.SYS) and many others. Like an operating system, Turbo can create several different kinds of files. You have already seen the Turbo editor use ordinary text files (.PAS), which can be used by any word-processing program. You have also seen binary files (.COM and .CMD), created by the compilation process. You know that Turbo has predefined logical files, which you have been using throughout the book in your READ and WRITE statements. They include INPUT, OUTPUT, LST, KBD, CON, and several others. These, however, are not true files, which appear in directories.

Turbo can create binary files, that is, files made up of bit patterns that cannot be interpreted by Turbo either as ASCII characters (.PAS or text files), nor as computer instructions (.COM, .CMD, and .CHN files). Binary files can be patterns of bits to display graphics, data collected from an analog-to-digital sampling device (counters, thermometers, barometers, anemometers, and so on), files encoded in "exotic" coding schemes (EBCDIC or TTS), or files that have been intentionally encrypted to prevent unauthorized access. In all these cases, Turbo will store, copy, open, close, read, and write these files, but it is the programmer's responsibility to keep track of their names and the type of information stored in them. Like every other data structure in Turbo, files have to be identified with an identifier and a data type.

If there is one concept that can help you master file management in Turbo it is this: while files may become vast and complex collections of data, the data must be manipulated one element at a time. Files of characters are read and written one character at a time; files of records are read and written one record at a time. Likewise, files of pure binary data are handled one byte at a time, and special untyped files are handled one block at a time. The lone exception to this consistent scheme is the text file, which can be read not only character-by-character, but line-by-line.

Lines

A line is not a data structure like a string or an array. Lines are purely a file-management convention, not a data element. They are neither declared nor do they use an identifier. They merely provide a form of "flow control" in what is essentially a character-oriented way of manipulating text files. A line, by Turbo definition, is a group of characters terminated by two special characters: the familiar carriage-return–line-feed (Control-M, Control-J) combination. Text files can be read character-by-character or line-by-line.

Operations on Files

Because these are such crucial—but neither obvious nor well-documented—concepts, it is worth repeating the points again. Files are complex data structures that must be identified and typed with whatever simpler data elements and structures make them up. It is only by its individual elements that a file can be read and written, and that process takes place one element at a time.

Files can be created, have their contents erased, or be deleted. Data can be read from, written to, or appended onto a file. In addition, files can be opened to begin some process, and closed at its termination. Some files can be read from and written to at the same time; other files must be closed and reopened before you can switch between reading and writing.

Turbo does not support the most common procedures of standard Pascal, GET and PUT. This omission is a blessing, because Turbo uses the same WRITE and READ procedures on files that it uses for all other I/O. The only disadvantage is that books on Pascal emphasize the GET and PUT procedures and shed no light on how Turbo does things.

Figure 4.25 shows the classic representation of a file.

All types of files are manipulated using the same set of consistent procedures. Just as you cannot directly input or output Boolean or user-created data, neither can you directly input or output to a file name. You must assign a file name to a file variable; this is done with the ASSIGN procedure. Figure 4.26 shows the right and wrong ways of assigning files.

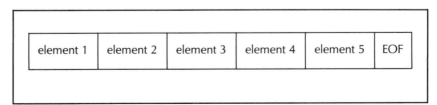

element 1	element 2	element 3	element 4	element 5	EOF

Figure 4.25 – Representation of a file.

Example A needs no operator interaction, while example B solicits input from the operator. Both will work well. Example C will only generate error messages, because you cannot reset a string; you can only use the RESET procedure on a file variable. RESET opens a file for reading only, and positions you at the beginning of the file. For writing to a file, you use the procedure REWRITE.

REWRITE will create a file if one with the requested name does not already exist. If you REWRITE a file that already exists, however, the REWRITE process will erase any data already in that file.

Once a file has been opened with either a RESET or a REWRITE procedure, it must be closed with the CLOSE procedure. If you forget to close a file after reading, Turbo will not give you an error message, and you do not generally have any problems. But if you do not close a file after writing, upon exiting from the program you will discover that you have an empty file (zero characters in the DOS or CP/M directory) with that name. The CLOSE command tells Turbo to do all housekeeping required by the the operating system to "put the file back" on disk and make the operating system aware of its new size and revision date.

Figure 4.27 is a summary of all the file-manipulation commands. Remember that Turbo does not conform to the standard Pascal usage of GET and PUT, so the operations on the chart are a realistic guide to what you will actually be doing in Turbo.

The first kind of file to consider is the sequentially accessed file—one in which each data element is accessed in order. It was, incidentally, the only kind of file supported in standard Pascal.

```
    (A)
        ASSIGN (FileVariable, ´HAMCLUB.LST´);
        RESET (FileVariable);

    (B)
        WRITE (´What is the input file name?  ´);
        READLN (FileName); {Accepts response typed by operator.}
        ASSIGN (FileVariable, FileName);
        RESET (FileVariable);

    (C)
        RESET (´HAMCLUB.LST´);
```

Figure 4.26 – Assigning a file name to a file variable.

In this figure the following abbreviations are used:

F	file variable
I	integer
ST	string

File-Handling Procedures and Functions:

APPEND (*F*) — Opens disk file *F* (like REWRITE), but the file pointer points to the end of the file. Elements can be added to the file, but not read from it. MS-DOS only.

ASSIGN (*F, ST*) — Assigns the valid file name included in the string *ST* to the file variable *F.*

CLOSE (*F*) — Asks the operating system to close disk file *F* and to perform all related housekeeping and directory updates.

EOF (*F*) — Returns Boolean TRUE if file pointer points beyond the last component of disk file *F.*

EOLN (*F*) — Returns Boolean TRUE if file pointer points at a carriage return character within text file *F.* Note that, in a text file, if EOF (*F*) is TRUE, then EOLN (*F*) must also be TRUE.

ERASE (*F*) — Disk file *F* is erased.

FILEPOS (*F*) — Returns current position of the file pointer in file *F.* Result is always an integer. Does not work on text files.

FILESIZE (*F*) — Returns the size of disk file *F,* measured in its constituent components (e.g., a file of records is counted in the number of records); result is always an integer. Does not work on text files.

Figure 4.27 – Procedures and functions for file manipulation (continues).

FLUSH (F)	(CP/M and CP/M-86 only). Empties internal sector buffer of disk file F. Normally this operation is done automatically, and this procedure is rarely invoked by a specific statement within the program. Does not operate on text files under these operating systems.
FLUSH (F)	(MS-DOS and PC-DOS only). Empties text file buffer of disk file F. Operates only on text files. Normally this operation is done automatically, and this procedure is rarely invoked by a specific statement within the program.
RENAME (F, ST)	Renames disk file F with the valid file name contained in string ST.
REWRITE (F)	Prepares file F for writing. Will erase any existing file F if one already exists or will create a new file if one does not already exist. File pointer points to the beginning of the file.
RESET (F)	Prepares file F for reading. File pointer points to the beginning of the file. Cannot create a file if one does not exist, so if you attempt to RESET a nonexistent file an error message is displayed.
SEEK (F, I)	Moves file pointer to point to component number I of disk file F. Does not work on text files.
SEEKEOF (F)	Returns Boolean TRUE if file pointer points beyond the last component of disk file F. Unlike EOF, SEEKEOF skips blanks, tab stops, and carriage returns before it tests for the end-of-file marker.
SEEKEOLN (F)	Returns Boolean TRUE if file pointer points at a carriage-return character within text file F. Unlike EOLN, SEEKEOLN skips blanks and tab stops before it tests for the carriage return. Note that, in a text file, if EOF (F) is TRUE, then SEEKEOLN (F) must also be TRUE.

Figure 4.27 – Procedures and functions for file manipulation (continued).

Figure 4.28 lists a sequential file-handling program written to help in the production of this book. I use the XyWrite word-processing package (XyWrite is to word processing what Turbo is to languages—the best and the fastest) but the publisher needed an ASCII file without any embedded XyWrite commands for their computer-based typesetting system. But my original file was full of XyWrite commands to generate neatly formatted hard copy and screen displays for my own editing (double-spacing, wide margins, neatly aligned tables, etc.). The program in Figure 4.28 reads the XyWrite file—which is a text file (not compiled, with no records or arrays, just thousands of characters)—character-by-character. It tests for the beginning of each XyWrite command ([) and the end of each command (]). Characters read after the start-of-command character are not written to the output text file until the program gets past the end-of-command character. Without nested commands, the program would have been much simpler. When the begin-command symbol was encountered, a Boolean variable (called a flag) would have been set. The program would read each character, and if the flag were set, would not output the character. When the end-command symbol was encountered, the flag would be cleared (its value would be reversed) and the program would resume outputting the characters. With nested commands, two or three intervening end-command delimiters might be encountered before the one paired with the opening command is found. The situation is shown below:

> . . . printable text [Overall command begins here [Nested command goes here*] overall command continues and ends here!] printable text continues . . .

A simple Boolean test would clear itself when it saw the first end-command character (shown above preceded with an asterisk) and would therefore print out part of the "enclosing" command string. We want the program to continue suppressing output until it sees the end-command symbol paired with the first begin-command character (indicated by the exclamation point). We must keep track of the number of begin-command characters encountered and not resume printing until an end-command character has been encountered to balance every begin-command character.

```
PROGRAM FilterXyWriteCommands;
VAR
    OneChar: CHAR;
    InFile, OutFile: TEXT;  {TEXT is a predefined file type.}
    SpecialChar: INTEGER;
    Inzie, Outzie: STRING[14];

PROCEDURE Initialize;
BEGIN
    WRITE ('What is the input file with the XyWrite commands?  ');
    READLN (Inzie);
    WRITE ('What is the stripped output file?  ');
    READLN (Outzie);
    ASSIGN (InFile, Inzie);
    ASSIGN (OutFile, Outzie);
    RESET (InFile);
    REWRITE (OutFile);
    SpecialChar:=0;
END;

PROCEDURE Stripper;
BEGIN
    WHILE NOT EOF (Infile) DO
        BEGIN
            READ (Infile,OneChar);
            IF OneChar = '[' THEN SpecialChar := SpecialChar + 1;
            IF OneChar = ']' THEN
              BEGIN
                 SpecialChar := SpecialChar-1;
                 READ (Infile,OneChar);
                 IF OneChar = '[' THEN SpecialChar := SpecialChar+1;
              END;
            IF SpecialChar = 0 THEN
              BEGIN
                 WRITE (OutFile,OneChar);
                 WRITE (OneChar);   {echo action to screen for debugging}
              END;
        END;
END;

BEGIN
    Initialize;
    Stripper;
    CLOSE (Infile);
    CLOSE (Outfile);
    WRITELN ('File processed successfully')
END.
```

Figure 4.28 – Program demonstrating use of text file for input and output.

The program uses a counter to keep track of begin-command and end-command pairs. It is typical of many real-world applications for text-file processing.

In the declaration section, you see that InFile and OutFile are file variables of the predefined file type TEXT. The following declarations are identical in effect:

```
InFile, OutFile : FILE OF CHAR;
InFile, OutFile : TEXT;
```

Inzie and Outzie are used to store the operator's keystrokes for the actual file name. It is possible to include the disk identifier in the string as well (for example: C:LETTER.TXT). The input file—which is only going to be read from—is begun with a RESET, while the output file is both created and begun with the REWRITE command. Both files are closed at the end of the program. Output is written to the disk file exactly as you would send it to a printer, screen, or any other device:

```
WRITE (OutFile, OneChar);
WRITE (OneChar); {Echoes output to screen.}
```

Incidentally, in writing programs to read and write files, the technique of echoing input and output to the screen is useful in monitoring what is (or is not) taking place during program execution. The lines that echo the process to the screen can be deleted when the program is debugged.

Figure 4.29 shows a typical XyWrite file, using square brackets to denote the normally nonprinting command delimiters. Figure 4.30 shows the output from running this file through the filter program.

The program uses READ and WRITE rather than READLN and WRITELN, in order to read the file character-by-character. READLN can be faster, but only if the lines in the text file fit completely within the size of the string variable into which you are reading them. Figure 4.31 lists a program to demonstrate the different ways of reading text files. In place of the file LETTER.TXT, substitute any short text file created with your word processor or a program like IBM's EDLIN line editor. Then alter the length of the string called OneLine from its current 255 (greatest permissible in Turbo) to much smaller values (5, 15, 40, 80) and run the program.

```
[RHA

[FC]Using Turbo Pascal
Introduction

][RFA


[FC]Page [PN]
[FL]
][FD66][PL60][LM17][RM70]
Introduction:
[IP5,0][LS2]
[MDBO]Why this book was written:
[MDNM]
This book was written to help readers develop, as quickly as
possible, the ability to write real-world, problem-solving
programs in[MDBO] TURBO[MDNM] Pascal. This should also develop an
[MDUL]understanding[MDNM] of structured programming along the
way. In Figure 1.2 you see a program.
[LM12][RM75][IP0,0]
[NB]/p/
[MDBO](Figure 1.2)[MDNM]
```

Figure 4.29 – *File produced by XyWrite with extraneous commands.*

```
Introduction:

Why this book was written:

This book was written to help readers develop, as quickly as
possible, the ability to write real-world, problem-solving
programs in TURBO Pascal.  This should also develop an
understanding of structured programming along the way.  In Figure
1.2 you see a program.

/p/
(Figure 1.2)
```

Figure 4.30 – *The file from Figure 4.29, as processed by the program in Figure 4.28.*

The program uses the Boolean standard identifiers EOF and EOLN (for End Of File and End Of Line). Because files are not of a predetermined size, these identifiers are the handiest way of knowing when you have come to the end of a file whose size you do not know in advance. They lend themselves to many program control structures in Turbo, producing an easy-to-use Boolean TRUE when the end-of-file or end-of-line is encountered. The EOF function is the most common way of controlling input from a file whose size you neither know nor care about. There are situations, however, in which you need to know exactly how many records make up a file—for example, in sorting programs. Techniques for determining file size will be covered shortly.

To save space, there isn't a screen display from this program; it is best if you run it with your own files. Incidentally, Turbo will not allow simultaneous reading from and writing to one text file. It must be closed and reopened before you can switch between these operations. This restriction does not apply to other files.

Nontext Files

This book has covered text files—a special case—before the more general kinds of files, because the ability to move characters to or from a file and then view the change (by using the DOS TYPE command to display the contents of an ASCII file) helps to develop an understanding of opening and closing files.

Nontext files are any files not of the predefined type TEXT. Figure 4.32 shows only those lines of code from the ham radio club roster program of Figure 4.22 that deal with writing and reading data files. The comments within the listing point out the critical processes.

Searching Files

One of the fastest ways of searching for a specific element in an ordered (sorted) group is the elegantly simple binary search. You compare your target item with a file element in the middle of the file. If your target is larger than this midfile sample, you know you don't have to look in the bottom half of the file, but only in the top half. You then compare your target with a file element from the midpoint of the upper half, and you can eliminate an additional quarter of the file. Even in lists of up to 16,000 elements, you can generally find

```
PROGRAM ReadSimpleTextFileWithLines;
VAR
      OneLine: STRING[255];
      OneChar: CHAR;
      InFile, OutFile: TEXT;
      PassCharThru: INTEGER;

PROCEDURE Initialize;
BEGIN
    ASSIGN (InFile, ´LETTER.TXT´);
    ASSIGN (OutFile, ´FINISHED.TXT´);
    RESET (InFile);
    REWRITE (OutFile);
    PassCharThru:=0;
END;

PROCEDURE LineReader;
BEGIN
    WHILE NOT EOF(Infile) DO
        BEGIN
            READ (Infile, OneLine);
            WRITE (OneLine);
            WRITE (OutFile, OneLine);
            READLN (InFile, OneLine);
            WRITELN (OneLine);
            WRITELN (OutFile, OneLine);
        END;
END;

PROCEDURE CharReader;
BEGIN
    WHILE NOT EOF(Infile) DO
        BEGIN
            READ (Infile, OneChar);
            WRITE (OneChar);
            WRITE (OutFile, OneChar);
        END;
END;

PROCEDURE CharReaderPlusLine;
BEGIN
    WHILE NOT EOF(Infile) DO
        BEGIN
            READ (InFile, OneChar);
            WRITE (OutFile, OneChar);
            WRITE (OneChar);
            IF EOLN (Infile) THEN WRITELN (´**end of line
encountered**´);
        END;
END;
```

Figure 4.31 – Program to demonstrate reading text files by character and by line (continues).

```
BEGIN
   Initialize;
   LineReader;
   CLOSE (Outfile);
   RESET (Infile);
   REWRITE (Outfile);
   CharReader;
   CLOSE (Outfile);
   RESET (Infile);
   REWRITE (Outfile);
   CharReaderPlusLine;
   CLOSE (InFile);
   CLOSE (OutFile);
   WRITELN ('File processed successfully');
END.
```

Figure 4.31 – Program to demonstrate reading text files by character and by line (continued).

```
PROGRAM DemonstrateRecords;

{Normal declaration section included definition of the record
HamOpRecord.}
.
.
.
VAR
   InFile, OutFile : FILE OF HamOpRecord;

{Note that we have defined our file as a file made up of records.
the records have been defined already.}
.
.
.
   WRITELN ('What file will contain all the names?');
   READLN (Response);
   ASSIGN (OutFile, Response);
   REWRITE (OutFile);

{Normal file assignment and opening for writing.}

   WHILE NOT AllDone DO
   BEGIN
     HamOp.Handle := Name;
     HamOp.CallSign := Call;
```

Figure 4.32 – Program excerpts to demonstrate writing records to a data file (continues).

```
{This section of code determined input for all the elements of a
single HamOp record.}
    .
    .
    .
      HamOp.VHF := FALSE;
      HamOp.Computer := FALSE;
      WRITE (OutFile, HamOp);

{Only when all the contents of a complete record have been
assembled is the record written to the output file, all at once.
A file of records is written one record at a time.}
    .
    .
    .
    CLOSE (OutFile);  {Don't forget this}
END;

PROCEDURE ReadExistingFile;
BEGIN
  WRITELN ('What file contains all the ham club records?');
  READLN (Response);
  ASSIGN (InFile, Response);
  RESET (InFile);
  WHILE NOT EOF (InFile) DO
  BEGIN
      READ (Infile, HamOp);
      WITH HamOp DO
        BEGIN

{The file is opened for reading with a RESET command. Because
there is no way of knowing how long the file is, the program uses
the EOF function to keep reading records sequentially until it
reaches the end of the file.  The data is read the same way it is
written--one record at a time.}
    .
    .
    .
  END;
 CLOSE (InFile);  {Don't forget this, either.}
 END;
    .
    .
    .
```

Figure 4.32 – *Program excerpts to demonstrate writing records to a data file (continued).*

your entry in less than 16 tries. To apply this technique to a file, you have to know precisely how many records are in the file. Figure 4.33 illustrates the application of the binary search to a huge array—the integers from 0 to 16,000—in memory. Figure 4.35 will apply this search technique to a large external data file using a function to determine the precise size of the file before beginning the search.

```
PROGRAM BinarySearchLogic;
    {Change Maximum from 10 to 100, 200, 500, 1000, 5000,
        10000 and 15000 and see how many additional passes it takes
        as the data base gets larger.}

VAR
    Minimum, Maximum, UnknownNumber, Turns, Guess :INTEGER;
    Found : BOOLEAN;

PROCEDURE Initialize;
BEGIN
    CLRSCR;
    Found := FALSE;
    Turns := 1;
    Guess := 0;
    Minimum := 0;
    Maximum := 16000; {Why should you avoid integers larger than 16383?}
    UnknownNumber := RANDOM (Maximum);
    WRITELN ('I am thinking of a number between 1 and ',Maximum,'
Can you guess it?');
END;

PROCEDURE PrintStatus;
BEGIN
    WRITELN ('On pass ', Turns:2,' you determined the target was
between ', Minimum:5,' and ', Maximum:5, '.');
END;

PROCEDURE GetAndEvaluateGuess;
BEGIN
        Guess := (Minimum + Maximum) DIV 2;   {Determines
midpoint of range.}
        WRITELN ('Your initial guess is ',Guess);
        WRITELN;
    WHILE NOT Found DO
      BEGIN
        IF Guess = UnknownNumber THEN
            BEGIN
                WRITELN ('The unknown number was ',UnknownNumber);
                Found := TRUE;
            END;
```

Figure 4.33 – Program to demonstrate fast binary search of a huge array (continues).

This program is so fast that many people think it is a trick and could not really do the search that quickly. You can prove to yourself that this program works. Change MaxElement and see what a slight difference in time it takes between searching 100 entries and 16,000. Figure 4.34 shows the screen displays from running the program twice.

Clearly, the binary search is very fast when searching data in memory. It is also quite fast in searching large external data files for individual records.

One approach to searching files is to read each record in turn and extract one key field (last name, customer number, etc.) from each, to be stored in memory as a two-dimensional array along with the record number. The array is then searched and the corresponding record number accessed. This works quite well, but

```
            IF Guess < UnknownNumber THEN     {Unknown number is in
upper half of range.}
            BEGIN
            Turns := Turns + 1;
            Minimum := Guess;  {New range becomes top half of old
range.}
            Guess := (Minimum + Maximum) DIV 2;
            PrintStatus;
            END;
            IF Guess > UnknownNumber THEN     {Unknown number is in
lower half of range.}
            BEGIN
            Turns := Turns + 1;
            Maximum := Guess;     {New range becomes bottom half
of old range.}
            Guess := (Minimum + Maximum) DIV 2;
            PrintStatus;
            END;

        END;
    END;

BEGIN
    Initialize;
    GetAndEvaluateGuess;
    WRITELN ('It took', Turns:3, ' tries to find the number.');
    WRITELN;
END.
```

Figure 4.33 – Program to demonstrate fast binary search of a huge array (continued).

only if the array itself fits into memory. Because Turbo limits the total amount of data it can manipulate to 64K, there is still a need for some kind of search that works on large files stored on disk.

The efficiency of the binary search lends itself to searching sequential files that can contain thousands of huge records. For the search to work on disk files, there must be procedures to determine the highest record number in the file without the tedium of reading and discarding each record in turn. In addition, there must be a procedure to access only the record that contains the target information.

```
I am thinking of a number between 1 and 16000 Can you guess it?
Your initial guess is 8000

On pass  2 you determined the target was between     0 and  8000.
On pass  3 you determined the target was between  4000 and  8000.
On pass  4 you determined the target was between  6000 and  8000.
On pass  5 you determined the target was between  6000 and  7000.
On pass  6 you determined the target was between  6500 and  7000.
On pass  7 you determined the target was between  6750 and  7000.
On pass  8 you determined the target was between  6875 and  7000.
On pass  9 you determined the target was between  6875 and  6937.
On pass 10 you determined the target was between  6906 and  6937.
On pass 11 you determined the target was between  6921 and  6937.
On pass 12 you determined the target was between  6921 and  6929.
On pass 13 you determined the target was between  6921 and  6925.
On pass 14 you determined the target was between  6923 and  6925.
The unknown number was 6924
It took 14 tries to find the number.

I am thinking of a number between 1 and 16000 Can you guess it?
Your initial guess is 8000

On pass  2 you determined the target was between  8000 and 16000.
On pass  3 you determined the target was between 12000 and 16000.
On pass  4 you determined the target was between 12000 and 14000.
On pass  5 you determined the target was between 13000 and 14000.
On pass  6 you determined the target was between 13000 and 13500.
On pass  7 you determined the target was between 13250 and 13500.
On pass  8 you determined the target was between 13250 and 13375.
On pass  9 you determined the target was between 13250 and 13312.
On pass 10 you determined the target was between 13250 and 13281.
On pass 11 you determined the target was between 13250 and 13265.
On pass 12 you determined the target was between 13257 and 13265.
On pass 13 you determined the target was between 13257 and 13261.
The unknown number was 13259
It took 13 tries to find the number.
```

Figure 4.34 – Screen display produced by the program in Figure 4.33.

Turbo offers tools for just these purposes. The function FILESIZE gives you the number of records in the file instantly. It is fast because it doesn't have to read them all—the operating system puts that information in the file control block. Similarly, the SEEK function tells what record number you want to read next within a file. The program in Figure 4.35 was written to maintain a mailing list for a local business with over a thousand names. In fact, it was the utter inability of BASICA on the IBM PC to begin to handle this task that got the author interested in Turbo in the first place.

The critical lines in the program are highlighted to emphasize the syntax of the FILESIZE, SEEK, and READ functions. FILESIZE and SEEK both need a file name as an argument; SEEK also requires a record number. The time it takes to seek any particular record number is negligible. A screen display of the operation of this program is useless as it does not convey any sense of speed. When you use this technique on your own data files, you will be pleasantly surprised by its speed.

Untyped Files

Turbo offers another type of file, called UNTYPED. Turbo allows you to move 128-byte long blocks from disk to a variable in an untyped file (using the BLOCKREAD and BLOCKWRITE procedures). This operation seems to violate Turbo's orientation toward strong typing, as it is effectively a mechanical transfer of bytes without any regard for their data types. It is an exotic application, for those writing their own I/O drivers, copy-protection schemes, and optimized programs that work intimately with the computer's operating system. It is beyond the scope of this book.

Files: Conclusion

File handling is fundamental to ambitious programs that address most common business, scientific, text-processing, and other concerns. The only way to master Turbo's unusual—but basically consistent—set of procedures is to experiment with small files and to dig into and modify the example programs in this chapter. All the fundamentals of creating, writing, and reading Turbo files have been covered.

```
PROGRAM DemonstrateBinarySearchWithFiles;

TYPE
  CustomerRecord =  RECORD
       LastName : STRING[13];
       FirstName : STRING[15];
       Street : STRING[30];
       Town : STRING[19];
       State : STRING[2];
       Zip : STRING[5];
    END;

VAR
  InFile : FILE OF CustomerRecord;
  Customer : CustomerRecord;
  SourceFile : STRING[14];
  SurName : STRING[14];
  RecNum, MaxRec : INTEGER;
  AllFinished : BOOLEAN;
  WhatsYourPleasure : CHAR;
  Minimum, Maximum, Fetch, LastFetch : INTEGER;
  Found, DoAnother : BOOLEAN;

PROCEDURE LookUpOneName;
BEGIN
   CLRSCR;
   WRITELN ('What file are we looking in? ');
   READLN (SourceFile);
   ASSIGN (InFile, SourceFile);
   RESET (InFile);
   Found := FALSE;
   MaxRec := FileSize (InFile) ;   {Finds file size for max in
binary search.}
   WRITELN ('FileSize = ', MaxRec);
   DoAnother := TRUE;
   WHILE DoAnother DO
     BEGIN
       Minimum := 0;
       Maximum := MaxRec;
       WRITELN ('What name are you looking for?');
       READLN (SurName);
       WHILE NOT Found DO
         BEGIN
           Fetch := (Minimum + Maximum) DIV 2; {Heart of the
binary search.}
           IF Fetch = LastFetch THEN  Minimum := MaxInt;
           LastFetch := Fetch;
           SEEK (InFile, Fetch);    {Points to the record.}
           READ (InFile, Customer); {Reads entire customer record.}
           IF SurName = Customer.LastName THEN
            BEGIN {Prints entire record when target record is
found.}
               Found := TRUE;
```

Figure 4.35 – Program to perform high-speed binary search on external data file (continues).

```
                        CLRSCR;
                        WRITELN (Customer.FirstName, ´ ´, Customer.LastName);
                        WRITELN (Customer.Street);
                        WRITE (Customer.Town, ´ ´, Customer.State);
                        WRITELN (´ ´, Customer.Zip);
                        WRITELN;
                        WRITELN (´Look up another name? Y/N  ´);
                        READ (KBD, WhatsYourPleasure);
                        IF (WhatsYourPleasure = ´Y´) OR (WhatsYourPleasure
    = ´y´) THEN
                          BEGIN
                             DoAnother := TRUE;
                             Found := FALSE;
                             CLRSCR;
                             WRITELN (´What name are you looking for? ´);
                             READLN (SurName);
                             Minimum := 0;
                             Maximum := MaxRec;
                          END
                             ELSE DoAnother := FALSE;
                        END;
                   IF Minimum < Maximum THEN    {Works only while search
       is valid.}
                        BEGIN
                           IF SurName > Customer.LastName THEN  Minimum := Fetch;
                           IF SurName < Customer.LastName THEN  Maximum := Fetch;
                        END
                        ELSE    {Tried all records and still have not gotten a hit.}
                          BEGIN
                             WRITELN (´I can not seem to find that name´);
                             WRITELN;
                             DoAnother := TRUE;
                             Found := FALSE;
                             WRITELN (´What name are you looking for? ´);
                             READLN (SirName);
                             Minimum := 0;
                             Maximum := MaxRec;
                          END;
                 END;
                 CLOSE (InFile);
          END;
       END;

    BEGIN
     LookUpOneName
    END.
```

Figure 4.35 – Program to perform high-speed binary search on external data file (continued).

The MS-DOS and PC-DOS version of Turbo Pascal supports an additional file-handling procedure. The APPEND procedure opens a file, automatically goes to the end, and allows you to add new records to the end of the file. The same results can be obtained in all versions of Turbo by using FILESIZE, SEEK, and WRITE.

Sets

Turbo Pascal uses the concept of *sets*. This concept is easily understood, but is limited in its practical applications. You already know that all identifiers must have a specified data type, but they can optionally be specified as belonging to a user-defined set as well. In turn, variables can be tested for membership within sets.

In theory, sets could be a powerful tool. In practice, they tend to be used infrequently, although, like so much of Turbo, their usefulness is a function of your ingenuity. With Turbo's range of capabilities, sets are often lost in the overabundance, and programmers tend not to master the concept.

Turbo restricts the maximum number of elements in a set to 256. Far more limiting, however, is the fact that sets can only be made up of nonstructured, scalar data types (but, as always, not real numbers), which have discrete predecessors and successors. This imposes severe restrictions. For example, you cannot make sets of strings. Nor can you make sets of things like ZIP codes (most ZIP codes exceed MAXINT) and many other numeric values. In fact, sets only come into their own when associated with a limited number of discrete elements, generally as tests and filters in character I/O.

Sets are useful when a limited range of valid input can be defined as a set. Input is tested for membership in the set with one statement, rather than by a tedious series of comparisons with each individual item. Another frequent application is in code-conversion programs, in which input may be compared with several sets, typically the set of text characters, the set of control characters, and the set of characters to be disregarded. After the program has tested for membership in a set, different processing procedures can be chosen.

However, there is nothing that can be done using sets that cannot be done using conventional tests and control structures. It is simply a question of finding those applications in which sets might be the most convenient way of doing things. The most common application of sets is in filtering out invalid keyboard input to a screen prompt. Figure 4.36 shows a traditional menu-response arrangement. Invalid input is taken care of by the ELSE clause in the CASE statement. Any input character that is not in the range 1 to 8 causes the ELSE clause to prompt for input again. The technique works extremely well and is very simple; it does not use sets.

This program has the additional benefit of exploiting the KBD standard file so that the operator does not have to hit the Enter key after making a selection. This operation is similar to $INKEY in BASIC, and was also illustrated in Figure 4.16.

This simple arrangement is useless when the range of menu choices exceeds the number that can be accommodated by a single character. Using an alphabetical key (A to Z) would be the logical choice for up to 26 choices (as shown in Figure 4.16). But if we need to interpret more than 26 choices, sets offer an alternative. Figure 4.37 shows the program from Figure 4.36 modified to use sets.

```
PROCEDURE InterpretChoice;   {Interprets menu selection.}
BEGIN
   READ (KBD, WhatsYourPleasure); {Avoids having to hit Return,
but can accept only one-character choice.}
   Option:=ORD (WhatsYourPleasure)-48; {Converts one ASCII
character to integer.}
   CASE Option OF             {All options accessible with one digit.}
        1: AcceptNewNames;
        2: LookUpOneName;
        3: AlphabetizeList;
        4: ProofListToScreen;
        5: ProduceLabels;
        6: CreateMailingListBook;
        7: GetDirectory;
        8: ExitProgram;
     ELSE
        BEGIN
          GOTOXY (19,22);
          WRITELN (#7,´*** Invalid choice, please try again ***´);
          GOTOXY (25,23); WRITELN (´WHAT NUMBER WOULD YOU LIKE?  ´);
          GOTOXY (55,23);
          InterpretChoice;
        END; {ends ELSE}
     END;   {ends CASE}
END;
```

Figure 4.36 – Filtering erroneous input using CASE/ELSE construction.

Pointers

Pointers are among the most complex and least understood of Turbo's data structures. Their operation is not obvious, nor is it analogous to natural structures the way arrays and strings are. Until you are writing programs that manipulate large and complex data files, you will find that arrays offer the simplest structure for sorting and accessing information quickly. It would be foolish to add the complexity of pointers to any program that could be served best by simple arrays.

```
PROCEDURE InterpretChoice;
VAR
   Choices: SET OF BYTE;
   Option, Result : INTEGER;
   WhatsYourPleasure : STRING[2];

BEGIN
    Choices := [1..8, 10, 15]; {Up to 256 discrete choices.}
    READLN (WhatsYourPleasure);   {You have to hit Return every time.}
    VAL (WhatsYourPleasure, Option, Result); {Converts input
string to integer.}
    IF (Option IN Choices) THEN
    BEGIN
    CASE Option OF
        1: AcceptNewNames;
        2: LookUpOneName;
        3: AlphabetizeList;
        4: ProofListToScreen;
        5: ProduceLabels;
        6: CreateMailingListBook;
        7: GetDirectory;
        8: ExitProgram;
       10: WRITELN ('Big 10');
       15: WRITELN ('Big 15');
    {You could have up to 256 different choices.}
    END; {end of CASE}
    END ELSE
    BEGIN
        GOTOXY (19,22);
        WRITELN (#7,'*** Invalid choice, please try again ***');
        GOTOXY (25,23); WRITELN ('WHAT NUMBER WOULD YOU LIKE?   ');
        GOTOXY (55,23);
        InterpretChoice;
    END; {End of ELSE clause.}
END;
```

Figure 4.37 – Procedure to demonstrate set membership as a control for illegal keyboard input.

But pointers are the only structure for accessing data elements that are related to each other, but cannot be found by simply adding or subtracting a known value from an index (as is the rule in using arrays).

In the previous section, we were forced to extend the concept of the binary search to disk file records when the size of the file size grew too large to fit into an array (or would simply take too long to load into memory for every search). We used a pointer-like device to do the binary search. In our binary search of a file, the record numbers that were determined by the FILESIZE function, and pointed to by the SEEK function, served as a form of pointer to the records we wanted. Turbo offers a data type to perform the same function on any data structure stored in memory. A *pointer* is a data type that contains the address of a variable. A pointer does not, however, contain the variable itself. Like all data types, pointers must be declared with an identifier and a type.

A *list* is not a formal data structure, so lists do not have to be identified and declared. Nonetheless, they are an important concept, intimately associated with pointers. A pointer is almost useless by itself. Pointers become important in determining the position of a variable in relationship to other variables. A *linked list* is a group of variables in which each variable contains a pointer to another variable. Pointers are the "links" tying one element to another.

Pointers are almost always used with records. In most applications, a record includes some data and at least one pointer, which contains the address of at least one other record. Records containing data and the address of their immediate predecessor or successor are called *singly-linked* lists. More complex *doubly-linked* lists include the address of both the successor and predecessor of the data. Even more complex structures, called *trees*, can include complex combinations of successors and predecessors with the data.

The most important fact about pointers is that they allow you to correlate some data with the addresses of other pieces of data. For simple alphabetical lists, pointers merely add complexity. They are invaluable, however, in creating sophisticated data bases. For example, in creating a true data-base manager for a business, you could file all records by customer number, but each customer's record could have a pointer to a related record—regardless of the primary sorting key. Thus, although all records were stored in ascending order by account number, each contract customer's record would have a pointer to the next contract customer; each cash customer would have a pointer to the next cash customer, and so on. There could also be pointers so that each customer in the eastern region had a pointer to the next customer in the eastern region. By adroitly traversing lists from pointer to pointer, complex data-base queries such as "Generate a list of all midwestern contract customers with an outstanding balance in excess of $300" can be handled more efficiently than by "brute force" searches, which read every record in the data base and perform a series of tests on each. As the size and complexity of the data base grows, the scope of application for pointers increases.

Two characteristics give pointers their unique place in the range of Turbo data structures. First, the lists linked by pointers can grow dynamically during the execution of a program. Where lists differ from files, however, is that files are disk-based structures. Lists are maintained in memory and are the only memory-resident data structure whose size can change dynamically during program execution. By contrast, although you may not fill every cell in an array, memory space for the entire maximum declared size of the array was allocated when the program began execution.

Second, a Turbo program can only be a maximum of 64K bytes long, and the total of all the data structures (all the variables and all the arrays) used in any one program can only be an additional 64K. On a computer with a total memory of 128K bytes, the largest possible Turbo program would use all the computer's memory. But on computers with more memory—say 256 or even 512K—there is extra memory available, if Turbo can take advantage of it. None of the programs in the book have been able to use this extra memory. But Turbo can access this extra space, through the use of the *heap*.

As its name suggests, the heap is the memory left over after space has been allocated to everything else. It is this heap space that Turbo uses to store the dynamically created pointer variables. In systems with less than 128K, there may still be some heap space. The heap will equal all the memory space "left over" from the size of your program and its data structures. For example, if a program occupies only 12K bytes and its data occupies only 4K bytes, there would be 112K bytes (128 − 16) of heap space.

Figure 4.38 shows all the procedures and functions available for

In this figure the following abbreviations are used:

I	integer
PTR	pointer variable

Procedures and functions:

DISPOSE (*PTR*)	Reclaims heap space of single variable *PTR*.
FREEMEM (*PTR, I*)	Reclaims *I* bytes of heap space previously allocated with GETMEM.
GETMEM (*PTR, I*)	Allocates *I* bytes of heap space to pointer variable *PTR*.
MARK (*PTR*)	Assigns heap pointer to *PTR*.
MAXAVAIL	Returns the size of the largest consecutive block of free space on the heap. Result is always an integer, but may need further interpretation if larger than MAXINT.
MEMAVAIL	Returns number of paragraphs (16 bytes) of free space on heap. MS-DOS only. Result is always an integer.
NEW (*PTR*)	Creates pointer variable *PTR*.
ORD (*PTR*)	Returns the address contained in pointer *PTR*. Result is always an integer. Note that ORD works entirely differently with a scalar argument.
PTR (*I*)	Function; converts integer value *I* to a pointer.
RELEASE (*PTR*)	Sets heap pointer to *PTR* (previously marked by the MARK procedure) in order to free dynamically allocated heap space from the specified pointer variable upwards.

Figure 4.38 – Standard procedure and functions for manipulating pointers and the heap.

manipulating pointers and the heap. Most of the functions are beyond the scope of this book, but are included here for reference.

Figure 4.39 is a short program that makes use of pointers. It uses the same string-manipulation techniques used in the program of Figure 4.11, this time taking a string consisting of the names of famous fictional detectives and creating a singly-linked list of names. In such a simple application, arrays would be a much more natural approach. However, handling a small amount of data makes the operation of the pointers and list more apparent.

Before we explore the operation of the pointers in Figure 4.39, look at Figure 4.40, which shows the screen display generated by the program. Seeing the screen output should make the relationship of the pointers clearer.

The procedure called Driver in Figure 4.39 parses the RawData string into individual detective names and creates a series of records, consisting of the detective name and a pointer to the record that describes the preceding detective. The procedure called PrintOut examines the last record, prints the detective's name, and goes on to examine each preceding record in turn.

Although the same operation could have been done with a simple array (and no pointers) or even with a simple text file (just keep reading to the EOF), it is important to see how the pointers are used. Once you understand how they work in a trivial program like this, you can see how meaningful pointers to related items could be added.

Pointers are declared, like any other data type, with an identifier and a type. However, they use an unusual syntax. The declaration section of our example program is shown below.

```
TYPE
   Name = STRING[17];
   PointerToDetectiveRecord = ^DetectiveRecord;
   DetectiveRecord = RECORD
      Detective : Name;
      PreviousDetective : PointerToDetectiveRecord;
      END;
CONST
   MaxElement = 5;
```

VAR
   Predecessor, CurrentDetectiveRecord, Temp : PointerToDetectiveRe-cord;
   I : INTEGER;
   OneName : Name;

The caret (^) denotes a pointer (Turbo uses this symbol for the unrelated purpose of denoting a control character). The identifier

```
PROGRAM PointerDemo;
TYPE
  Name = STRING[17];
  PointerToDetectiveRecord = ^DectectiveRecord;
  DectectiveRecord = RECORD
      Detective : Name;
      PreviousDetective : PointerToDetectiveRecord;
      END;
CONST
  MaxElement = 5;
VAR
  Predecessor, CurrentDetectiveRecord, Temp : PointerToDetectiveRecord;
  I : INTEGER;
  OneName : Name;

PROCEDURE Driver; {String manipulation similar to Figure 4.11.}
VAR
   FirstChar, Slash, CharsLeft : INTEGER;
   RawData : STRING[72];
BEGIN
  RawData := ^SHERLOCK HOLMES/MISS MARPLE/HERCULE POIROT/NERO
WOLFE/INSPECTOR MAIGRET/^;
  FirstChar := 1;
  Slash := 1;
  Predecessor := NIL;   {Initialize list, first pointer points to
the end.}
  FOR I := 1 TO MaxElement DO
  BEGIN
     CharsLeft := LENGTH (RawData);
     Slash := POS (^/^, RawData);
     OneName := COPY (RawData, FirstChar, (Slash - 1));
     RawData := COPY (RawData, (Slash + 1), (CharsLeft - Slash));
     NEW (CurrentDetectiveRecord);
     CurrentDetectiveRecord^.Detective := OneName;
     CurrentDetectiveRecord^.PreviousDetective := Predecessor;
     Predecessor := CurrentDetectiveRecord; {The predecessor now
points to the current record.}
     WRITELN (^The current detective is:
^,CurrentDetectiveRecord^.Detective);
   END;
END;
```

Figure 4.39 – Program to create a singly-linked list using pointers (continues).

PointerToDetectiveRecord is defined as a pointer to DetectiveRecord. In turn, DetectiveRecord is defined like any record. Pointer declarations are the only case in which Turbo allows the use of a term prior to its declaration. In this case ^DetectiveRecord is used before DetectiveRecord has been declared.

```
PROCEDURE PrintOut;
BEGIN
  WRITELN;
  WRITELN ('The names read by traversing the series of pointers are:');
  WRITELN;
  Temp := CurrentDetectiveRecord;
  WHILE Temp <> NIL DO
  BEGIN
    WRITELN (Temp^.Detective);
    Temp := Temp^.PreviousDetective;
  END;
  WRITELN; WRITELN; WRITELN;
END;

BEGIN
  CLRSCR;
  Driver;
  PrintOut;
END.
```

Figure 4.39 – Program to create a singly-linked list using pointers (continued).

```
The current detective is: SHERLOCK HOLMES
The current detective is: MISS MARPLE
The current detective is: HERCULE POIROT
The current detective is: NERO WOLFE
The current detective is: INSPECTOR MAIGRET

The names read by traversing the series of pointers are:

INSPECTOR MAIGRET
NERO WOLFE
HERCULE POIROT
MISS MARPLE
SHERLOCK HOLMES
```

Figure 4.40 – Screen display produced by the program in Figure 4.39.

PointerToDetectiveRecord is just an address; it does not contain the record data. Turbo will give an I/O error if asked to print a pointer to the screen. To print the data to which a pointer points, you use the following syntax:

WRITELN (PointerToDetectiveRecord ^.Detective);

This line prints the detective name stored in the record to which the pointer refers. The syntax is like that used to access the data elements within ordinary records.

The standard identifier NIL is used to flag the last pointer in a list. The program begins by initializing the first pointer to this value. The following four lines create the pointers and assign values to them:

NEW (CurrentDetectiveRecord);
CurrentDetectiveRecord ^.Detective : = OneName;
CurrentDetectiveRecord ^.PreviousDetective : = Predecessor;
Predecessor : = CurrentDetectiveRecord; {the predecessor now points to the current record}

The NEW procedure allocates space in the heap for the record to be indicated by the pointer, which it also creates. Unlike the dimensioning of arrays, the NEW procedure is not done only once for the entire list. Each additional pointer-and-record combination is created dynamically and individually, with the NEW procedure used each time. Figure 4.38 lists several procedures for allocating specific amounts of space at one time, but they are used in applications beyond the scope of this book.

Once the pointer is created by NEW, data is written to the record. In the example program, a detective's name is parsed into the variable OneName, which is then assigned to CurrentDetective-Record ^.Detective. (In a more ambitious program, the record could have more fields.) The next line of code sets the pointer within the current record to point to some other record. Setting the pointer is the most critical step in using pointers. For simplicity, the example loads the address of the predecessor record into this pointer. In this way, each new record contains a pointer to a preceding record. The first record containing a detective's name (Sherlock Holmes) has a pointer towards a dummy record (Predecessor), which has a pointer to NIL. This identifier flags the end of the list to Turbo.

If we used buffers and additional pointers in each record, every record could point to its successor as well as its predecessor, but that would make for an unacceptably complex example program.

The PrintOut procedure is initialized with the last record (Temp := CurrentDetectiveRecord) and uses a loop, first to print the detective name and then to find the next record. It uses the test for NIL much like EOF, to continue reading the list of unknown length.

This discussion can only scratch the surface of the many uses for lists and pointers. They are an advanced topic, which deserves an entire book to explore its real power.

Graphics
and
Sound

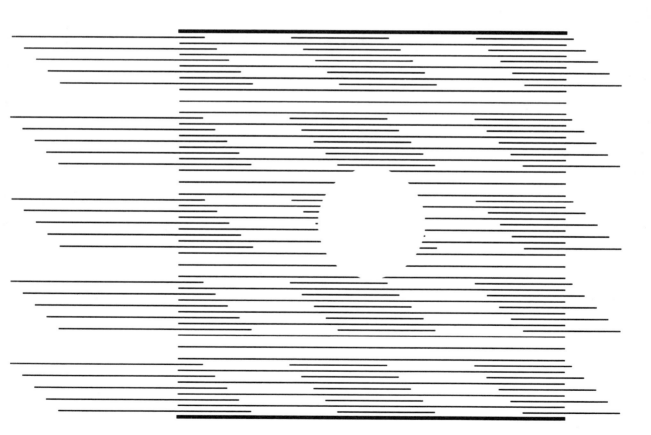

Chapter 5

Overview

This chapter deals with what are often called "bells and whistles": sound and graphics. Much of the graphics capability of Turbo Pascal depends on the capabilities of the computer hardware. Obviously, Turbo's commands to control color display are useless on a monochrome monitor. Similarly, most of the enhanced graphics capabilities require a high-resolution graphics card. Several other commands function only within the MS/PC-DOS system. It would be impossible to do justice to all the graphics options in every Turbo implementation without devoting a book to this topic.

This chapter discusses only those commands included in all Turbo implementations, with a few observations on one IBM-specific feature, Turtlegraphics. Features that rely on optional hardware are summarized in tables for easy reference by those who have the required hardware. CompuServe and many bulletin boards around the country offer many excellent programs using the full range of Turbo graphics options. If you have a computer equipped for color and graphics, these bulletin boards are an excellent source for fascinating programs you can modify for your own applications.

Sound

Turbo can sound the computer beeper by writing a Control-G (ASCII #7) character to the screen. Sound is useful for alerting an operator when a long task has been accomplished, such as a lengthy alphabetization, or when an error has occurred. For an example of this technique, look at the last few lines of the program listed in Figure 4.38 and you will see the line:

WRITELN (#7,'* * * Invalid choice, please try again * * *');

Writing the ASCII #7 to the screen sounds a beep before printing the error message.

There are many times when you wish to control both the pitch and the duration of the beep. Turbo gives you complete control over both of these parameters. Of course, the internal speaker in most personal computers does not lend itself to creating great music, but it can be amusing to play with this process. There are programs on some bulletin boards that play different songs and programs that let the operator generate songs; they all use variations on the simple steps shown in Figure 5.1. This program demonstrates the process for generating tones of specific pitch and duration using three predefined Turbo procedures. The procedure SOUND accepts as an argument the desired frequency stated in Hertz. The sound is terminated by the procedure NOSOUND. The duration of the tone is determined by the DELAY procedure, which takes a duration—in milliseconds—as its argument.

The program in Figure 5.1 plays a high, middle, and low C for 0.75, 1, and 1.5 seconds respectively. Figure 5.2 shows the approximate frequencies for two octaves, rounded to the nearest integer.

Just for fun, try the program listed in Figure 5.3, which plays the first four bars of "O Canada!" It uses two simple procedures, called Play and Anthem, and a table of constants to streamline the somewhat tedious process of generating a series of notes. The pitch and the duration of the notes (quarter, half, three-quarter, and whole notes) are stored in a table of constants, a technique chosen both to save typing and to make the program's operation more obvious. To save repeated typing of the SOUND/DELAY/NOSOUND sequence, these steps are put into a very simple procedure—Play— to which the calling procedure merely passes the identifier (A, B, C, and so on) for a note pitch and the identifier for a note duration (Q for quarter note, H for half note, and so on).

Control of the Screen Display

Turbo offers several straightforward procedures and functions to control the screen display; they are particularly useful in making the user interface of your programs more inviting. Figure 5.4 shows the screen-manipulation tools available in all releases of Turbo. Most of the features are self-explanatory.

GOTOXY has already been explained as a technique to print output anywhere on the screen. NORMVIDEO, LOWVIDEO, and

```
PROGRAM DemoSound;

BEGIN
    WRITELN ('High C');
    SOUND (523);
    DELAY (750);
    NOSOUND;
    WRITELN ('MIDDLE C');
    SOUND (262);
    DELAY (1000);
    NOSOUND;
    WRITELN ('Low C');
    SOUND (131);
    DELAY (1500);
    NOSOUND
END.
```

Figure 5.1 – Short program to play three musical notes.

HIGHVIDEO are used to make lines on the screen appear in bold, normal, or dim video (if available on your computer). Each video mode remains in effect until superseded by another command. Advanced programmers can use Turbo's terminal-installation program to define the video attribute associated with each command. One could, conceivably, make LOWVIDEO blink the screen or even make all characters disappear. This procedure is covered in the Borland documentation.

DELLINE, INSLINE, CLREOL, and CLRSCR operate exactly as

All frequencies are rounded to the nearest integer and are expressed in Hertz.

Low C	131
C#	139
D	147
D#	156
E	165
F	175
F#	185
G	196
G#	208
A	220
A#	231
B	247
Mid C	262
C#	277
D	294
D#	311
E	330
F	350
F#	370
G	392
G#	415
A	440 (exactly)
A#	466
B	494
C	523

Figure 5.2 – Approximate frequencies for two octaves.

described in Figure 5.4. Many of the programs throughout this book make liberal use of the clear-screen procedure, CLRSCR. Versions 1 and 2 of Turbo Pascal automatically clear the screen at the beginning of every program. Because many users objected to this, Borland modified the program so that version 3 no longer does this initial automatic CLRSCR. If you want your program to begin with a cleared screen (and the cursor positioned in the upper-left corner), you have to invoke this procedure in your program.

CRTINIT and CRTEXIT are normally issued automatically by Turbo and are used rarely within a program. They serve as safety valves in

```
PROGRAM OCanada;
CONST
  Q = 300;  {Quarter-note.}
  H = 600;  {Half-note.}
  T = 900;
  W = 1200;

  C = 262;  {Portion of scale.}
  D = 294;
  E = 330;
  F = 350;
  G = 392;
  A = 440;

PROCEDURE Play (Note, Time : INTEGER);
BEGIN
    SOUND (Note);
    DELAY (Time);
    NOSOUND;
END;

PROCEDURE Anthem;
BEGIN
    Play (E, H);   {Plays E for half-note duration.}
    Play (G, H);
    Play (G, Q);   {Plays G for quarter-note duration.}
    Play (C, T);
    Play (D, Q);
    Play (E, Q);
    Play (F, Q);
    Play (G, Q);
    Play (A, Q);
    Play (D, W);
END;

BEGIN
  Anthem;
END.
```

Figure 5.3 – Program using constants and procedure to play "O Canada!"

In this table the following abbreviations are used:

I	integer
V	any variable
VAL	either a character or byte data type

Procedure	Purpose
CLREOL	Clears all screen characters from cursor position to the end of the current line, without changing the cursor position.
CLRSCR	Clears the screen and then repositions the cursor to the upper-left corner of the screen. Works only in text-display, not in graphics, mode.
CRTINIT	Sends the terminal initialization string to the screen. Used very rarely.
CRTEXIT	Sends the terminal reset string to the screen. Used very rarely.
DELLINE	Deletes the line upon which the cursor is positioned. Moves all lines below the cursor position up one linespace.
FILLCHAR (*V, I, VAL*)	Fills *I* bytes of memory starting with the first byte of variable *V*. *VAL* (either a character or byte data type) defines the value that will be used to fill the bytes. Primarily used to initialize "image planes" for graphics, but can also be used to initialize data structures.
GOTOXY (*X, Y*)	Moves the cursor to the screen coordinates *X, Y*. *X* is a horizontal position and *Y* is a vertical position. Both are integer values measured from the upper-left corner of the screen.
HIGHVIDEO	Sets screen display for high video as defined in terminal-installation procedure (usually bold).
INSLINE	Inserts a blank line at the cursor position.
LOWVIDEO	Sets screen display for low video as defined in terminal-installation procedure.
MOVE (*V1, V2, I*)	Does a block copy within memory of *I* bytes, beginning with the first byte of variable *V1* and moving them to the portion of memory beginning with the first byte of variable *V2*. Primarily used to swap screen images for high-speed graphics (image planes).
NORMVIDEO	Screen display is set for normal video as defined in terminal-installation procedure.

Figure 5.4 – Standard procedures and functions in Turbo Pascal for screen manipulation.

debugging complex graphics programs—particularly programs that can direct output to either a monochrome or a color monitor—to reset the graphics monitor (giving you a fresh start) without having to start the entire program over again.

FILLCHAR and MOVE are used primarily in connection with advanced techniques of memory addressing.

IBM PC Graphics

The majority of Turbo's other graphics features are supported only on the IBM PC and some of its highly compatible clones.

Capabilities unique to the IBM PC include the creation of screen windows (not available on version 1), extensive high-resolution graphics for drawing and plotting curved and straight lines, manipulation of foreground and background colors, and determination of the current cursor position. By including a special external file of graphics procedures, you can get an even more extensive collection of graphics functions and an implementation of Turtlegraphics. All of the IBM PC-specific capabilities are summarized in Figure 5.5.

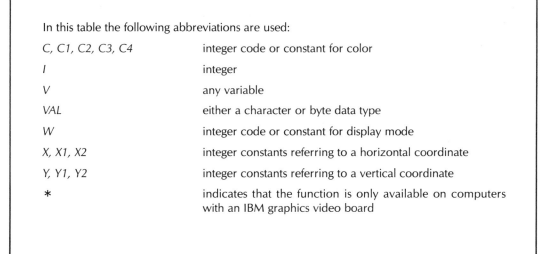

In this table the following abbreviations are used:

C, C1, C2, C3, C4	integer code or constant for color
I	integer
V	any variable
VAL	either a character or byte data type
W	integer code or constant for display mode
X, X1, X2	integer constants referring to a horizontal coordinate
Y, Y1, Y2	integer constants referring to a vertical coordinate
*	indicates that the function is only available on computers with an IBM graphics video board

***Figure 5.5** – Graphics procedures and functions in Turbo Pascal available only for the IBM PC and some compatibles (continues).*

Color and display mode controls:

TEXTCOLOR (C)   Selects color for character display depending on the value of C. C can be either the integer code or the predefined constant (that is, the color name) associated with that code in the color table. The integer codes and predefined constants for colors are:

Integer	Constant
0	Black
1	Blue
2	Green
3	Cyan
4	Red
5	Magenta
6	Brown
7	LightGray
8	DarkGray
9	LightBlue
10	LightGreen
11	LightCyan
12	LightRed
13	LightMagenta
14	Yellow
15	White
16	Blink (add 16 to any other constant to make it blink)

TEXTBACKGROUND (C)   Selects background color depending on the value of C. C can take on only the values 0–8 from the color table.

TEXTMODE (W)   Sets screen display to 25 lines of depth and either 40 or 80 characters of width, depending on the value of W. W can be either the integer code or the predefined constant from the list below.

Figure 5.5 – *Graphics procedures and functions in Turbo Pascal available only for the IBM PC and some compatibles (continues).*

Integer codes and constants for monochrome display widths:

Width	Integer	Constant
40 characters	0	BW40
80 characters	2	BW80

Integer codes and constants for color display widths:

Width	Integer	Constant
40 characters	1	C40
80 characters	3	C80

Graphics and Windows

∗CLEARSCREEN

Clears the active window in graphics mode and in Turtle-graphics. (Use CLRSCR in text mode.)

∗DRAW
(X1, Y1, X2, X2, C)

Draws a line in the color designated by *C*, between the points defined by the pairs of coordinates *X1, Y1* and *X2, Y2*.

∗GRAPHCOLORMODE

Sets display for 320 × 200 resolution color graphics. Clears the screen in the graphics mode. All colors in the color table are available.

∗GRAPHBACKGROUND
(C)

Selects background color in graphics mode depending on the value of *C*. *C* can be either the integer code or the predefined constant from the color table.

∗GRAPHWINDOW
(X1, Y1, X2, Y2)

In any graphics mode, defines the active portion of the screen for all text and graphics display. Unlike the coordinates for text windows, coordinates for graphic windows are for dots, not characters (e.g., 640 is the maximum *X* coordinate in high-resolution graphics). *X1, Y1* are the coordinates of the upper-left corner of the window, and *X2, Y2* are the coordinates of its lower-right corner.

Figure 5.5 – Graphics procedures and functions in Turbo Pascal available only for the IBM PC and some compatibles (continues).

*GRAPHMODE	Sets display for 320 × 200 resolution monochrome graphics. Clears the screen in the graphics mode. With an RGB color monitor, supports the limited selection of colors described under the PALETTE procedure.
*HIRES	Sets display for 640 × 200 graphics (high resolution) using black and one additional color. Clears the screen in the graphics mode. Background color is always black, but drawing color can be selected from the color table using the HIRESCOLOR procedure.
*HIRESCOLOR (C)	Selects drawing color in high-resolution graphics mode depending on the value of C. C can be either the integer code or the predefined constant from the color table.
*PALETTE (C)	Selects one of the four standard color palettes depending on the value of C. Each palette is defined as containing three colors plus the background color as defined in the palette table. When using an RGB Monitor after invoking GRAPHMODE (which is ordinarily used with monochrome monitors), C determines the palette from the limited palette table.

Integer codes to access full-range predefined palettes.

COLOR:	0	1	2	3
PALETTE				
0	Background	Green	Red	Brown
1	Background	Cyan	Magenta	LightGray
2	Background	LightGreen	LightRed	Yellow
3	Background	LightCyan	LightMagenta	White

Integer codes to access limited-range predefined palettes when using an RGB monitor in black and white graphics mode.

COLOR:	0	1	2	3
PALETTE				
0	Background	Blue	Red	LightGray
1	Background	LightBlue	LightRed	White

Figure 5.5 – Graphics procedures and functions in Turbo Pascal available only for the IBM PC and some compatibles (continues).

*PLOT (X, Y, C)	Plots a single point on the screen at the coordinates indicated by *X* and *Y*, in the color designated by *C*.
WHEREX	Function; returns the *X* coordinate of the cursor position. Result is always an integer. Does not require graphics board.
WHEREY	Function; returns the *Y* coordinate of the cursor position. Result is always an integer. Does not require graphics board.
WINDOW (X1, Y1, X2, Y2)	In text mode only, defines the active portion of the screen in which all text will be displayed. *X1, Y1* are the coordinates of the upper-left corner of the window, and *X2, Y2* are the coordinates of the lower-right corner of the window. Does not require graphics board.

Extended Graphics (Requires the use of include file Graph.P, which contains the definitions for the assembly-language routines stored in file Graph.Bin.) All operations require a graphics card.

| ARC (X, Y, ANG, RAD, C) | Draws an arc from the starting point described by coordinates *X* and *Y* and of a radius specified by *RAD*. The angle is determined by the value of *ANG*. A positive value generates clockwise rotation from the starting point, and a negative angle generates counterclockwise rotation. *C* determines the color (0–3) from the color palette currently in effect. A value of − 1 for C accesses a color from the color translation table specified by the COLORTABLE procedure. All parameters must be integers. |
| CIRCLE (X, Y, RAD, C) | Draws a circle from the starting point described by coordinates *X* and *Y* and of a radius specified by *RAD*. *C* determines the color (0–3) from the color palette currently in effect. All parameters must be integers. A value of − 1 for C accesses a color from the color translation table specified by the COLORTABLE procedure. This procedure draws an ellipse rather than a circle when used in the 320 × 200 low-resolution graphics mode. |

Figure 5.5 – Graphics procedures and functions in Turbo Pascal available only for the IBM PC and some compatibles (continues).

COLORTABLE (C1, C2, C3, C4)	Used in conjunction with the PALETTE procedure to define an alternative palette, or translation table. Each color code in the palette is assigned a second color (from the same palette), and when a given point on the screen is written again, its current color code determines the new color. Current color 0 in the palette will be converted to the color defined by C1, current color 1 will be converted to the color defined by C2, etc.
FILLPATTERN (X, Y, X2, Y2, C)	Fills a rectangular area defined by the coordinates X1, Y1 (upper-left corner) and X2, Y2 (lower-right corner) with the pattern defined by the PATTERN procedure. C specifies the color of the bits whose value is 1 (see PATTERN).
FILLSCREEN (C)	Fills the active screen window with the color C from the currently selected color palette.
FILLSHAPE (X, Y, C1, C2)	Fills an area of any shape with the color specified by C1. The area to be filled is the closed shape that contains the "sample" spot designated by the coordinates X and Y and is surrounded by color C2. Both C1 and C2 are values from the currently selected color palette.
GETDOTCOLOR (X, Y)	Function; returns the integer color code for the dot at screen coordinates X and Y. The integer value returned will be from the color table or the current color palette, or will be − 1 if the dot is outside the currently defined window.
GETPIC (V, X1, Y1, X2, Y2)	A rectangular area defined by the coordinates X1, Y1 (upper-left corner) and X2, Y2 (lower-right corner) is copied into a variable V.
PATTERN (DESIGN)	Defines the pattern to be used by the FILLPATTERN procedure. DESIGN is an identifier for an 8 × 8 array of data type byte. The sequence of binary digits 1 and 0 in each byte determines the pattern of bits that will be displayed in color C by the FILLPATTERN procedure.
PUTPIC (V, X, Y)	Reverses process of GETPIC, copies a graphics image from a variable V into a screen area whose lower-left corner is defined by the coordinates X and Y.

Figure 5.5 – Graphics procedures and functions in Turbo Pascal available only for the IBM PC and some compatibles (continues).

Turtlegraphics. Requires the use of include file Graph.P, which contains the definitions for the assembly-language routines stored in file Graph.Bin. All Turtlegraphics commands require a graphics board. Unlike X and Y coordinates in all other Turbo graphics modes, which are relative to the upper-left corner of the screen, all Turtlegraphics coordinates are relative to the center of the screen. X coordinates above this point are positive; those below this point are negative. Similarly, Y coordinates to the right of this point are positive; those to the left are negative. Coordinates are stated in dots (e.g., plus or minus 320 would be the maximum X coordinate using a 640 × 200 dot display mode).

BACK (*I*)	Moves turtle *I* dots in the direction opposite to its current heading. Draws a line corresponding to this movement.
CLEARSCREEN	Clears the active window and returns turtle to the home position (0,0).
FORWARD (*I*)	Moves turtle *I* dots in the direction it is currently heading. Draws a line corresponding to this movement.
HEADING	Function; returns direction in which the turtle is heading. The value returned is always an integer in the range 0 to 359, corresponding to the degrees in a circle. Predefined constants are NORTH (0), EAST (90), SOUTH (180), and WEST (270).
HIDETURTLE	"Hides" the turtle so that it is no longer displayed on the screen.
HOME	Locates turtle in the home position (0,0) and resets HEADING to 0.
NOWRAP	Disables screen wrapping (see WRAP). This is the default condition.
PENDOWN	Initiates plotting of lines corresponding to turtle movement. Default condition.
PENUP	Disables plotting of lines corresponding to turtle movement.
SETHEADING (*I*)	Sets the heading for turtle movement. *I* is an integer and is described under HEADING.

Figure 5.5 – Graphics procedures and functions in Turbo Pascal available only for the IBM PC and some compatibles (continues).

SETPENCOLOR (C)	Selects color to be used in drawing lines corresponding with turtle movement. C selects a color from the color palette.
SETPOSITION (X, Y)	Jumps turtle to the point described by the coordinates X and Y. If you are in the PENDOWN mode, no line will be plotted for this jump.
SHOWTURTLE	Displays turtle position. Because the turtle is hidden at the beginning of a program, SHOWTURTLE must be invoked at the beginning of each session. The turtle is displayed as a triangle.
TURNLEFT (I)	Alters the heading by I units. Positive values turn left; negative values turn right.
TURNRIGHT (I)	Alters the heading by I units. Positive values turn right; negative values turn left.
TURTLETHERE	Returns Boolean TRUE if the turtle is visible anywhere within the current Turtlewindow.
TURTLEWINDOW (X, Y, WIDTH, HEIGHT)	Defines the active screen window for Turtlegraphics. X and Y are the coordinates of the center of the Turtlegraphics window. WIDTH and HEIGHT are integer values defining the width and height of the rectangular window.
XCOR	Returns the integer value of the X coordinate of the turtle's current position (whether visible or hidden).
YCOR	Returns the integer value of the Y coordinate of the turtle's current position (whether visible or hidden).
WRAP	Enables "wrapping" of turtle movement. As the turtle moves beyond the edge of the active window, wrapping makes the turtle (and the line it draws) reappear at the opposite edge.

Figure 5.5 – Graphics procedures and functions in Turbo Pascal available only for the IBM PC and some compatibles (continued).

As noted in Figure 5.5, to exploit the extended set of IBM PC graphics (including Turtlegraphics), application programs must use the compiler option:

{$I GRAPH.P}

This *include file* contains the Turbo definitions for a collection of assembly-language routines contained in another special file, called GRAPH.BIN. Include files are explained more fully in Chapter 6. Both the file GRAPH.P and the binary file GRAPH.BIN must be present on the disk when the graphics program is compiled. Once the application program is compiled, however, the compiled program is self-contained and does not need the external files.

Turtlegraphics

Among the extended graphics options available on the IBM PC through the include file called GRAPH.P is an implementation of Turtlegraphics. This program is a series of procedures for plotting graphics, intended for users unfamiliar with the usual algebraic and Cartesian orientation of most computer graphics software. The goal of Turtlegraphics is primarily to promote computer literacy through a seductively comfortable user interface. Turtlegraphics is fun, particularly for children.

Unlike other graphics schemes, which are based on the Cartesian concept of two separate displacement values (X and Y) measured from the upper-left corner of the screen, Turtlegraphics plot movement in any direction from the center of the screen. Lines are created by giving an imaginary turtle (represented by a small triangle on the screen) a series of movement instructions. In the interest of user-friendliness, most commands are ordinary English words. Each instruction tells the turtle what direction to move and what distance to cover. To those with formal math training, the parallels with vector theory will be apparent. In fact, Turtlegraphics might be more appropriately discussed in a tutorial on vector-oriented CAD/CAM (computer assisted design/computer assisted manufacturing) systems than one on Turbo. It is not, however, particularly useful for serious programming and is peripheral to the main goal of this book: enabling readers to write useful programs in Turbo Pascal as quickly as possible.

Advanced Features

Chapter 6

Compiler Options

Every Pascal compiler differs from every other compiler; some operations and options vary dramatically. The implementation-specific chapters of the Turbo *Reference Manual* are the only source of information on Turbo's compiler operation. That is unfortunate, because there are several powerful, but almost unknown, debugging capabilities available to the programmer simply by choosing various options. Even many advanced Turbo programmers ignore these options because so much of the information is buried in the documentation or must be gleaned entirely by trial and error.

The Turbo compiler is the heart of Turbo Pascal. Borland has crammed an unbelievably fast and powerful compiler into less than 40 kilobytes of memory. Its speed and capability are absolutely unprecedented and are already being held up as a standard of performance for other compilers.

Borland has done several things to make the compiler fast. We have already discussed the fact that programs are edited, run, and debugged entirely in RAM memory. We have also seen that Turbo has streamlined the compilation process by not generating listings and cross-reference tables. Yet another way in which Borland has improved the speed of its compiler (and each version of Turbo seems to be faster than the preceding one) is by a set of compilation conditions chosen for optimum day-in, day-out performance. For the majority of the programs you are likely to write, the Turbo compiler is preset for optimum speed. You do not normally have to choose any compiler options before running a program in the Turbo environment. You simply type the keystroke R to request the compile-and-run option of the Turbo editor. And to make a .COM or .CMD file, you merely have to ask for the C option before compiling the program.

Turbo offers many options in the compilation process, which you can choose when you need them. Most of the options are tools to help in program debugging. Generally they slow down program execution—sometimes drastically—to check for errors. When a program has been debugged, you can recompile it with these speed-reducing diagnostic processes turned off.

Other compiler options are like the 78 RPM switch on some stereo record players. All LP records today operate at 33 RPM, so most of us use this setting almost exclusively, with perhaps the odd single or children's record played at 45 RPM. It would be silly to have a turntable that required you to set the speed at 33 RPM before playing each and every LP record. Many people might never use any other setting for years. But suppose you came across a box of rare, old 78 RPM records in the attic or at a flea market—you would certainly want the option of setting your turntable to 78 RPM in order to play them. Changing the speed of the turntable to an infrequently needed setting is directly analogous to several of the once-in-a-blue-moon compiler options. When you need them, you really need them.

Unlike Turbo, most Pascal compilers require you to answer a series of questions for every compilation. Many also require that you manually initiate two separate processes for each compilation. The process is tedious, especially when you recall that for every misplaced semicolon in the program, you have to repeat the entire process. This is certainly more of a nuisance than resetting your stereo for 33 RPM before playing every record, but it was the state of the art until Turbo came along.

Turbo compiler options, then, fall into two main categories: diagnostic options to help in debugging programs and support for unusual conditions. Figure 6.1 lists every directive available from the Turbo compiler. It also lists the default conditions for all options. By *default,* we mean the value the compiler assumes for any directive if you do not specifically request a value. Remember that Borland has chosen these default values to produce the fastest program, so you should not override a default without a good reason.

All compiler options are set with compiler directives—comment lines within programs, whose unique syntax tells Turbo they are not really comments, but commands to the compiler. Compiler directives all begin with the dollar sign ($). Most are simple one-character codes with a plus (+) to enable an option or a minus (−) to disable it. In addition, most of them can be turned on and off throughout a program. However, a few (such as B, C, and U) must apply to the entire program. The point is not made clear in the documentation, but these options either do not work at all or work erratically unless they are invoked in the first line following the program header.

Several compiler options merit individual explanations.

Default I/O devices (B) Normally, the standard files INPUT and OUTPUT are associated with the console logical device (CON:), with full buffering and screen echo. When disabled (B−), these files are associated with the terminal logical device (TRM:). Recall that the terminal device does not buffer keystrokes and suppresses the screen echo of most control (but not text) characters. This option cannot be altered within a program once it has been set.

Keyboard control during program execution (C and U) During program execution, the default setting of the C option (C+) allows you to suspend screen output by typing Control-S and continue output with another Control-S. This option is useful when a program prints output faster than you can read it. Similarly, typing Control-C will abort the program—another handy feature for stopping a program in a loop or for stopping a long printout after you have found the information you needed. When it is disabled (C−), neither Control-C nor Control-S have any effect on the program. By default, the C option is enabled. The U option has no effect on the operation of Control-S, but when U is enabled (U+) a Control-C will abort the program. The default condition for C allows the operation of Control-C, while the default condition for U does not. The net effect

CODE	DEFAULT	DESCRIPTION
B	B+	**Default I/O devices** Selects logical devices to be associated with standard files INPUT and OUTPUT. B+ uses CON: and B− uses TRM:.
C	C+	**Keyboard control during program execution** C+ allows Control-C to abort a running program and Control-S to toggle output to the screen. C− instructs Turbo to ignore these sequences.
I	I+	**I/O error checking** Checks all I/O for errors and generates the relevant Turbo (not operating system) error message. I− ignores errors.
I	none	**Include external file during program execution** The I directive followed by a file name (e.g., {$I LIBRARY.PAS}) will merge the named file with the current file, forming a compiled program including every line of both programs.
R	R−	**Range checking on array indices and scalars** When active (R+), checks that all array indices and scalar values are within their declared bounds.
U	U−	**Keyboard control during program execution** U+ allows Control-C to interrupt a running program at any time. Unlike the C option, it has no effect on Control-S.
V	V+	**Length checking of strings passed as variable parameters** Checks to make sure that strings passed as variable (VAR) parameters are exactly the same length as those defined within the called procedure.

Figure 6.1 – Compiler directives and options available on all versions of Turbo Pascal.

of these contradictory defaults is that Control-C will abort a program. By using the two options together, however, you can get three different possible operating conditions:

C+,U−   Default condition, both Control-S and Control-C will control program.

C−,U−   Neither Control-S nor Control-C have any effect.

C−,U+   Control-S will have no effect on operation, but Control-C will abort the program.

U and C cannot be altered within a program once they have been set. Disabling this option causes a negligible increase in program speed, because Turbo does not have to check for keyboard activity.

I/O error checking (I+ and I−)   All I/O operations are checked by Turbo for errors. When an error is encountered, the program is aborted and the appropriate I/O error message is generated. In advanced programming, you can disable (I−) this automatic error checking to prevent a program from aborting because of an error. If you choose to disable this option, your program should have an error-handling routine (using the standard function IORESULT) to analyze errors and prompt for remedial action from the user. Disabling the option without a substitute error-handler can result in unpredictable program operation and can crash the operating system as well. In programs written by expert Turbo programmers, you may see error checking disabled for a few lines of code and then enabled again for the rest of the program. This technique can be handy for avoiding certain trivial I/O errors, but you have to know what you are doing before attempting it.

Include external file during program execution (I with a file name)   The I directive within a program (called the *working* program by the Turbo editor) instructs the Turbo compiler to open the indicated file and insert its contents into the compiled version of the working program. Once the working program is compiled, it includes every line of the include file and does not need the include file for any further operation. There is no limit to the number of files that can be included in one calling program. As a result, this becomes the most common way to access several libraries of procedures and functions for special applications.

There are two bugs in the include directive. The TLIST program will print an error message, and will not print out the contents of an include file, if you use the standard syntax:

{$I LIBRARY.PAS}

However, the problem disappears and TLIST will print both the main and included files if you omit the space before the file name, as shown below:

{$ILIBRARY.PAS}

In some versions of Turbo, to function reliably, the name of the file to be included must be at least eight characters long or must have a file extension. Trying to include a file using the following syntax will not work:

{$I TAB}

However, adding a file extension to this file name will work:

{$I TAB.XXX}

Include files are normally just collections of declarations, procedures, and functions. They cannot be complete programs. If you try to include a complete program into another file, Turbo will see two BEGIN/END pairs and will generate an error message. Thus, include files are never compiled independently, but only stored on disk. To aid in debugging, most include files contain a short "stub" program that calls the functions and procedures to test their operation. When the functions have been tested, the stub is usually commented out. In that way it will not be seen by the compiler when the file is included, but can be easily reinserted if further testing is ever required. Looking ahead to the program in Figure 6.11, you'll see that the comments there indicate the lines that would be commented out of this file to convert it from a working, self-contained program into a suitable include file.

Check range on array indices and scalars (R) When active, (R+), Turbo checks all array indices to be sure each is within its declared range of values. It also checks the values assigned to scalars to make sure they are within the bounds of both the standard and user-defined limits. Index checking slows down program execution, and Borland has chosen to disable this option as a default condition. Some competitors have alleged that by disabling run-time range checking, Turbo appears fast but only by an unfair comparison with Pascals that enable range checking as the default condition. With or without range checking, Turbo is very fast. Serious programmers sometimes activate range checking while debugging programs and disable it for fastest execution of the finished program. Most casual programmers find that even with the option in its default state, Turbo does enough error checking to meet their debugging needs.

Strict length checking of strings passed as variable parameters (V)   When this option is enabled, Turbo checks to see that strings passed as variable (VAR) parameters are exactly the same length as those defined within the called procedure. In the disabled state (V −), Turbo allows the passage of strings of any length to the procedure, but the results may be unpredictable if the string is too long for the target procedure. You can minimize potential problems by writing the target procedures so that they can handle the longest possible string they might need to process (255 characters overall, 80 characters for strings based on line input, 14 for strings to hold MS DOS file identifiers, and so on).

There are several additional compiler directives depending on your computer's operating system. They are of interest primarily to programmers writing programs to do nonstandard types of I/O. They are included in the table in Figure 6.2 merely for reference.

The EXECUTE Procedure

Turbo offers two other techniques for interaction between files. The EXECUTE procedure allows one Turbo program to run another. You cannot, however, run a program that was not created by Turbo. Do not confuse the EXECUTE procedure with the concept of an include file. When you execute one program from another, the original program is replaced in memory by the second program. Both files remain independent. When the second program has completed execution, operation cannot revert to the first program because it is no longer in memory.

To demonstrate the EXECUTE procedure, compile the program in Figure 5.3 to create a .COM (or .CMD) file. On the author's development system, the compiled task is called TUNE.COM. We will modify the Shell sort program in Figure 4.1 to play "O Canada!" when the sort is completed. This example is not contrived. It grew out of the author's experience with a program to alphabetize a huge mailing list. The process could take from seven to twelve minutes, during which time I hovered around the computer waiting for the "done"

MS-DOS, PC-DOS, and CP/M-86 only:

CODE	DEFAULT	DESCRIPTION
K	K+	Checks to make sure there is sufficient room on the stack to accommodate variables used in subprograms.

MS-DOS and PC-DOS only:

G	G0	Defines file buffer for standard file INPUT.
P	P0	Defines file buffer for standard file OUTPUT.
D	D+	Performs automatic checking to determine whether an output file is a device (line printer, screen, modem, etc.) rather than a disk file. If output is directed to a device rather than a disk file, it is sent character-by-character rather than buffer-by-buffer.
F	F16	Sets the maximum number of files which may be open simultaneously.

CP/M-80 (8-bit systems) only:

A	A+	Prevents the generation of recursive code.
W	W2	Sets maximum depth of nesting WITH constructions.
X	X+	When an array is generated, selects whether the code will be optimized for speed (X+) or for minimum memory space usage (X−).

Figure 6.2 – Compiler directives and options that are specific to computer operating systems.

message. I modified the sort program to call TUNE.COM, so I would be alerted to the completion of the sort without having to constantly check the screen. Playing a tune is much more pleasant than simply sounding the PC's beeper.

A follow-up application of the EXECUTE procedure had the alphabetization program execute a separate, all-purpose spooling program to print the mailing list on gummed labels. (*Spoolers,* incidentally, are programs designed to control output to a relatively slow output device. Orginally designed to buffer output so that fast computers did not have to slow down to accommodate mechanical output devices, spoolers are most commonly used today to exploit the formatting controls of modern line printers. TLIST, used to print out Turbo listings, is a typical spooling program that controls line spacing, margins, underlining, and both line-numbering and page numbering.)

We used the EXECUTE procedure rather than simply call a spooling procedure because EXECUTE replaces the calling program with the called program in memory. Both programs were quite large and we could not have fit one omnibus program in memory at one time.

Returning to the example, modify the program from Figure 4.1 to include the three new lines shown in Figure 6.3.

You must know the name of the program to be executed, and it must be a .COM or .CMD file. The file name must be assigned to a file variable using the usual ASSIGN procedure. The straightforward syntax of the EXECUTE procedure is illustrated in Figure 6.3. You must declare a variable of the type FILE (AlertFile in the example). Next, you must ASSIGN the name of the file you want to have executed to this (TUNE.COM in the example) file variable. Finally, you must EXECUTE this file variable. You cannot test the execution of a program by another program while within the Turbo environment. The initiating program must also be compiled and run outside of Turbo for the EXECUTE procedure to work. If you compile the program in Figure 6.3 and run it from DOS (or CP/M), you will see it print out all the messages from the Shell sort program and automatically start playing "O Canada!" When the tune is over, operation will revert to the operating system and you will see its prompt. With a little imagination, you can do some interesting tricks with programs initiating other programs—perhaps even linking back to the original program.

The CHAIN Procedure

Much more complex than the EXECUTE and include-file processes is the CHAIN procedure. You have probably noticed that even the smallest Turbo program, when compiled, is over 9000 bytes long. But you have also noticed that as your Turbo .PAS file gets much longer, the length of the compiled program increases much more slowly. That is because the Turbo compiler automatically includes the Turbo run-time library. This library includes a copyright notice and the definitions for the dozens of standard identifiers and standard procedures. Once all 9000 or so bytes of this information are included in your compiled file, however, each additional procedure you write may be converted into only a few additional bytes of compiled code after Turbo converts your lengthy identifiers to simple addresses, strips out your comments, and so forth.

```
{Note: The only change to the program in Figure 4.1 are the
addition of the three lines noted.}

PROGRAM ShellSort;
{Demonstrates Shell sort of 500 random numbers.}
CONST
  MaxElement = 500;
VAR
  Nums : ARRAY[1..500] OF INTEGER;
  Temp, I, J, Pass, Gap : INTEGER;
  AlertFile : FILE;    {This line is added.}
  .
  .     {All the code in the middle of the program remains
untouched.}
  .
BEGIN
  WRITELN ('Turbo Shell sort program begins now');
  GenerateInput;
  WRITELN ('Array of ', MaxElement, ' values is all loaded and
the sort is about to begin');
  Sort;
  WRITELN ('The sort is completed. Here are the ', MaxElement, ' values
in order:');
  PrintOut;
  ASSIGN (AlertFile, 'TUNE.COM');   {This line is added.}
  EXECUTE (AlertFile);              {This line is added.}
END.
```

Figure 6.3 – Modifications to Shell sort program in Figure 4.1 to EXECUTE the program called TUNE.COM.

With the CHAIN procedure, you instruct Turbo to compile your program without including the Turbo run-time library in the compiled file. Without the library, though, the chained file cannot run by itself. However, when it is called (with the CHAIN procedure) by a program that does include the library, it will run perfectly.

Chaining, then, is a variation on the concept of the include file. Some people consider it an intermediate step between an include file, which not only cannot be run independently but cannot even be compiled, and completely independent .COM files (like TUNE.COM in the example above), which can be and are run independently.

Chaining is not always an automatic process in Turbo, and you have to make sure that the chained file fits into the amount of memory allocated for the calling program. If the chained program is smaller than the calling program, the chain process is totally automatic and works well. To demonstrate this, recompile the "O Canada!" program from Figure 5.3, but instead of choosing the C (compile) menu option, chose the H (for cHain) option. Using a source file called TUNE.PAS this produced a file called TUNE.CHN. Go back to the modified Shell sort program and change these two lines:

```
ASSIGN (AlertFile, 'TUNE.COM');    {This line is added.}
EXECUTE (AlertFile);               {This line is added.}
```

to use chain files and the CHAIN, rather than the EXECUTE command:

```
ASSIGN (AlertFile, 'TUNE.CHN');    {Uses .CHN, not .COM.}
CHAIN (AlertFile);
```

Compile the Shell sort program using the C menu option to produce a .COM file. Exit from Turbo and run the program. It should perform the sort and then play "O Canada!"

So far the operations of EXECUTE and CHAIN seem almost identical. What is the difference? Figure 6.4 is a directory excerpt showing the sizes of three different versions of the program file listed in Figure 5.3. It shows that the ASCII source file (.PAS), including all our identifiers and comments, is 516 bytes long. The command file (.COM), which includes the Turbo run-time library, is 11,459 bytes long—but remember that it is a self-contained file that can run out-side the Turbo environment. The chain file (.CHN) is clearly the smallest of all, with only 269 bytes. Yet in conjunction with another .COM file it, too, operates outside of Turbo. The file SHELL.COM (the name of the compiled Shell sort program) is 11,924 bytes long whether it uses EXECUTE or CHAIN.

It is obvious that the savings in memory, even for an unambitious program like TUNE, can be significant between an executable format (11,459 bytes) and a chainable format (269). Obviously, in memory-sensitive situations, or in applications requiring a large library of alternative modules, this memory conservation can be significant.

One chaining situation requires vigilance. As is the case with EXECUTE, the called program takes the place in memory of the calling program. This process has two phases. The code parts of the program (the instructions)—except for the Turbo run-time library, which remains in memory—are swapped. Similarly, the data parts of the program (storage for variables) are swapped—except for variables clearly intended to be global to both segments. (It is possible to pass variables between the original and the chained programs. To do this, both programs must be compiled to be the same size. Also, whatever variables are to be common to both programs must be declared in both programs, in the identical order, and before any noncommon variables are declared. When Turbo swaps the programs, if it sees two variables with the same name (one declared in each program) in the same place in memory, it will not automatically initialize the variables. Thus, whatever value is stored in a variable by the first program will be retained in memory for use by the second program.) If the initial program is larger than the chained program, there is no problem. If the chained program is larger than the calling program, the chained program will not run. When

TUNE	CHN	269
TUNE	PAS	516
TUNE	COM	11459
SHELL	COM	11924

Figure 6.4 – Directory excerpt showing length of source, chain, and command files for the program in Figure 5.3.

TUNE.CHN was compiled, the compiler displayed the information shown in Figure 6.5.

This display told us the size of the code and data segments—273 and 32 bytes, respectively. When SHELL.COM was compiled the compiler displayed the information shown in Figure 6.6.

This display told us that the size of the code and data segments for SHELL.COM were 736 and 1120 bytes respectively. Had the chain segments been larger than the SHELL segments, when we did the SHELL compilation we could have set the values of the code and data segments to values at least as large as the chain file. Whenever you choose the C option from the menu, Turbo allows you to change these values. Figure 6.7 is a copy of the screen display listing the options. If you type O or D, Turbo will prompt for a new value. The value you type must be larger than the default value (hexadecimal 2CC) of the Turbo run-time library, it must equal at least this 2CC plus the size of the chain file. Determining this value takes some awkward calculations, and the requirement is not well documented. The fact that memory is allocated in 16-byte paragraphs also complicates the process.

```
Compiling --> C:\PASCAL\TUNE.CHN
   38 lines

Code:         0011 paragraphs (    272 bytes), 0D23 paragraphs free
Data:         0002 paragraphs (     32 bytes), 0FDA paragraphs free
```

Figure 6.5 – Compiler statistics displayed after compiling TUNE.CHN.

```
Compiling --> C:\PASCAL\SHELL.COM
   67 lines

Code:         002E paragraphs (    736 bytes), 0D06 paragraphs free
Data:         0046 paragraphs (   1120 bytes), 0F96 paragraphs free
Stack/Heap:   0400 paragraphs (  16384 bytes) (minimum)
              A000 paragraphs (655360 bytes) (maximum)
```

Figure 6.6 – Compiler statistics displayed after compiling SHELL.COM.

```
                 Memory
       compile -> Com-file
                 cHn-file


       minimum cOde segment size:    0000 (max 0D34 paragraphs)
       minimum Data segment size:    0000 (max 0FDC paragraphs)
       mInimum free dynamic memory:  0400 paragraphs
       mAximum free dynamic memory:  A000 paragraphs


       Find run-time error   Quit
```

Figure 6.7 – Options displayed by Turbo compiler.

Overlays

Turbo (except for version 1) offers yet another technique for moving compiled programs in and out of memory. Just a few years ago, computer memory was vastly more expensive than programmer time. As a result, computer memory was at a premium and programmers had to devote days of programming time to the task of shoehorning complex programs into only 4K, 16K, or 32K of computer memory. To fit real computer applications into such limited memory took constant swapping of sections of the program between disk and memory. *Overlays* are portions of a computer program that are swapped between disk and memory. Until recently, it took tedious and clever programming to exploit this capability. The programmer had to know exactly what segments of the program were in memory at any time, and also had to attend to all the details of program and overlay size to prevent an overlay being accidentally written on top of some other part of the program. With overlays, the calculations were far more complex than those needed to make certain that the .COM file allocated sufficient room for the .CHN file.

Most personal computers today have at least 128K of memory, and many have as much as 512K. As a result, overlays are needed much less than ever before. With Turbo, you do not even need to consider the use of overlays until the size of your compiled program

(.COM or .CMD) exceeds 64K. As you have already seen, once space is allocated for the Turbo run-time library, the Turbo compiler is very stingy with memory, converting thousands of bytes of source code into only hundreds of bytes of compiled code.

Nonetheless, Turbo supports a system of overlays for large programs. Turbo does not require the programmer to calculate any space allocations for the overlays—Turbo does all space calculations and all overlay management automatically. Using Turbo overlays is painless.

In the .PAS source file, simply insert the reserved word OVERLAY before the reserved word PROCEDURE for each procedure you want stored as an overlay outside the main file. It is only common sense, however, to keep the most often used procedures in memory all the time, and to relegate infrequently used procedures to the overlay file, in which they will be swapped into memory only when needed.

You can add as many consecutively declared procedures as you wish to the same overlay file. If a source program contained ten procedures, you could consign the first two and last two to overlay files, and leave the fourth to the eighth in memory all the time. Turbo would put each group of consecutive procedures into separate overlays. Thus the first two procedures would become overlay file .000 and the last two procedures would become overlay file .001. The presence of any intervening nonoverlay procedures tells Turbo to close an overlay file.

When you compile the program, Turbo automatically creates the overlay file (or files). Overlay files use the same file name as the main program, but with sequential file extensions.

Figure 6.8 is a directory showing a program compiled with and without overlays. The file called MAIL.PAS is the source file for a

```
MAIL       PAS      13468
MAIL       COM      17598
MAILOVER   PAS      13508
MAILOVER   COM      16546
MAILOVER   000       1536
```

Figure 6.8 – Directory excerpt showing overlay files.

large mailing list file, similar to the one in Appendix B. It is 13,468 bytes long. When compiled without overlays, it produces a .COM file that is 17,598 bytes long. Clearly there is no need for overlays with this file, as it fits well within the Turbo maximum of 64 kilobytes. To demonstrate the use of overlays, however, we copied our source file into a file called MAILOVER.PAS and proceeded to edit it, turning the five procedures used for alphabetization into OVERLAY procedures. The edited file became 13,508 bytes long, reflecting the addition of the word OVERLAY five times. When MAILOVER was compiled, it produced two output files: MAILOVER.COM and MAILOVER.000, the latter is the overlay file. Comparing the size of the two .COM files, you can see that by using overlays we reduced the size of the MAIL.COM file by 1052 bytes. These bytes, along with some additional ones (called overhead) required by Turbo to manage the overlays, appear in the file called MAILOVER.000.

From the user's point of view, MAIL and MAILOVER operate identically. Large programs can be slowed somewhat while Turbo reads overlay files from disk. But by putting only the least-used procedures in overlays, and using RAM disks and hard disks, these delays are minimized. Turbo further allows the creation of multiple overlay files. Again, Turbo takes care of accessing the correct file when it is needed.

Accessing Operating-System Routines

The array of tools and techniques covered so far is enough to handle a wide range of programming tasks. Turbo's dazzling speed and its set of control structures, data structures, and custom-designed functions give you capabilities that exceed those of most other personal-computer-based languages.

The first five chapters of this book covered only about two-thirds of the total Turbo capability. You have to master the fundamentals of Turbo—data types, control structures, and manipulating its data structures—before you can exploit Turbo's advanced features. Moreover, many of the advanced Turbo features require a thorough understanding of your computer's operating system and access to the computer manufacturer's documentation. Topics such as direct memory addressing and manipulation, BIOS and BDOS calls, interrupt handling, port addressing, and bit manipulation all require computer-specific knowledge and a healthy inclination toward experimentation. These capabilities are extraordinarily powerful, but their power requires a strong caveat. A little bit of knowledge in this area can be dangerous.

For many programmers who still bear the scars of their experience with assembly-language programming, one of the attractions of Turbo is that it offers speed and power without forcing them to immerse themselves in these arcane, computer-specific studies. They appreciate the fact that you can write powerful programs without having to care about low-level computer manipulation.

It would be impossible (and dangerous) for this book to do anything more than catalog these additional features. It will, however, demonstrate some of the most useful (and least risky) hooks into the computer's operating system, and point you in the right direction for further exploration. CompuServe and many bulletin boards abound with example programs for further exploration.

BIOS, BDOS, and INTR

All four of the common PC-oriented operating systems (MS-DOS, PC-DOS, CP/M and CP/M-86) are similar in philosophy and operation, although the syntax of parallel functions differs between them. One thing they have in common is a collection of operating-system routines to perform a wide range of basic functions, all of which are available to the assembly-language programmer. Now they are available to the Turbo programmer as well. These routines are lumped into two categories: BIOS (basic input and output system) routines and BDOS (basic disk operating system) routines. There is no rigid division between the two, but together they control—and give access to—every facet of the computer's operation, including elementary character I/O with the disk, CPU, and communication ports, error handling and time keeping, and even making the screen blink.

To use these capabilities, you need the documentation supplied with your computer's operating system and a good understanding of the internal operation of the computer. If terms like *register, status flag, file-attribute table, interrupt,* and *vector* are unfamiliar to you, go no further. But, if you are familiar with these terms and your operating system, read on.

Figure 6.9 summarizes the assortment of procedures available with MS-DOS, PC-DOS, CP/M, and CP/M-86. In most cases the operation is similar. You create a record consisting of variables that will contain the values stored in each of the relevant computer registers. In some cases, you load critical values into the particular registers; in other cases you merely read the values returned in these registers; and in some cases you do both. Generally, the record is passed as a parameter, along with an integer that refers to a system interrupt number or function call number. The chart in Figure 6.9 lists the specific syntax and definition of each procedure. Just by glancing at the table, you can see that Turbo offers truly painless hooks into the operating system for those familiar with operating-system function calls.

Turbo does not offer commands to fetch and print the system date or time similar to Microsoft BASIC's DATE$ and TIME$ commands. However, all four of the operating systems mentioned can provide this information as a standard BDOS function. Figure 6.10 shows a short but thoroughly commented program, which creates a function called Date. This function will fetch the date from MS DOS and convert it from DOS's internal format into a form that can be printed and manipulated easily in a Turbo program. This program, incidentally, is one I use frequently and store in a library include file, along with a refined version of the Tab procedure from Chapter 3.

The function called Date uses the Turbo interrupt procedure INTR. The syntax of this procedure calls for two parameters: an interrupt number and the name of a record from which DOS can load values into registers and into which DOS can return values to Turbo. The program uses a record called RegisterRecord for this purpose. In MS-DOS, interrupt 21 (hex) is the "door" through which 45 different functions can be performed, based on initial values loaded into different registers. In addition, values between 24 and 26 (hex) give access to additional functions to intercept the DOS error handler, and to perform absolute disk reads and writes. Needless to say, using these interrupts can lead to catastrophic results.

Among the functions accessed by interrupt 21 are four safe and useful functions—function 2A (hex) gets the system date, and function 2C (hex) gets the time. Similarly, functions 2B and 2D set the

In this table the following abbreviations are used:

FUNC	operating system BIOS or BDOS function number
I	integer
X	special value explained below

Procedures and functions used only with CP/M or CP/M-86:

BDOS (*FUNC, I*)	Procedure; invokes the CP/M BDOS call indicated by the integer *FUNC*. *I* is an optional integer value loaded into the DE registers prior to the call. A call to address 5 invokes this procedure.
BDOS	Function; returns the integer value loaded into the A register by the CP/M BDOS invoked with the BDOS or BDOSHL procedures.
BDOSHL (*FUNC, I*)	Procedure; invokes the CP/M BDOS call indicated by the integer *FUNC*. *I* is an optional integer value loaded into the HL registers prior to the call. A call to address 5 invokes this procedure.
BDOS (*X*)	Function; performs a CP/M-86 BDOS call. *X* is a record made up of the values to be loaded into the relevant system registers. Results of the call (changed flags and register values) are returned in the same record. Note that the desired BDOS function code is included in register pair CL and not as a separate parameter (as is the case with an MS-DOS call).
BIOS (*FUNC, I*)	Procedure; invokes the CP/M BIOS call indicated by the integer *FUNC*. *I* is an optional integer value loaded into the BC registers prior to the call.
BIOS	Function; returns the integer value loaded into the A register by the CP/M BIOS invoked with the BIOS or BIOSHL procedures.
BIOSHL (*FUNC, I*)	Procedure; invokes the CP/M BIOS call indicated by the integer *FUNC*. *I* is an optional integer value loaded into the HL registers prior to the call.

Figure 6.9 – Standard procedures and functions in Turbo Pascal for access to BIOS and BDOS operating-system routines (continues).

Functions used only with MS-DOS and PC-DOS:

INTR (*I, X*)   Makes software interrupt number *I* once it has loaded values into (or initialized) the system registers. *X* is a record made up of the values to be loaded into all the registers and flags.

MSDOS (*X*)   Performs DOS system call. *X* is a record made up of the values to be loaded into all the registers and flags. Unlike INTR, MSDOS does not use a separate parameter to indicate the desired system call number. The call is chosen by loading a value in the appropriate register within record *X*. Most commonly, this involves loading a value in the high-order byte of the AX register; but other registers are used by some system calls.

Figure 6.9 – Standard procedures and functions in Turbo Pascal for access to BIOS and BDOS operating-system routines (continued).

date and time. DOS determines which of the 45 functions to perform based on the value loaded into the AH register. Thus, to get the date, we invoke interrupt 21 (hex) and we load a value of 2A (hex) into register AH (within the record of registers called Register-Record). DOS returns the date information by returning integer values in the following registers:

CX = Year (1980 – 2099)
DH = Month (1 – 12)
DL = Day (1 – 31)

All this information—interrupt numbers, function access numbers, and the values to be expected in individual registers—can be found in the documentation for your computer's operating system.

It is easier to use INTR than to explain it. The two lines of code below show the mechanics of loading the date function value ($2A) into the AX register within the RegisterRecord record:

```
RegisterRecord.AX := $2A00;  {AX register includes hex 2A, the DOS
    function to get date.}
INTR ($21, RegisterRecord);  {Hex $21 is the DOS interrupt for many
    functions}
```

```
PROGRAM DateFunction; {Comment out the first 3 lines to make this
an include file.}
TYPE
  DateString = STRING[40];

FUNCTION Date: DateString; {Returns decoded date to calling
program.}
TYPE
  Registers = RECORD
              AX, BX, CX, DX, BP, SI, DS, ES, Flags : INTEGER;
            END;
VAR
  RegisterRecord :  Registers;  {This is needed for any system
call.}
  Month : STRING[8];  {Holds decoded output.}
  Day :   STRING[2];  {Holds decoded output.}
  Year :  STRING[4];  {Holds decoded output.}
  DX,CX : INTEGER;    {Holds values returned by DOS before being
decoded.}

BEGIN
  RegisterRecord.AX := $2A00; {AX register includes hex 2A: DOS
function to get date.}
  INTR ($21, RegisterRecord); {Hex $21 is the DOS interrupt for
many functions}
  WITH RegisterRecord DO
    BEGIN
      STR (CX, Year);   {Converts integer value in register CX to a
string called Year.}
      STR (LO (RegisterRecord.DX), Day); {Alternative approach to
conversion in line above.}
      CASE (HI (RegisterRecord.DX)) OF {Converts month numerical
value to appropriate string.}
        1 : Month := 'January';
        2 : Month := 'February';
        3 : Month := 'March';
        4 : Month := 'April';
        5 : Month := 'May';
        6 : Month := 'June';
        7 : Month := 'July';
        8 : Month := 'August';
        9 : Month := 'September';
       10 : Month := 'October';
       11 : Month := 'November';
       12 : Month := 'December';
    END;
  END;
  Date := Month +' ' + Day +', ' + Year; {Concatenates strings
into familiar format.}
END;
BEGIN     {This program stub exercises the function. Comment it
out to make this program an include file.}
  WRITELN (Date);
END.
```

Figure 6.10 – Program to fetch, decode, and print date using DOS interrupt.

Two points to remember are that almost every value moving to and from the operating system is expressed in hexadecimal and that when reading or writing values that fill only one byte of the 16-bit (two-byte) register, you must be careful to read the correct byte. That is precisely why $2A was padded out to become $2A00 when loaded into the AX register.

The program converts the numeric information returned by DOS into a string, to make it easier for insertion into reports and printing on the screen. The following lines of code convert the year (an integer value stored in both bytes of the CX register) into a string, then convert the date (stored in the low-order byte of the DX register) into a string, and finally convert the month (stored in the high-order byte of the DX register) into a string spelling out the name of the month.

```
WITH RegisterRecord DO
BEGIN
    STR (CX, Year);    {Converts integer value in CX register to a string
called Year.}
    STR (LO (RegisterRecord.DX), Day);    {Alternative approach to con-
version in line above.}
    CASE (HI (RegisterRecord.DX)) OF    {Converts month numerical
value to appropriate string.}
        1: Month : = 'January';
        2: Month : = 'February';
        3: Month : = 'March';
        4: Month : = 'April';
        5: Month : = 'May';
        6: Month : = 'June';
        7: Month : = 'July';
        8: Month : = 'August';
        9: Month : = 'September';
        10: Month : = 'October';
        11: Month : = 'November';
        12: Month : = 'December';
    END;
END;
```

Once you understand how the INTR function works, the operation of all the functions listed in Figure 6.9 should just be variations on the same principles. Figure 6.11 shows the application of the

```
PROGRAM ShellSortWithElapsedTimeDisplay;
  {Gets time from DOS and computes elapsed time of Shell sort.}
CONST
  MaxElement = 300;
VAR
  Nums : ARRAY[1..MaxElement] OF INTEGER;
  Temp, I, J, Pass, Gap : INTEGER;
  B, M, E : REAL;


PROCEDURE CountTheSeconds (VAR TotalTimeInHundredths : REAL);
  {Gets time from DOS and converts to a total of hundreds of
seconds.}
TYPE
  RegisterRecord = RECORD
      AX, BX, CX, DX, BP, SI, DS, ES, Flags : INTEGER;
    END;
VAR
  Regs: RegisterRecord;
  Hours, Mins, Secs, Hundredths : REAL;
BEGIN
   WITH Regs DO
   BEGIN
      AX := $2C00; {Hex 2C gets the time.}
      MSDOS (Regs);{We could just as easily have used the INTR function.}
      Hours := HI (CX);
      Mins  := LO (CX);
      Secs := HI (DX);
      Hundredths := LO (DX);
   END;
 TotalTimeInHundredths := ((18000 * Hours) * 2) + (6000 * Mins) +
(100 * Secs) + Hundredths;
END;

PROCEDURE Driver;
BEGIN
  CLRSCR;
  WRITELN ('The sort program begins operation NOW!');
  FOR I := 1 TO MaxElement DO
     BEGIN
       Nums[I] := RANDOM (5000);
     END;
END;

PROCEDURE PrintOut;
BEGIN
  FOR I := 1 TO MaxElement DO
  BEGIN
  WRITE (Nums[I]);
  WRITE ('   ');
  END;
  WRITELN; WRITELN;
END;
```

Figure 6.11 – Program to print elapsed time for Shell sort program (based on Figure 4.1) by getting system time from DOS (continues).

```
PROCEDURE FlipFlop;
BEGIN
  Temp := Nums[J];
  Nums[J] := Nums[J+Gap];
  Nums[J+Gap] := Temp;
END;

PROCEDURE Sort;
BEGIN
   Gap := MaxElement DIV 2;
   WHILE Gap > 0 DO
   BEGIN
    FOR  I := (Gap + 1) TO MaxElement DO
       BEGIN
          J := I-Gap;
          WHILE J > 0 DO
             BEGIN
               IF Nums[J] > Nums[J+Gap] THEN
               BEGIN
                 FlipFlop;
                 J := J-Gap;
               END
               ELSE J := 0;
             END;
       END;
       Gap := Gap DIV 2;
     END;
END;

BEGIN
   Driver;
   CountTheSeconds (B);
   Sort;
   CountTheSeconds (M);
   PrintOut;
   CountTheSeconds (E);
   E := (E-B)/100;
   WRITELN ('It took  ', E:3:2,' seconds total time for the
sorting and printing of ',MaxElement,' numbers.');
   M := (M-B)/100;
   WRITELN ('It took  ', M:3:2,' seconds for just the sorting (no
printing) of ',MaxElement,' numbers.');
END.
```

Figure 6.11 – *Program to print elapsed time for Shell sort program (based on Figure 4.1) by getting system time from DOS (continued).*

MSDOS function in place of the INTR. The program is another modification to the Shell sort program from Figure 4.1. In its current form, the program calculates and prints out the time it takes for the entire program to run and how much of that time is used for the Shell sort. The routine acts as a built-in stop watch, and has many other applications as well.

The program gets the system time from DOS (by loading a value of $2C in the AX register, rather than the $2A used to get the date) and converts it into the number of seconds elapsed since midnight. By getting and comparing the time at critical points within the program, we can compute elapsed time between points.

Turbo
Resources

Thanks to the great popularity of Turbo Pascal, users of this language have a wide range of resources.

Borland International

Borland must rank as one of the most responsive of all software vendors. They answer questions via phone, mail, and CompuServe promptly. They also provide a continuing series of new releases of Turbo as well as extensions for special purposes. Currently, they offer Turbo extensions for exploiting the 8087 math coprocessor and for handling binary-coded decimals. Packages of optimized subroutines for graphics, complex database management, and unusual screen installations are also offered.

Borland International, Inc.
4585 Scotts Valley Drive
Scotts Valley, CA 95066
(408) 438-8400

Turbo Users' Group

Turbo also boasts an excellent users' group, independent of Borland. Every other month, they produce a newsletter, *TUG Lines,* which ranks as one of the most impressive users' group publications available. It is a treasure trove of proven programs, bug work-arounds, new products, and interesting correspondence. It carries no advertising and is a genuinely independent source of information. The users' group also provides a clearinghouse for members to help each other. There is a nominal membership fee.

Turbo Users Group
Box 1510
Poulsbo, WA 98370

Borland SIG on CompuServe

CompuServe subscribers can join the Borland special interest group (SIG), which includes a forum and a message board to communicate not only with other users but with Borland personnel as well. There is an ever-expanding collection of programs available for downloading and experimentation. This is an invaluable source of help from other users in tackling difficult problems.

CompuServe subscribers can access the SIG by typing GO BOR at any system prompt.

CompuServe, Inc.
5000 Arlington Centre Blvd.
Box 20212
Columbus, OH 43220

Bulletin Boards

Many of the bulletin board systems catering to IBM PC and to CP/M users are including more and more Turbo programs. Several, in fact, have separate download directories dedicated exclusively to Turbo. Although any list of bulletin boards is subject to constant change, *PC World* magazine, and *Computer Living/New York* both periodically run lists of bulletin boards, and the message section of the Borland SIG on CompuServe frequently reports the number of a new bulletin board. Some computer-store staffers are also good sources for local bulletin board numbers, as are local computer clubs. Almost every bulletin board has a list of other boards, so you only have to find one to get the numbers for other active bulletin boards.

Further Reading

There is no shortage of books about Pascal and structured programming. Although this book has pointed out the idiosyncracies of Turbo Pascal, many good ideas found in other books on standard Pascal can be translated into Turbo.

Brooks, Frederick P. *The Mythical Man-Month: Essays on Software Engineering.* Reading, Mass.: Addison-Wesley, 1975.

While not a book on Pascal, this is an amusing exploration of the pitfalls of traditional programming. No other book makes quite so clear how many problems are overcome by Turbo.

Feuer, Alan R. and Gehani, Narain (editors). *Comparing and Assessing Programming Languages: Ada, C and Pascal.* Englewood Cliffs, N.J.: Prentice-Hall, 1984.

Gives a great insight into the ways in which Turbo (not even mentioned in the text, incidentally) has addressed many of the weaknesses of popular implementations of these structured languages.

Hergert, Richard and Hergert, Douglas. *Doing Business with Pascal.* Berkeley, Calif.: SYBEX, 1983.

Excellent examples of applying Pascal structures to solving real-world problems.

Knuth, Donald E. *The Art of Computer Programming. Vols. 1 and 3.* Reading, Mass.: Addison-Wesley, 1973.

Not for the casual programmer! These are the standard reference works on computer programming regardless of the programming language involved.

Ledgard, Henry and Singer, Andrew. *Elementary Pascal.* New York: Vintage, 1982.

The fundamental concepts of Pascal explained in the enjoyable context of Sherlock Holmes and Dr. Watson. This is a very readable book. It is particularly appropriate to Turbo enthusiasts because all example programs use a simplified generic dialect of Pascal.

Vile, Richard C. *Programming Your Own Adventure Games in Pascal.* Blue Ridge Summit, Penna.: TAB, 1984.

This book demonstrates innovative uses of Pascal's unique data structures to create an adventure environment. It contains a wealth of ideas that can be applied to programs other than adventure games.

Wirth, Niklaus. *Algorithms + Data Structures = Programs.* Englewood Cliffs, N.J.: Prentice-Hall, 1976.

The ultimate source for anyone studying Pascal; Wirth is the creator of the language.

Zaks, Rodnay. *Introduction to Pascal (Including UCSD Pascal).* Berkeley, Calif.: SYBEX, 1981.

As noted in the Acknowledgments, this is still the best book on Pascal in the microcomputer world.

The
Mailing-List
Program

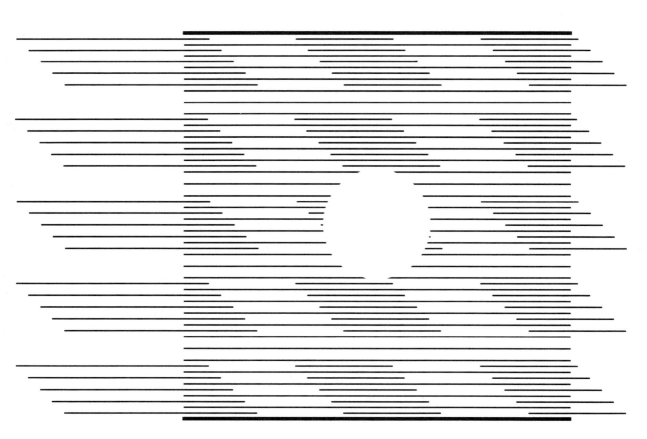

Appendix B

Following is the complete mailing-list program, portions of which have appeared (in slightly different form) in Chapter 4.

This program illustrates many of the topics covered in this book: modular structure, sorting, searching, arrays, files, records, user interaction, error trapping, an include file for common routines, and most of the common control structures. Most importantly, it demonstrates these features not in small, contrived examples, but in a working program. The program is used monthly to produce mailing labels for a small business.

Although this program is not elegant, it is an example of a good, workmanlike program that gets the job done. While no program is ever complete—there is always room for a nicer interface, better support for possible errors, and so on—the purpose of programming is to solve problems today, rather than developing the ultimate program tomorrow.

This program does not use any obscure logic or tricky algorithms, but almost always uses the simplest or most obvious programming approach, rather than one that might offer slightly more speed but with increased complexity.

The program is entirely self-documenting, with prompts telling the user what to do at each step.

```pascal
PROGRAM Mailing_List;
   {Uses inclue file called COMMON.PAS for common routines.}
CONST
  C = 'C';     {Controls tab positioning: centered, left, or right.}
  L = 'L';
  R = 'R';
TYPE
  CustomerRecord =  RECORD
       LastName  : STRING ;
       FirstName : STRING ;
       Street    : STRING ;
       Town      : STRING ;
       State     : STRING ;
       Zip       : STRING ;
     END;
  Name  = STRING ;
  Words = STRING ;

  NameAndKey = RECORD
       ZipAndName : STRING ; {Concats zip and name for sort within sort.}
       Key : INTEGER;
       END;

VAR
  InFile, OutFile : FILE OF CustomerRecord;
  Customer : CustomerRecord;
  Sort : ARRAY  of NameAndKey;
  TempHold : NameAndKey;
  Correx    : STRING ;
  SourceFile, TargetFile : STRING ;
  SirName : STRING ;
  LastName : Name;
  RecNum, Index, MaxRec, I, J : INTEGER;
  LinesDone, Option: INTEGER;
  AllFinished, Swap : BOOLEAN;
  WhatsYourPleasure : CHAR;
  Minimum, Maximum, Fetch : INTEGER;
  Delete, Found, DoAnother : BOOLEAN;

{$I Common.Pas}    {COMMON.PAS holds Tab, Date, and Canada (tune) procedures.}
```

```
PROCEDURE DisplayMenu;
{All basic program options are chosen from this menu.  After every process}
{the menu is displayed again.}
VAR
   Today : STRING ;
BEGIN
   Today := Date;     {Gets today's date to center on screen with line below.}
   Tab (Today, 80, C);
   CLRSCR;
   GOTOXY (26,2);  WRITELN ('Turbo Pascal Mailing List Program');
   WRITELN (Today);
   GOTOXY (35,5);  WRITELN ('Command Menu');
   GOTOXY (30,7);  WRITELN ('1. ACCEPT SOME NEW NAMES');
   GOTOXY (30,9);  WRITELN ('2. LOOK UP OR CHANGE AN ENTRY');
   GOTOXY (30,11); WRITELN ('3. SORT LIST ALPHABETICALLY OR BY ZIP CODE');
   GOTOXY (30,13); WRITELN ('4. PROOF LIST TO THE SCREEN');
   GOTOXY (30,15); WRITELN ('5. OUTPUT LIST TO THE ACTUAL LABELS');
   GOTOXY (30,17); WRITELN ('6. CREATE BOOK NOW OR SPOOL LISTING');
   GOTOXY (30,19); WRITE   ('7. COPY FILE ');
                   WRITELN ('OR MERGE NEW NAMES INTO MAIN LIST');
   GOTOXY (30,21); WRITELN ('8. EXIT PROGRAM');
   GOTOXY (25,23); WRITELN ('WHAT NUMBER WOULD YOU LIKE?  ');
   GOTOXY (55,23);
END;

PROCEDURE ErrorHandler;
{Could be made more elaborate.  Merely provides a graceful way to return to}
{the menu if one does not type a valid menu choice.}
BEGIN
   WRITELN ('Error Condition');
   DELAY (700);      {Enough time to read the message.}
END;

PROCEDURE CopyFile;
{Copies contents of one file to another while filtering out those records}
{that have been flagged to be deleted.  This procedure is used by other}
{procedures and does not do its own file initialization like RESET, REWRITE,}
{and ASSIGN--these tasks are done by the calling procedure.}
BEGIN
   WHILE NOT EOF (InFile) DO
   BEGIN
      READ (Infile, Customer);
      IF Customer.FirstName <> '@' THEN WRITE (OutFile, Customer);
   END;
   CLOSE (InFile);
   CLOSE (OutFile);
END;
```

```
PROCEDURE AcceptNewNames;  {Choice #1.}
{During initial entry of new names, this procedure puts the new names into}
{a temporary file for easiest proofreading and correction.  When the file}
{is correct, it prompts the user to append this list to the master list.}
VAR
    AllDone : BOOLEAN;
BEGIN
    CLRSCR;
    WRITELN ('What file should hold the new names temporarily?');
    WRITELN ('Hit enter to use  NEWNAMES.TMP ');  {Default temporary file.}
    READLN (TargetFile);
    IF TargetFile = '' THEN ASSIGN (OutFile, 'NEWNAMES.TMP')
      ELSE ASSIGN (Outfile, TargetFile);

{The following routine handles the situation in which the default temporary}
{file does not exist.  In that case the I/O error "File does not exist" would }
{abort the program.  This routine turns off error checking just for the one}
{line in which this error might occur.  If the file does exist, operation}
{continues unaffected and error checking is turned on again.  If the file}
{does not exist, the function IORESULT changes from a value of 0 to 1.}
{We test for a value other than 0.  If the error has occurred the program}
{uses REWRITE to create the file NEWNAMES.TMP.  It then turns error checking}
{back on again.}

    {$I-}   {Turn off error checking to catch if NEWNAMES.TMP does not exist.}
    RESET (Outfile);  {Try to reset file.}
    {$I+}   {Turn on error checking again.}
    IF IORESULT <> 0 THEN REWRITE (OutFile);  {Create file if necessary.}

    MaxRec := FILESIZE (OutFile);  {Determine last record number.}
    SEEK (Outfile, MaxRec);        {Put any entry at the end of the file.}
    AllDone := FALSE;              {Initialize loop to get a new name.}
    WHILE NOT AllDone DO
    BEGIN
        WITH Customer DO
        BEGIN
            WRITELN ('Type an asterisk (*) to end this input session.');
            WRITELN;
            WRITELN ('What is the customer FIRST NAME:  ');
            READLN (FirstName);
            IF FirstName <> '*' THEN
            BEGIN
                WRITELN ('What is the customer LAST NAME:  ');
                READLN (LastName);
                WRITELN ('What is the STREET ADDRESS:  ');
                READLN (Street);
                WRITELN ('What is the CITY:  ');
                READLN (Town);
                WRITELN ('What is the STATE:  ');
                READLN (State);
                WRITELN ('What is the ZIP CODE:  ');
                READLN (Zip);
                WRITE (Outfile, Customer);
            END
            ELSE AllDone := TRUE;
        END;  {END processing one complete record.}

    END;  {END loop if and only if AllDone is TRUE.}
    CLOSE (OutFile);
END;  {Procedure.}
```

```
PROCEDURE InputFromExternalFile;
{Part of choice #3, Alphabetize File.}
{Initializes for sorting either just alphabetically or primarily  by}
{ZIP code and then alphabetically by last name within each ZIP code.  This}
{procedure loads a two-dimensional array consisting of a key--the}
{concatenation of the ZIP code and last name--and the record number of that}
{entry within a disk file.  This gives the speed of an array sort with the}
{huge amount of data which can be stored in an external disk file.}
VAR
    AlphaOnly : BOOLEAN;
    AlphaOrZip : CHAR;
    Number : STRING ;
BEGIN
    CLRSCR;
    AlphaOnly := FALSE;
    WRITELN ('What file would you like to sort?  ');
    READLN (SourceFile);
    ASSIGN (InFile, SourceFile);
    WRITELN ('Sort alphabetically (A) or by zip code (Z) ?');
    READLN (AlphaOrZip);
    AlphaOrZip := UPCASE (AlphaOrZip);
    IF AlphaOrZip = 'A' THEN AlphaOnly := TRUE;
    WRITELN ('What file will contain the sorted output?' );
    READLN (TargetFile);
    ASSIGN (OutFile, TargetFile);
    RESET (InFile);
    RecNum := 0;
    WHILE NOT EOF (InFile) DO     {Loads array called SORT with keys.}
        BEGIN
            READ (Infile,Customer);
            RecNum := RecNum + 1;
            Number := Customer.Zip;

{This is a useful programming trick for a sort within a sort.  By}
{concatenating a zipcode and name the system sorts an entry like}
{06457Smith before 94211Adams, and 07011Davis before 07011Dover.}
{When we want just an alphabetical sort, ignoring ZIP codes, we}
{set the ZIP code--just in the key, not in the file record--of}
{everybody to 0.  This means that 0Adams will come before 0Smith.}

            IF AlphaOnly THEN Number := '0';
            Sort.ZipAndName := Number + Customer.LastName;
            Sort.Key := RecNum;
        END;
    MaxRec := RecNum;
    CLOSE(Infile);
END;
```

```
PROCEDURE WriteNewFile;
{Part of choice #3, Alphabetize File.}
{Once the array of keys and record numbers has been sorted, the records}
{are read in their new, correct order, and written to the output file.}
{On long files thi can take several minutes due to the relative slowness}
{of the mechanics of doing so much disking.  It still is much faster than}
{doing an entirely disk-bound sort.  The time can be halved by using a}
{RAM disk or rewriting the procedure to use pointers.}
VAR
   NameKey : NameAndKey;
BEGIN
   ASSIGN (InFile, SourceFile);
   RESET (Infile);
   ASSIGN (OutFile, TargetFile);
   REWRITE (OutFile);
   FOR I:= 1 to MaxRec DO
     BEGIN
        NameKey := Sort;
        RESET (Infile);
        SEEK (Infile, NameKey.Key-1); {READ entire record from infile.}
        READ (Infile, Customer);
        WRITE (OutFile, Customer);    {Write this record to the output file.}
     END;
   CLOSE (InFile);
   CLOSE (OutFile);
END;


PROCEDURE ByeBye;
{Part of choice #3, Alphabetize File.}
{Just alerts operator to completion of sort with a message and by calling}
{the procedure to play "O Canada".}
BEGIN
   CLRSCR;
   WRITELN ('File called ', TargetFile, ' created.');
   WRITELN ('It contains contains ',MaxRec,' names.');
   Canada; {Plays O Canada to alert that program is done sorting.}
END;


PROCEDURE FlipFlop;
{Part of choice #3, Alphabetize File.}
{Does the swap of elements within the array.  It has been extracted from}
{the larger sort routine simply to make the operation of both routines}
{clearer.}
BEGIN
   TempHold := Sort ;
   Sort  := Sort ;
   Sort  := TempHold;
   Swap  := TRUE;
END;
```

```
PROCEDURE SortProg;
{Part of choice #3, Alphabetize File.}
{Shell sort applied to the array of ZIP code-and-name records.}
VAR
   Pass, Gap : INTEGER;
BEGIN       {SortProg}
   FOR Pass := MaxRec DOWNTO 2 DO
      BEGIN
        Swap := TRUE;
        IF Swap THEN
        BEGIN              {While swap flag set.}
          I := 1;
          Swap := FALSE;
          WHILE  I < MaxRec DO
            BEGIN             {Actual swap.}
              IF Sort.ZipAndName > Sort .ZipAndName THEN FlipFlop;
              I := I+1;
            END;
        END;    {While swap flag is set.}
      END;  {FOR Pass...}
END;  {SortProg}

PROCEDURE AlphabetizeList;
{Choice #3.  Because this is such a complex operation, it has been broken up}
{into several clearly-defined procedures.}
BEGIN
   InputFromExternalFile;
   SortProg;
   WriteNewFile;
   ByeBye;
END;
```

```
PROCEDURE CorrectAName;
{Called by the TestName procedure.  Allows user to correct an existing}
{record in a disk file.  Also, by changing the first name to "@" the user}
{can flag a record to be deleted.  This is a nicely polished routine}
{which prompts the user to change just the specific items within the record}
{which are incorrect, while leaving the correct elements.  It also keeps}
{prompting for additional changes.}
BEGIN
   WITH Customer DO
   BEGIN
      WRITELN (FirstName);
      WRITELN ('Change to: ');
      READLN (Correx);
      IF Correx <> '' THEN FirstName := Correx;
      WRITELN (LastName);
      WRITELN ('Change to: ');
      READLN (Correx);
      IF Correx <> '' THEN LastName := Correx;
      WRITELN (Street);
      WRITELN ('Change to: ');
      READLN (Correx);
      IF Correx <> '' THEN Street := Correx;
      WRITELN (Town);
      WRITELN ('Change to: ');
      READLN (Correx);
      IF Correx <> '' THEN Town := Correx;
      WRITELN (State);
      WRITELN ('Change to: ');
      READLN (Correx);
      IF Correx <> '' THEN State := Correx;
      WRITELN (Zip);
      WRITELN ('Change to: ');
      READLN (Correx);
      IF Correx <> '' THEN Zip := Correx;
      SEEK (InFile, Fetch); {Nullifies automatic pointer advance.}
      WRITE (InFile, Customer);
      WRITELN ('Correct another name Y/N?  ');
      READ (KBD, WhatsYourPleasure);
      WhatsYourPleasure := UPCASE (WhatsYourPleasure);
      IF WhatsYourPleasure = 'Y' THEN
      BEGIN
         DoAnother := TRUE;
         Found := FALSE;
         CLRSCR;
         WRITELN ('What name are you looking for? ');
         READLN (SirName);
         Minimum := 0;
         Maximum := MaxRec;
         END ELSE DoAnother := FALSE;
         END;
      END;
```

```
PROCEDURE DeleteEntry;
{Part of TestName procedure. Changes first name to "@" and prompts for}
{additional records to be deleted.  When the operator says that there are}
{no more records to be deleted, this procedure sets the Delete flag to TRUE}
{and calls the CompressFile procedure to purge this file of the records}
{flagged for deletion.}
BEGIN
   Customer.FirstName := ´@´;
   SEEK (InFile, Fetch);
   WRITE (InFile, Customer);
   Delete := TRUE;
   CLRSCR;
   WRITELN (´Delete another name Y/N?  ´);
   READ (KBD, WhatsYourPleasure);
   WhatsYourPleasure := UPCASE (WhatsYourPleasure);
   IF WhatsYourPleasure = ´Y´ THEN
    BEGIN
      DoAnother := TRUE;
      Found := FALSE;
      CLRSCR;
      WRITELN (´What name are you looking for? ´);
      READLN (SirName);
      Minimum := 0;
      Maximum := MaxRec;
      END
    ELSE DoAnother := FALSE;
   END;

PROCEDURE CompressFile;
{Used by TestName procedure.  In turn, uses CopyFile to copy the file}
{while filtering out records flagged for deletion.  This procedure uses}
{the RENAME and ERASE procedures to create a temporary scratch file for}
{the copy procedure and than to give the new, compressed file, the same}
{name as the original, uncompressed file.  This is a handy technique when}
{when you need to create intermediary working files but want the operator}
{to see only the results of the operation.  In this case the input and}
{output file appears to have the same file name.}
 BEGIN
    WRITELN (´Deletion process can take several minutes.  Wait for tune.´);
    RENAME (InFile, ´@@.@@@´);
    RESET (InFile);
    ASSIGN (OutFile, ´TEST.TMP´);
    REWRITE (OutFile);
    CopyFile;
    RENAME (OutFile, SourceFile);
    ERASE (InFile);
    Canada;   {Play tune to alert that update procedure is finished.}
 END;
```

```
PROCEDURE TestName;
{Part of FindOneName procedure.  This does most of the work of the binary}
{search for one name within a large file.  This procedure calls several}
{other procedures to set up for changing and deleting entries and to handle}
{the mechanics of creating a new file without deleted records.  The actual}
{binary search has been covered in the text.}
VAR
   LastFetch : INTEGER;
BEGIN {Procedure.}
 Delete := FALSE;
 WHILE NOT Found DO
   BEGIN {NOT FOUND loop.}
      Fetch := (Minimum + Maximum) DIV 2;  {Heart of the binary search.}
      IF Fetch = LastFetch THEN  Minimum := MaxInt;
      LastFetch := Fetch;
      SEEK (InFile, Fetch);
      READ (InFile, Customer);
      IF SirName = Customer.LastName THEN
      BEGIN
         Found := TRUE;
         CLRSCR;
         GOTOXY (1,12);
         WRITELN (Customer.FirstName,´ ´, Customer.LastName);
         WRITELN (Customer.Street);
         WRITE (Customer.Town,´ ´, Customer.State);
         WRITELN (´ ´,Customer.Zip);
         WRITELN;
         WRITE (´ (L)ook up another, (D)elete entry,´);
         WRITELN (´ (C)orrect entry, (R)eturn to Menu? ´);
         READ (KBD, WhatsYourPleasure);
         WhatsYourPleasure := UPCASE (WhatsYourPleasure);
         CASE WhatsYourPleasure OF
         ´L´:
            BEGIN
               DoAnother := TRUE;
               Found := FALSE;
               CLRSCR;
               WRITELN (´What name are you looking for? ´);
               READLN (SirName);
               Minimum := 0;
               Maximum := MaxRec;
            END; {L compound statement.}
         ´D´: DeleteEntry;
         ´C´: CorrectAName;
         ´R´: DoAnother := FALSE;
         END;    {END CASE construction.}
      END; {END procedure when SirName matches.}
```

```
      IF Minimum < Maximum THEN    {Works only while search is valid.}
      BEGIN
         IF SirName > Customer.LastName THEN
         BEGIN
            Minimum := Fetch;
         END;
         IF SirName < Customer.LastName THEN
         BEGIN
            Maximum := Fetch;
         END;
      END ELSE    {Tried every record and still have not gotten a hit.}
            BEGIN
               WRITELN ('I can not seem to find that name');
               WRITELN;
               DoAnother := TRUE;
               Found := FALSE;
               WRITELN ('What name are you looking for? ');
               READLN (SirName);
               Minimum := 0;
               Maximum := MaxRec;
            END; {IF Min < Max compound statement.}
      END; {NOT FOUND loop.}
      CLOSE (InFile);
      IF Delete THEN CompressFile;
END; {Procedure.}

PROCEDURE LookUpOneName;
{Choice #2.}
{Initializes for use of binary sort to READ records on disk.  This procedure}
{works entirely with records in an external file. It uses several other}
{procedures.}
BEGIN
   CLRSCR;
   WRITELN ('What file are we looking in? ');
   READLN (SourceFile);
   ASSIGN (InFile, SourceFile);
   RESET (InFile);
   Found := FALSE;
   MaxRec := FileSize (InFile) ;    {Find max for binary search.}
   WRITELN ('FileSize = ', MaxRec);
     DoAnother := TRUE;
     WHILE DoAnother DO
     BEGIN
       Minimum := 0;
       Maximum := MaxRec;
       WRITELN ('What name are you looking for?');
       READLN (SirName);
       TestName;
   END;
END;
```

```
PROCEDURE ProofListToScreen;
{Choice #4.}
{Handy procedure to check on initial keyboard input as well as to confirm}
{the operation of the sorting routines.  Makes extensive use of the TAB}
{procedure for most attractive screen display.}
VAR
  L1, L2, L3, L4 : STRING ;
 BEGIN
   CLRSCR;
   WRITELN ('What file would you like to have displayed?   ');
   READLN (TargetFile);
   ASSIGN (OutFile, TargetFile);
   RESET (OutFile);
        WHILE NOT EOF(OutFile) DO
          BEGIN
            READ (Outfile, Customer);
            WITH Customer DO
              BEGIN
                L1 := FirstName +  ' ' + LastName;
                Tab (L1, 26, L);
                L2 := Street;
                Tab (L2, 26, L);
                L3 := Town;
                Tab (L3, 19, L);
                L4 := State + ' ' + Zip;
                Tab (L4, 8, L);
                WRITELN (L1, L2, L3, L4);
              END;
          END;
   CLOSE (Outfile);
   WRITELN;
   WRITELN ('Hit ENTER to return to menu');
   READ (WhatsYourPleasure);
   IF KeyPressed THEN;  {Does not really care what specific key is hit.}
 END;
```

```
PROCEDURE ProduceLabels;
{Choice #5.}
{The primary purpose for writing this program was to generate mailing labels}
{every month.  This procedure takes a pre-sorted file, sets the line printer}
{for the one-inch high labels, and prints the file.  In addition, to conform}
{with the Post Office bulk mailing regulations, the customer requested that}
{the program give a count of labels within the town--Clifton, NJ--which are}
{mailed at one rate, and a total for all non-local addresses that are mailed}
{at a higher rate.  Clifton has several ZIP codes so testing for one ZIP}
{code--a simpler approach--did not work.}
VAR
  Clifton, NonClifton, Total, Result : INTEGER;
  Zippy : REAL;
BEGIN
  Clifton := 0;
  NonClifton := 0;
  Total := 0;
  CLRSCR;
  WRITELN ('What file contains the names?  ');
  READLN (TargetFile);
  ASSIGN (OutFile, TargetFile);
  RESET (OutFile);

  {The codes for setting the line printer are those for the NEC Spinwriter}
  {using one-inch labels.  Different printers require different}
  {initialization strings.}

  WRITE (LST, #27, #67, #6);   {Sets Spinwriter for six line deep labels.}
  WHILE NOT EOF(OutFile) DO
    BEGIN
      READ (Outfile, Customer);
      WITH Customer DO
      BEGIN
         WRITELN (LST);
         WRITELN (LST, FirstName,' ', LastName);
         WRITELN (LST, Street);
         WRITELN (LST, Town,' ', State,' ', Zip);
      END;
      WRITELN (LST, #12);   {Sends form feed.}

  {The following routine totalled the Clifton labels.  It is not an}
  {elegant approach--but it shows how quickly you can modify a Turbo}
  {program to respond to an ad hoc programming request.}

      VAL (Customer.Zip, Zippy, Result);
      IF (Zippy >= 7010) AND (Zippy <= 7015) THEN Clifton := Clifton + 1;
      Total := Total + 1;
    END;
    CLOSE (Outfile);
    NonClifton := Total - Clifton;
    WRITELN (LST, Date);
    WRITELN (LST,'    Clifton Names = ', Clifton);
    WRITELN (LST,'Non-Clifton Names = ', NonClifton);
    WRITELN (LST,'      Total Names = ', Total);
    WRITELN (LST, #12);
END;
```

```
PROCEDURE CreateMailingListBook;
{Choice #6.}
{In addition to producing labels monthly, the shopkeeper requested that}
{the program also produce the mailing list in book format to be kept}
{at the shop and in which she could make corrections and additions for}
{the monthly update session.  This procedure prints a pre-sorted file}
{allowing for margins on all sides of the paper and printing a running}
{head on each page.  In addition, it can either print the book immediately}
{or it can create a file--with all the headers and form feeds--which can}
{be spooled to the line printer at some more convenient time}
{The technique for choosing immediate output or redirection}
{of output to a file is handy for many applications.}
VAR
   Spool :  TEXT;
   PrintNow : BOOLEAN;
   OneLine : STRING ;
   L1, L2, L3, L4 : STRING ;
BEGIN
   CLRSCR;
   WRITELN ('What file contains the names?  ');
   READLN (SourceFile);
   ASSIGN (InFile, SourceFile);
   RESET (InFile);
   WRITE ('Type a FILE NAME only if you want');
   WRITELN (' this stored for printing later.');
   WRITELN ('To print it right now, just hit ENTER');
   READLN (TargetFile);
   IF TargetFile <> '' THEN
   BEGIN
     ASSIGN (Spool, TargetFile);
     REWRITE (Spool);
     PrintNow := FALSE;
   END
   ELSE
   BEGIN
    ASSIGN (Spool, 'TEMP');
    REWRITE (Spool);
    PrintNow := TRUE;
    END;

{Again, the initialization strings here are just for the NEC Spinwriter--}
{they initialize the printer, set the pitch, page length, etc.  Different}
{printers need different initialization strings.}

   WRITE (Spool, #27, #67, #66);  {Sets page length on Spinwriter.}
   WRITE (Spool, #27, '$A', #27, #85, #1, #27, #87, #82); {Initializes NEC.}
```

```
      Ll := 'TURBO PASCAL MAILING LIST';
      Tab (Ll, 80, C);
      WRITELN (Spool, Ll);
      Ll := Date;
      Tab (Ll, 80, C);
      WRITELN (Spool, Ll);
      WRITELN (Spool, #10, #10, #10); {Linefeed characters for top border.}
      LinesDone := 7;
      WHILE NOT EOF(InFile) DO
        BEGIN
        IF LinesDone < 59 THEN    {Test for full page.}
        BEGIN
          WITH Customer DO
             BEGIN
               READ (Infile, Customer);

{This routine makes good use of the TAB procedure to format the printed page}
{to put the most information on each page while still being easy to read.}

               Ll := FirstName +  ' ' + LastName;
               Tab (Ll, 26, L);
               L2 := Street;
               Tab (L2, 26, L);
               L3 := Town;
               Tab (L3, 19, L);
               L4 := State +  ' ' + Zip;
               Tab (L4, 8, L);
               WRITELN (Spool, Ll, L2, L3, L4);
               LinesDone := LinesDone + 1;
             END;    {Printed one record.}
        END {First part of IF...completed one page.}
        ELSE
        BEGIN {Print new page header.}
          LinesDone := 8;
          WRITELN (Spool, #12, #10, #10);
           {Sends form feed and two line feeds to printer.}
          Ll := 'TURBO PASCAL MAILING LIST';
          Tab (Ll, 80, C);
          WRITELN (Spool, Ll);
          Ll := Date;
          Tab (Ll, 80, C);
          WRITELN (Spool, Ll);
          WRITELN (Spool, #10, #10, #10);
        END;
      END;  {End WHILE...the input file has been completely read.}
   CLOSE (Infile);
   CLOSE (Spool);
     IF PrintNow THEN       {If not spooled, print it right now.}
     BEGIN
       RESET (Spool);
       WHILE NOT EOF (Spool) DO
       BEGIN
         READLN (Spool, OneLine);
         WRITELN (LST, OneLine);
       END;
     END;
   END;
```

```
PROCEDURE CopyOrMerge;
{Choice #7.}
{This procedure can either add the list of new names to the main file or}
{it can be used to make backup copies of a file.  It uses the CopyFile}
{procedure.}
BEGIN
   CLRSCR;
   WRITE ('Do you want to (C)opy a file ');
   WRITELN ('or (M)erge new names into the master list? ');
   READ (KBD, WhatsYourPleasure);
   WhatsYourPleasure := UPCASE (WhatsYourPleasure);
   CASE WhatsYourPleasure OF
      'C':
         BEGIN
            WRITELN ('What file is the source?  ');
            READLN (SourceFile);
            WRITELN ('What file should it be copied to?  ');
            READLN (TargetFile);
            ASSIGN (InFile, SourceFile);
            RESET (InFile);
            ASSIGN (OutFile, TargetFile);
            REWRITE (OutFile);
            CopyFile;
         END;
      'M':
         BEGIN
            WRITELN ('What file has JUST the new names?' );
            READLN (SourceFile);
            WRITELN ('What is the master file will all the names? ');
            READLN (TargetFile);
            ASSIGN (InFile, SourceFile);
            RESET (InFile);
            ASSIGN (OutFile, TargetFile);
            RESET (OutFile);
{This procedure appends new names to the end of the master file.  This}
{procedure works well in all versions of Turbo.  It does not, however,}
{automatically alphabetize the file.  This must be done separately to get}
{the added names into the proper alphabetical position.}

            MaxRec := FILESIZE (OutFile);  {Getlast record number.}
            SEEK (Outfile, MaxRec);  {Put any entry at the end of the file.}
            WHILE NOT EOF (InFile) DO
            BEGIN
               READ (InFile, Customer);
               WRITE (OutFile, Customer);
            END;
            CLOSE (InFile);
            CLOSE (OutFile);
            END;
      ELSE CopyOrMerge;
   END;
END;


PROCEDURE ExitProgram;            {Choice #8.}
BEGIN
   AllFinished := TRUE;
END;
```

```
        PROCEDURE InterpretChoice;  {Interprets menu selection.}
        BEGIN
           READ (KBD, WhatsYourPleasure);
           Option:=ORD (WhatsYourPleasure)-48; {Protects against alpha input.}
           CASE Option OF
              1: AcceptNewNames;
              2: LookUpOneName;
              3: AlphabetizeList;
              4: ProofListToScreen;
              5: ProduceLabels;
              6: CreateMailingListBook;
              7: CopyOrMerge;
              8: ExitProgram;
              ELSE ErrorHandler;
           END;
        END;

        BEGIN
        {Actual program execution begins here.  This is typical of most Turbo}
        {programs. After a procedure completes its operation, the menu is}
        {re-displayed unless the procedure has set the AllFinished flag to TRUE.}

           AllFinished:=FALSE;
           WHILE NOT AllFinished DO
              BEGIN
                 DisplayMenu;
                 InterpretChoice;
              END;
        END.
```

The Include File
Common.Pas

```
{The following three routines make up the include file Common.Pas.}
{The
 first function, called DATE, fetches the date from DOS and converts}
{the informtion from integers into strings.}
TYPE
  InputString  =  STRING;
  DateString = STRING; {returns decoded date to calling program}

FUNCTION Date: DateString;
{Utility function to get the date from DOS and convert it into a useful}
{string format simply by a call to  "Date".}
TYPE
  Registers = RECORD
                AX, BX, CX, DX, BP, SI, DS, ES, Flags : INTEGER;
              END;
VAR
  RegisterRecord :  Registers;  {needed for any MSDOS call}
  Month : STRING;
  Day :   STRING;
  Year :  STRING;
  DX,CX : INTEGER;

BEGIN
  RegisterRecord.AX := $2A00; {AX register includes hex 2A: DOS function to get date}
  INTR ($21, RegisterRecord); {Hex $21 is the DOS interrupt for many functions}
  WITH RegisterRecord DO
  BEGIN
    STR (CX, Year);    {converts integer value in CX register to a string called Year}
    STR (LO (RegisterRecord.DX), Day); {different approach conversion in line above}
    CASE  (HI (RegisterRecord.DX)) OF  {converts month numerical value to appropriate string}
      1 : Month := ´January´;
      2 : Month := ´February´;
      3 : Month := ´March´;
      4 : Month := ´April´;
      5 : Month := ´May´;
      6 : Month := ´June´;
      7 : Month := ´July´;
      8 : Month := ´August´;
      9 : Month := ´September´;
     10 : Month := ´October´;
     11 : Month := ´November´;
     12 : Month := ´December´;
    END;
  END;
  Date := Month +´ ´ + Day +´, ´ + Year;
END;
```

```
{The next procedure, called TAB, controls horizontal positioning of}
{strings for screen or line printer output.}

PROCEDURE Tab (VAR Phrase : InputString; Field : INTEGER; Pos : CHAR);
{Procedure to position any input string anywhere within a field of any length}
{up to 80 characters wide.  Applies to screen or line printer.}
VAR
  LSpaces, RSpaces : STRING;
  I, LeftSideSpaces, RightSideSpaces, SpaceOnLine : INTEGER;
BEGIN
  LSpaces := '';
  RSpaces := '';
  LeftSideSpaces := 0;
  SpaceOnLine := Field - Length (Phrase);
  IF (Pos = 'C') OR (Pos = 'c') THEN      {centering}
  BEGIN
    LeftSideSpaces := SpaceOnLine DIV 2;
    RightSideSpaces := (SpaceOnLine DIV 2) + (SpaceOnLine) mod 2;
    FOR I := 1 TO LeftSideSpaces DO LSpaces :=  LSpaces + ' ';
    FOR I := 1 TO RightSideSpaces DO RSpaces :=  RSpaces + ' ';
  END;
  IF (Pos = 'R') OR (Pos = 'r') THEN      {flush right}
  BEGIN
    LeftSideSpaces := SpaceOnLine;
    FOR I := 1 TO LeftSideSpaces DO LSpaces :=  LSpaces + ' ';
  END;
  IF (Pos = 'L') OR (Pos = 'l') THEN      {flush left}
  BEGIN
    RightSideSpaces := SpaceOnLine;
    FOR I := 1 TO RightSideSpaces DO RSpaces :=  RSpaces + ' ';
  END;
  Phrase := LSpaces + Phrase + RSpaces;
END;
```

```
{The third procedure, called CANADA plays the first four bars of}
{"O Canada".}

CONST
  Q = 300;  {Quarter-note}
  H = 600;
  T = 900;
  W = 1200;

  LowC = 262;  {Portion of scale}
  D = 294;
  E = 330;
  F = 350;
  G = 392;
  A = 440;

PROCEDURE Play (Note, Time : INTEGER);
BEGIN
    SOUND (Note);
    DELAY (Time);
    NOSOUND;
END;

PROCEDURE Canada;
{Plays four bars of "O Canada" simply by calling "Canada".  Useful to alert}
{operator to the completion of long process.}
BEGIN
    Play (E, H);
    Play (G, H);
    Play (G, Q);
    Play (LowC, T);

    Play (D, Q);
    Play (E, Q);
    Play (F, Q);
    Play (G, Q);
    Play (A, Q);
    Play (D, W);
END;
```

Index

Selections from
The SYBEX Library

Pascal

INTRODUCTION TO PASCAL
(Including UCSD Pascal™)
by Rodnay Zaks
420 pp., 130 illustr., Ref. 0-066
A step-by-step introduction for anyone
who wants to learn the Pascal language.
Describes UCSD and Standard Pascals.
No technical background is assumed.

THE PASCAL HANDBOOK
by Jacques Tiberghien
486 pp., 270 illustr., Ref. 0-053
A dictionary of the Pascal language,
defining every reserved word, operator,
procedure, and function found in all major
versions of Pascal.

APPLE® PASCAL GAMES
**by Douglas Hergert and
Joseph T. Kalash**
372 pp., 40 illustr., Ref. 0-074
A collection of the most popular computer
games in Pascal, challenging the reader
not only to play but to investigate how
games are implemented on the computer.

PASCAL PROGRAMS FOR
SCIENTISTS AND ENGINEERS
by Alan R. Miller
374 pp., 120 illustr., Ref. 0-058
A comprehensive collection of frequently
used algorithms for scientific and technical applications, programmed in Pascal.
Includes programs for curve-fitting, inte-
grals, statistical techniques, and more.

DOING BUSINESS WITH
PASCAL
**by Richard Hergert and
Douglas Hergert**
371 pp., illustr., Ref. 0-091
Practical tips for using Pascal programming in business. Covers design consid-
erations, language extensions, and
applications examples.

Other Languages

FORTRAN PROGRAMS FOR
SCIENTISTS AND ENGINEERS
by Alan R. Miller
280 pp., 120 illustr., Ref. 0-082
This book from the "Programs for Scientists and Engineers" series provides a
library of problem-solving programs while
developing the reader's proficiency in
FORTRAN.

A MICROPROGRAMMED APL
IMPLEMENTATION
by Rodnay Zaks
350 pp., Ref. 0-005
An expert-level text presenting the complete conceptual analysis and design of
an APL interpreter, and actual listing of
the microcode.

UNDERSTANDING C
by Bruce H. Hunter
320 pp., Ref 0-123
Explains how to program in powerful C
language for a variety of applications.
Some programming experience
assumed.

FIFTY PASCAL PROGRAMS
by Bruce H. Hunter
338 pp., illustr., Ref. 0-110
More than just a collection of useful programs! Structured programming techniques are emphasized and concepts
such as data type creation and array
manipulation are clearly illustrated.

PROGRAMMING THE 68000™
by Steve Williams
250 pp., illustr., Ref. 0-133
This book introduces you to micropro-
cessor operation, writing application programs, and the basics of I/O
programming. Especially helpful for own-
ers of the Apple Macintosh or Lisa.